Diasporas and
Development

Diasporas and Development

Exploring the Potential

EDITED BY
Jennifer M. Brinkerhoff

LYNNE
RIENNER
PUBLISHERS

BOULDER
LONDON

Published in the United States of America in 2008 by
Lynne Rienner Publishers, Inc.
1800 30th Street, Boulder, Colorado 80301
www.rienner.com

and in the United Kingdom by
Lynne Rienner Publishers, Inc.
3 Henrietta Street, Covent Garden, London WC2E 8LU

Library of Congress Cataloging-in-Publication Data
Diasporas and development : exploring the potential / Jennifer M.
Brinkerhoff, editor.
    p. cm.
 Includes bibliographical references and index.
 ISBN 978-1-58826-603-3 (hardcover : alk. paper)
1. Emigration and immigration—Economic aspects. 2. Emigrant remittances.
3. Immigrants. 4. Economic development. I. Brinkerhoff, Jennifer M., 1965–
 JV6035.D515 2008
 338.9—dc22

                                                        2008009263

British Cataloguing in Publication Data
A Cataloguing in Publication record for this book
is available from the British Library.

Printed and bound in the United States of America

Printed on 30% postconsumer recycled paper

The paper used in this publication meets the requirements
of the American National Standard for Permanence of
Paper for Printed Library Materials Z39.48-1992.

5 4 3 2 1

Contents

Preface

After the events of September 11, 2001, led to the US military action in Afghanistan, I was very moved by the efforts of the Afghan diaspora to contribute to the reconstruction of their homeland. Along with my colleague Lori Brainard, who specializes in online communities, we initiated a research program on digital diasporas. While the digital angle is fascinating work, I became increasingly eager to learn more about diasporas' contributions beyond the virtual world. And so I embarked on a project to do just that, one result of which is this book.

I have an agenda. For too long, policymakers and development practitioners, if they were interested at all, have primarily been interested in diasporas with regard to the volume of remittances or "brain drain." But the issues and potential contributions of diasporas to development are far richer. As an international development specialist, my main concern has always been how to bring as many resources to bear as possible to address global poverty and improve quality of life around the world. To that end, my first book looked at partnerships among governments, nongovernmental organizations, multinational corporations, and donors (Brinkerhoff 2002). Now, I see diasporas as one of the least recognized yet significant potential contributors.

The role of diasporas in development is a growing area of interest for research, policy, and practice. While the International Organization for Migration (IOM) has long explored the potential contributions of diasporas to their homelands, the primary focus until recently has been on repatriation. The IOM has dramatically expanded its thinking vis-à-vis diasporas and is more strategically investigating diasporas' potential development contributions, with or without repatriation. Issues related to migration, diasporas, and development also are slowly being mainstreamed into development policy agendas and activities. Related programming can be found, for example, at the United Kingdom's Department for International Development (DFID), the Dutch Ministry of Foreign Affairs, the Canadian International Development Agency, and the United States Agency for International Development, among the bilaterals; the Asian Development Bank, the Inter-American Development Bank, and the World Bank, among the multilaterals; and multiple UN agencies (notably the United Nations Development Programme) and foundations.

To date, most programming is research-oriented and exploratory and/or remains primarily focused on remittances, though some development agencies and diaspora communities are far ahead in innovating with respect to diasporas and international development. For example, the Dutch Ministry of Foreign Affairs regularly consults with diasporas, including consultations related to country-assistance strategies. It has invested in capacity building and other partnership approaches to both create and facilitate diasporans as international development actors (DGIS 2007). Some of its support to diasporans is channeled through Oxfam-Novib, which in early 2007 facilitated the formation of the Diaspora Forum for Development, a network of twenty-three Netherlands-based diaspora organizations representing twenty countries of origin.

As early as 1997, DFID made a commitment to "build on the skills and talents of migrants and other ethnic minorities within the UK to promote the development of their countries of origin" (DFID 1997). It has continued its focus on engaging with the diaspora for policy consultation and selected project support (DFID 2007). Connections for Development is a network of black and minority ethnic (BME) communities whose mission it is to ensure that "UK BME communities, and the organisations they are involved in here, are supported in the process of shaping and delivering policy and projects that affect their countries of origin or interest—collectively 'our world'" (Connections for Development 2007). Connections for Development disseminates DFID's country action strategies to appropriate country constituencies, who provide feedback and commentary to DFID.

Home-country governments have also demonstrated significant innovation. As of 2000, approximately eighty-nine countries allowed for dual citizenship or included migrants as official members of their political communities (Renshon 2000). The Mexican government has created positions for elected diaspora representatives in state parliaments, and Mexico's Institute of Mexicans Abroad, housed in the federal Secretariat of Foreign Relations, provides advocacy training to Mexican diaspora organizations and includes a Consultative Council of 105 elected representatives of immigrant groups in the United States and Canada (see Ayón 2006). The government of the People's Republic of China maintains diaspora-related institutional structures, policies, program activities, and official websites (see Biao 2006).

And the government of India has created a special status for "Non-Resident Indians"; it consulted with NRIs to modify the policy framework in support of India's software industry (Saxenian 2002b).

Despite these innovations, many other countries and development actors remain far behind in acknowledging diasporas' importance to development and in exploring ways to tap them as important resources for development policy and practice. While the 2006 UN High Level Dialogue on Migration and Development and, more recently, the first Global Forum on Migration and Development have placed the topic of migration and development squarely on international agendas, there remains a tremendous gap between the promise of this attention and coherent policy and programming.

This book seeks to advance and deepen our understanding of diasporas and development by highlighting the broad range of diasporas' potential contributions and inspiring a more systematic effort to capture this potential. Country, diaspora, and organization examples inform analytic frameworks and provide demonstrations that other actors may choose to explore. The aim is to open minds and encourage further creativity regarding how to match the complex phenomenon of diasporas to conventional development understandings, policy, and programming.

*   *   *

It has been a privilege over the last few years to meet and study inspiring individuals and organizations from various diasporas. This book is dedicated to the many diaspora members who endeavor to improve their own quality of lives—often in an adopted country—at the same time that they support family, community, and country back home.

The book would not be possible without the many scholars and practitioners who contributed chapters, who participated in conference discussions, and who live diasporas and development every day. Thanks also go to the George Washington University Center for the Study of Globalization and its director, John Forrer; GW's Center for International Business Education and Research; the Trachtenberg School of Public Policy and Public Administration; and the Elliott School of International Affairs. A special acknowledgment goes to my colleagues Stephen Lubkemann and Liesl Riddle, with whom I cofounded the interdisciplinary Diaspora Research Program at GW.

Special thanks also go to Lynne Rienner, who encouraged me to produce an integrated book that could have a meaningful impact on our understanding, policy, and practice related to diasporas and development; and to my husband, Derick Brinkerhoff, who supports me in everything.

—*Jennifer M. Brinkerhoff*

1

The Potential of
Diasporas and Development

Jennifer M. Brinkerhoff

One long-standing and universally accepted role of foreign aid in development is to leverage and enable private initiatives, whether these concern foreign direct investment, more targeted private-sector development activities, or the development of important inputs into economic growth, such as knowledge and skills. While this general role has not changed and is not expected to, new—or at least newly recognized—avenues exist for foreign aid to support or at least avoid inhibiting private efforts. Specifically, donors can partner and coordinate with diaspora organizations, and possibly enhance, support, and channel the contributions of diasporas to development. At a minimum, the development industry will need to account for diasporas and their activities in policy analysis, needs assessment, and development programming.

Governments, international organizations, and donors increasingly recognize diasporas as important actors in peace and conflict and development, but policymakers have few, if any, guidelines or formal policies on how best to incorporate diasporas into peace and development strategies. A lack of understanding of the nature of these contributions, how to mobilize them, and the circumstances that are most likely to yield positive results hamper policymakers' ability to maximize this expanding resource. There is a risk that without a deep understanding of these dynamics, donors' interventions can stifle, prevent, or interfere with their potential.

Diasporas may be very important to the development of their homelands, yet related research remains scarce, apart from attention to remittances and continuing concerns about brain drain. Are diasporas a solution to poverty alleviation and national development? A growing body of literature explores the impact of remittances in receiving countries (see, for

1

example, Özden and Schiff 2005). Such remittances are an important component of diasporas' potential contributions. Yet money alone will not ensure development. Much attention has been focused on remittances' application to consumption as opposed to savings and investment, though the direct relationship to enhanced options at the household level and their impact on household and community development remain relatively underexplored. Furthermore, research shows that the largest recipients of remittances are not the poorest of the poor but households of relative poverty and low income who can afford to send members abroad (Massey et al. 1999). Similarly, the term *brain drain* has been part of the development lexicon almost since the inception of the industry. Historically, the emphasis in the migration and development literature and among its scholars has been on the negative impacts of migration almost to the total exclusion of potential for positive returns. Attention to economic remittances and brain drain has overshadowed the growing impact of diasporas related to social and political contributions and economic development (e.g., transnational entrepreneurism and diaspora homeland investment).

Focusing on diasporas' potential constructive contributions to development of the homeland, this book provides a more nuanced view of how diasporas contribute specifically to homelands emerging from conflict (Part 1), to private sector development in the homeland (Part 2), and, looking beyond remittances, to development of the homeland on a national scale (Part 3). In each of these areas specific subthemes are explored both to illustrate diaspora potential and to explore specific means to maximize it. Each chapter is grounded empirically with examples from one or more diaspora cases. All together, the book explores in depth seven different diasporas and their homelands, and includes examples from a host of others.

Following a review of diasporas, their potential impact on the homeland—both negative and positive—and their motivations, this introduction provides a brief overview of diasporas' contributions to economic development and knowledge transfer (with diaspora philanthropy included in both) in support of homeland development. The introductions to Parts 1–3 provide more detailed reviews. This introduction also reviews the remainder of the book and closes with a comment on the implications for foreign aid.

Diasporas: For Worse, or for Better?

Modern diasporas are "ethnic minority groups of migrant origins residing and acting in host countries but maintaining strong sentimental and material links with their countries of origin—their homelands" (Sheffer 1986, 3). Migration has kept pace with global population rates, doubling from 75 million in 1965 to 150 million in 2000 (IOM 2000), and rising to 185 million in

2005 (IOM 2005). Coupled with increased ease of communication and transportation, these numbers suggest that diasporas are likely to continue to be important players on the global stage. Diasporas attract attention for a variety of reasons. Beyond security concerns related to terrorism and civil unrest, in the international development arena, developing country governments and international donors are taking notice of diasporas' potential contributions to economic development. Here, attention has primarily focused on the impressive totals of economic remittances, whose global estimates in the twenty-first century outpace official development assistance: $70 billion per year in 2004, and estimated at $125 billion in 2005 and $167 billion in 2006 (World Bank 2004b, 2005b, 2006a). This attention, alone, is a significant evolutionary development, since historically national governments mainly focused on the security risks posed by organized diasporas, and, along with the development community, emphasized the brain drain phenomenon of out-migration.

Neither of these issues has been eliminated. Security remains a concern. Collier and Hoeffler (2001) posit that diasporas substantially impact the risk of renewed conflict; after five years of postconflict peace, they claim, the presence of diasporas increases the likelihood of renewed conflict sixfold. As for brain drain, Özden and Schiff (2005) identify four positive externalities that are lost to the sending country as a consequence of skilled migration: (1) spillover productivity of other workers, (2) public service provision (e.g., education and health), (3) tax revenues, and (4) public debate and policy and institution influence. The consequences of brain drain are most commonly noted with respect to health care. Public health systems in Africa are a case in point (see Schrecker and Labonte 2004). The loss of nurses in the Philippines (Alburo and Abella 2002) and Jamaica (Thomas-Hope 2002) pose serious challenges. Docquier and Marfouk (2005) confirm high brain drain levels in poor and isolated small countries in Africa and the Caribbean.

An alternative perspective sees migrants—or diasporas—as assets that can be mobilized (Meyer et al. 1997). Potential resource gains include remittances as well as skills and knowledge. Recent perspectives on remittances promote attention to a broader perspective that includes social remittances, that is, skills transfer, and cultural and civic awareness/experience (Nyberg-Sorensen 2004b). The potential gains to the homeland derive not only from skills and knowledge from the diaspora itself but also from the "socio-professional" networks these migrants have joined overseas (Meyer and Brown 1999). The International Organization for Migration (2005) confirms that these extended diaspora networks can yield investments in new technology, market intelligence, and business contacts (see also Hunger 2002). At the macroeconomic level, migration can reduce unemployment (IOM 2005), provide access to foreign exchange (Lowell, Findlay, and

Stewart 2004; Gamlen 2005), and yield other benefits through more sophisticated financial flows (Lowell and Findlay 2002). The latter can include strengthening the portfolios of home country banks through the purchase of remittance-backed bonds and the holding of foreign currency accounts (Lowell, Findlay, and Stewart 2004).

Until shortly before the turn of the twenty-first century, the drain-or-gain question was almost exclusively answered with the former. Now diasporas' contributions and potential contributions to the development of their homelands are increasingly recognized by beneficiary communities, homeland governments, and development practitioners and policymakers. Experimentation to recruit and foster such contributions is at an early stage, in part inhibited by a full appreciation and understanding of the breadth of the potential.

Diasporas, Identity, and Motivation

Beyond individual household remittances, several features common to diasporas bind their members and suggest a potential for collective action. Cohen (1997, 515) identifies a range of these, including

- A collective memory and myth about the homeland. . . .
- An idealization of the putative ancestral home and a collective commitment to its maintenance, restoration, safety and prosperity, even to its creation.
- The development of a return movement which gains collective approbation.
- A strong ethnic group consciousness sustained over a long time and based on a sense of distinctiveness, a common history and the belief in a common fate. . . . [and]
- A sense of empathy and solidarity with co-ethnic members in other countries of settlement.

These features contribute to the development of communities of identity, where members reinforce in one another their links to the home culture and associated values. Allegiance to the home country "provides emotional support and identity resources" (Kastoryano 1999, 198).

Immigrants neither wholly accept their host country culture nor automatically embrace their homeland culture to the exclusion of other influences. Many diaspora members may come to share civic and other values of the host country, learned through exposure and/or social pressure, or consciously sought (sometimes through elective migration). US-based diasporas are believed to embrace US values of pluralism, democracy, and human rights. Based on the integrationist pluralist model, it is anticipated that such diasporas "prefer, express, and adhere to the same democratic values when

allowed to flourish and attain the best that is in them"; and they are expected to "extend to others the same rights they themselves claim" (Shain 1999,
26). While this may not be universally true, an important benefit of diaspora
organizations is the opportunity to negotiate cultural identity (Brinkerhoff
2004; Brainard and Brinkerhoff 2004), exploring these dimensions, and to
enact it through communication and collective action.

In his research on diasporas in the United States, Shain (1999) argues
that the US tolerance for "hyphenization"—that is, African-American,
Asian-American, and Arab-American—affords diasporas a greater opportunity to pursue their cultural identity, within the context of their American
selves, as well as their identity-based political agendas. Shain (1999) con-
tends that diasporas can both "humanize" and "Americanize" US foreign
policy, combating isolationist tendencies, on the grounds of American values of freedom and democracy. In doing so, they can contribute meaningfully to the quality of life in their home territories (e.g., through lobbying for
foreign assistance, economic remittances, and/or informing policy and programs). John F. Kennedy's famous inaugural speech, "Ask not what your
country can do for you. Ask what you can do for your country," seems to
have broad appeal across many US-based diaspora groups. They apply it as
a call to serve, not their home of residence where it was inspired, but the
now distant homeland.[1]

Diaspora members mobilize, in part, to express their identities, and
these identities can be reinforced through activity on behalf of the homeland. Some may be motivated by a sense of obligation or guilt, as they seek
to reconcile their preference for the adopted homeland with their allegiance
to a suffering homeland (see Brinkerhoff forthcoming). The felt need to
actively express identity may derive from various forms of marginalization
(social, economic, political, or psychic), confusion, and a sense that the
homeland identity will be lost without proactive expression, or may simply
be a response to social reinforcement and perhaps pride (Brinkerhoff forthcoming). Diasporas may proactively promote and re-create homeland identities, and these efforts may be more acute in the absence of a physical
homeland (see Koslowski 2005b; Brinkerhoff 2006b). The form diasporas'
mobilization takes may represent an expression of their hybrid identity,
which may encompass liberal values.

Not all diaspora activity, however, may be directed to the homeland,
and not all migrants mobilize based on a homeland identity (or even consider themselves to be a part of a diaspora). Diaspora groups and members may
be more or less inclined to concern themselves with quality of life and policies vis-à-vis their home countries. Political activism resulting from cultural
identity, whether targeted to home or host country, is likely to be driven by
"interests and obligations that result from migrants' simultaneous engagement in countries of origin and destination" (Nyberg-Sorensen, Van Hear,

and Engberg-Pedersen 2002). The higher the cost to status and security in their adopted country, the greater the likelihood that the diaspora community will split and/or fail to support the homeland (Esman 1986).

Scholars have identified several factors conducive to diaspora participation in home country development. Esman (1986) identifies three: the material, cultural, and organizational resources available; the "opportunity structures" available in host countries; and "their inclination or motivation to maintain their solidarity and exert group influence" (336). Economic resources are especially critical to remittances and sometimes repatriation. Organizational resources affect the ability to mobilize for political action and for independent development activities, such as hometown associations, and the ability to access host-country and international decisionmaking structures (see Shain 1999). The importance of organizational resources also depends on the size and diversity of the diaspora community. The most commonly identified factor necessary for effective mobilization is the creation of a sense of solidarity and community identity (see, for example, King and Melvin 1999; Shain 1999). But what, specifically, might diasporas mobilize for?

Economic Effects of Diasporas

A discussion of the economic impact of diasporas must necessarily begin with an overview of remittances, since these are the focus of much attention and policy, and remain more prominent in terms of data collection and research than other potential contributions. Economic remittances have grown substantially in recent years. As noted above, they now significantly outpace global overseas development assistance (Nyberg-Sorensen, Van Hear, and Engberg-Pedersen 2002), with estimates of $70 billion per year in 2004, $125 billion in 2005, and $167 billion in 2006 (World Bank 2004b, 2005b, 2006a). The US Agency for International Development estimates that of all US international assistance (public and private), individual remittances comprise more than 30 percent, and they more than doubled in the 1990s (USAID 2002).

Economic remittances, however, do not automatically contribute to national development. According to the International Organization for Migration (IOM), remittances tend to follow three spending phases, with regard to (1) family maintenance and housing improvement, (2) conspicuous consumption, and (3) productive activities (Nyberg-Sorensen, Van Hear, and Engberg-Pedersen 2002, 14–15). A large percentage of remittances do not extend to phase three. Furthermore, such remittances often do not reach the poorest of the poor, who may be less likely to have links to diaspora communities (Massey et al. 1999); and remittances to socioeconomically unequal societies may further polarization (Gardner 1995). In their study of Mexico, Mora and Taylor (2005) found that remittances have an equalizing effect on incomes only in high migration areas.

While there is cause to be cautious in making assumptions about the household use of remittances and their consequent productive contributions, the IOM (2005) finds that recipients do have a high propensity to save, and remittances may pave the way to accessing investment capital. They can also more directly provide capital for small businesses when channeled through credit cooperatives and microenterprises. The highly skilled are not necessarily the largest remitters, but they are more likely to make productive investments (Lowell, Findlay, and Stewart 2004). In its research in the early 2000s, the World Bank reports that remittances can (1) reduce recipient household poverty, with spillover to other households; (2) increase investment in education and health as well as other productive activities; (3) reduce child labor; and (4) increase entrepreneurship (Özden and Schiff 2005). With respect to poverty reduction, remittances are especially important for addressing the *severity* of poverty, for example, in Guatemala (Adams 2005). In Chapter 3 of this volume, Stephen C. Lubkemann explores the role and forms of remittances in war-torn societies and post-conflict recovery through an examination of Liberia and its diaspora.

While development planners would naturally like to view remittances as programmable resources, the fact remains that most household remittances constitute family transfers. Should they be counted as development resources? Is it appropriate to lament their application to consumption goods? If so, under what circumstances? This is an issue the development industry seems to overlook in its eagerness to maximize diaspora potential: how to reconcile economic development objectives with the rights of self-determination and ownership of what is, basically, family income. Some have rightly pointed out that better documentation of regular remittances has potential to assist households and nations better to access credit. Clearly, the scope for research and policy experimentation with respect to remittances is wide open.

Diasporas, themselves, are concerned with development beyond the household. Seeking to better channel and coordinate remittances for development purposes, diasporas form hometown associations (HTAs) or regional clubs, and other philanthropic diaspora organizations. Through such associations, resources can be channeled to specific development projects, sometimes identified by the targeted communities themselves, and/or coordinated with government funds and expertise (see Orozco 2003; Orozco with Lapointe 2004; see also Smith 2001; Shain 1999). HTAs in Mexico, for example, usually begin with health and education, sports and cultural projects, and then focus on physical infrastructure. HTAs have also begun to explore more targeted productive activities, such as job creation and direct investments (Orozco 2003; see also Landolt 2001). The US Agency for Development has sought proposals for collaborative ventures with HTAs (Lowell, Findlay, and Stewart 2004). Beyond HTAs, diasporas have created regional- and national-level development initiatives, sometimes in direct partnership with homeland governments. These initiatives may concern specific sectors for development, such as national infrastructure (the subject of Natasha Iskander, Chapter 8), or more general national development planning (as described by Thomson Fontaine with Jennifer M. Brinkerhoff in Chapter 9).

Regarding development objectives more generally, diasporas also organize philanthropic activities targeted to the homeland, either through diaspora organizations and faith communities/organizations or less formally and individually. Janelle A. Kerlin, in Chapter 2, outlines an impressive array of Afghan American philanthropic organizations and activities. Some diaspora organizations have evolved into professional nonprofits and international development NGOs (nongovernmental organizations), competing alongside more traditional development actors and participating in the international development industry (e.g., Coptic Orphans, Afghan-American Reconstruction Council). Almost half of the Afghan American nonprofits Kerlin studied work in some way with other development entities ranging from other Afghan diaspora organizations and international charitable institutions to US government and United Nations agencies. Associations of diaspora professionals organize humanitarian tours and contributions—for example, providing health services and training teachers. The latter is an example of diaspora knowledge transfer.

The scale of diaspora philanthropy is growing and merits attention. In addition to the few wealthy millionaires—such as Kirk Kerkorian of the Armenian diaspora, who founded the Lincy Foundation (discussed in Chapters 5 and 6—many individual diaspora members give regularly on small scales, which add up. For example, according to Opiniano and Castro (2006), Filipino diaspora remittances of approximately $218 million were sent through the formal banking system as gifts and donations (not including remittances to families) in 2003 (Association of Foundations 2005), a five-year high, according to data from the balance of payments of the Bangko Sentral ng Pilipinas.

Beyond remittance-related efforts, diasporas contribute to the economic development of their homelands through foreign direct investment and transnational entrepreneurship, including support for entrepreneurs and small businesses in the homeland. These are the subjects of Part 2. In her introduction to Part 2, Liesl Riddle provides a more detailed overview than presented here of the literature and state of knowledge of diasporas' contribution to the homeland private sector. The United Nations Development Programme's (UNDP's) Commission on Private Sector Development notes that diasporas are "supporting entrepreneurs in their homelands with remittances, informal financing of small businesses, and business advice and mentorship" (Commission 2004, 30). Diaspora members may be much more effective investors. First, they may be more likely to invest in economies that others would consider high-risk, simply because they have better knowledge and relationship opportunities that other investors lack (Gillespie, Sayre, and Riddle 2001; Gillespie et al. 1999). Second, they can combine this knowledge with the skills, knowledge, and networks they have cultivated abroad, yielding important synergistic advantages.[2] India's information technology success story is a widely cited case, where diaspora members have networked with their returned counterparts, contributing an estimated 16 percent of total foreign investment (Margolis et al. 2004; see also Saxenian 2002a).

More specifically, a substream of the literature on transnationalism and international migration has begun to examine transnational entrepreneurs. For example, Landolt and Associates (1999; see also Landolt 2001) developed a framework of transnational enterprises, identifying four types. Circuit firms concern themselves with the transfer of goods and remittances between countries; they include informal couriers as well as large formal enterprises. Cultural enterprises depend upon contacts within the home country for the purpose of importing cultural goods. Ethnic enterprises are based in the host country and provide goods imported from the home country. Finally, return migrant microenterprises are created by returned migrants who depend upon their former-host-country contacts for their business. Transnational enterprises may rely on kin networks both in the home country and in the diaspora (see, for example, Portes and Sensenbrenner 1993). These various enterprises are conduits for diasporas' economic contributions through consumption, described more fully by Orozco in Chapter 10.

Diaspora Knowledge Transfer

While this volume focuses on the constructive contributions of diasporas to development in their homelands, as noted above, much of the research on migration and development to date has emphasized brain drain. As a consequence, policy has emphasized migration management, including efforts to prevent the migration and to promote the repatriation of the highly skilled. Skilled migrants are most commonly defined as "those in possession of a tertiary degree or extensive specialized work experience" (Vertovec 2002, 2). The ability of homelands to tap diaspora knowledge and skills resources has been limited by the misconception promoted by the human capital approach. Meyer (2001) discusses how brain drain and the human capital approach "refer to a substantialist view of skills as a stock of knowledge and/or abilities embedded in the individual" (95). This perspective ignores the fact that knowledge is not static, nor is it represented by only the credentials the migrants achieved (whether prior to or after migration). That is, the host society (or adopted homeland) may provide the experience necessary to enhance the migrants' skills and the context and relationships to support them. A *total* human capital approach accounts for tacit knowledge, including interpersonal skills and self-confidence (Williams and Baláz 2005). The receiving country may also provide the experience and context necessary to enhance the migrants' skills. For example, in response to disgruntled compatriots' questions about why he left Italy, Italian-born astrophysicist and 2002 Nobel laureate Riccardo Giacconi responded: "Scientists are like painters. Michelangelo became a great artist because he had been given a wall to paint. The US gave me my wall" (qtd. in Margolis et al. 2004, 30).

Meyer and Brown (1999) elaborate on what this "wall" might mean, noting scientific migrants' work environment in the industrialized host country, which tends to be far superior to the developing country homeland in terms of funding, technical support, equipment, scientific networks, and experimental conditions. They apply the sociology of science and technology to further argue that the process of knowledge creation, transmission, and application requires not only social and institutional communities but also sociocognitive ones, which are rarely replicable because they rely upon local conditions and collective tacit knowledge built through daily group practice.

Beyond technical knowledge and skills, then, diasporas may contribute new understandings acquired in the host country, cultural competencies and associated intermediary roles, and tacit knowledge that encompasses hybrid identities and transnational experience. Sometimes the most important contribution a diasporan may bring to the homeland is belief in the possibility of change. Especially in fragile or postconflict states, citizens may be demoralized and passive. For example, Coptic Orphans, a US-based diaspora organization, inspires its Egyptian staff to reject passive acceptance and seek to redress the injustices children face, such as in the education system. The founder also brings her engineering background to create systems of organization and accountability to ensure effectiveness and efficiency in their work (Brinkerhoff 2008b).

Diaspora members offer unique advantages vis-à-vis other development actors in their efforts to contribute to the homeland. Recipients of knowledge transfer/exchange in both China and the Philippines note the advantages of diaspora-specific contributions deriving from the absence of language and culture barriers, and more specifically, their ability to better understand and thus more effectively adapt foreign approaches and technology to the homeland context (Wescott and Brinkerhoff 2006). In short, where knowledge exchange is concerned, diaspora members can act as important interlocutors between the technology and its originating context and the homeland recipients and culture. In the Philippines, beneficiaries also noted the greater potential, vis-à-vis other foreign nationals, to persuade diaspora members to extend short-term stays and contributions (Opiniano and Castro 2006). Opportunities and efforts for diaspora knowledge exchange can be motivated and also framed to appeal to economic and career incentives as well as philanthropy.

Diaspora knowledge transfer occurs in tandem with other diaspora contributions, and both the skills and knowledge at the time of departure and those acquired after migration are important potential resources for homeland development. Diaspora members can contribute these through not only permanent repatriation but also short-term or even virtual (in cyberspace) return. Some may engage in circular migration, with periodic movement back and forth, or even maintain a transnational lifestyle, maintaining residency in both the homeland and an adopted country, as Lubkemann describes in Chapter 3, noting Liberians' "house with two rooms." Information technology (IT) has emerged as an essential enabler of diaspora knowledge transfer (see, for example, Pellegrino 2001). Through IT, knowledge transfer projects can be proposed, designed, and vetted. IT also enables diaspora knowledge contributions without necessitating short-term return or repatriation.

Diaspora knowledge transfer is often embedded in broader networks of resource exchange. As the chapters in Part 3 illustrate, sometimes these networks—inclusive of diaspora associations, professional networks, and other development actors—can lead to important economic investments and development in particular sectors; in other instances these networks and partnerships may evolve to encompass national development objectives, including national planning.

Overview of the Book

This book is organized into three parts. Part 1 addresses the question, How do diasporas respond to homelands in crisis? Following a general introduction, the answers are discussed in Chapters 2–4. Diasporas organize and raise money for relief, reconstruction, and development (Chapter 2). They remit to support subsistence and later livelihoods, and mobilize to participate in postconflict reconstruction through repatriation, lobbying, and/or philanthropy (Chapter 3). And they participate in the development industry's reconstruction efforts (Chapter 4). Together, these chapters consider the experiences of Afghanistan, Liberia, and Iraq.

Liesl Riddle introduces Part 2, "Mobilizing Diaspora Homeland Investment." Esman provides an overview of key issues determining diaspora contributions to homeland investment (Chapter 5), focusing on characteristics of both the diaspora and the homeland. Based on his analysis of three diaspora experiences—the overseas professional Chinese, Armenian, and Irish Catholic US diasporas—he identifies three factors: diasporas' capability, their inclination, and the investment climate in their homeland. The remaining chapters in Part 2 are operational in nature, focusing on the specific actions and strategies actors from the diaspora and the homeland might take to maximize diaspora investment and effectiveness. Kate Gillespie and Anna Andriasova (Chapter 6) take capability and inclination for granted, focusing on strategies for ensuring the effectiveness of diaspora investment that has already been mobilized. They examine the efforts of three Armenian diaspora organizations—the Armenian Business Corporation, the Lincy Foundation, and the Izmirlian Foundation—and develop an institutional framework for comparatively analyzing varied strategies in terms of implementing agents (control set), contributing investors (input set), and targeted audiences (output set). In Chapter 7, Riddle and Marano focus on diaspora inclination and consider strategies for recruiting for diaspora investment. Specifically, they examine export promotion organizations (EPOs) and investment promotion agencies (IPAs). After discussing the general role these agencies play in fostering economic development, they consider the case of Afghanistan and propose how the work of EPOs and IPAs should be modified in order better to target and recruit homeland participation and investment from diasporas.

Part 3 looks "Beyond Remittances" to consider "Knowledge and Networks for National Development." Jennifer Brinkerhoff's introduction provides an overview of homeland government policy options, and the importance of networks and diaspora organizations. The more specific treatments and case studies demonstrate diasporas' potential to contribute to development on a national scale, and far beyond the volume of remittances. Chapters 8 and 9 focus on diaspora-initiated activities targeted to national development. Iskander (Chapter 8) challenges the notion that remittances are vectors of change and introduces the concept of "constituted remittances." The value and impacts of remittances, she argues, derive from the actions of diaspora members. Thus, the true vectors of change are "the social processes through which actors infuse remittances with meaning and choose how they will use them" (pp. 163–164). She examines how the Moroccan diaspora in France mobilized technical experts, policymakers, and public agencies in order to provide electrification and road infrastructure to remote mountainous areas of Morocco. Thomson Fontaine with Jennifer Brinkerhoff (Chapter 9) explore the initiatives and roles diasporas can take for homeland national planning as they consider the case of a small island nation with one of the highest rates of out-migration (skilled and unskilled) in the world: Dominica. They detail how the Dominican diaspora has organized international conferences of the diaspora for the purpose of planning and consolidating small individual contributions for Dominica's national development. Resulting initiatives include the creation of the Dominica Academy of Arts and Sciences, which created a database of skilled and professional Dominicans, and the Dominica Sustainable Energy Corporation (DSEC). The evolving experience of Dominica and its diaspora suggests a path of escape for those countries caught in the vicious cycle of remittance dependence and brain drain.

The book closes with an exploration of some of the impediments to diasporas' development contributions. Manuel Orozco (Chapter 10) examines why, to date, diasporas' contributions have not been effectively linked to formal development industry policy, planning, and programming. He identifies the limits of the contribution of diasporas' economic practices to development, and specifies issues that prevent the development industry from more effectively engaging with diasporas.

What Role for Foreign Aid?

Before donors can begin fully to capitalize on potential diaspora contributions, they need first to recognize the full depth and breadth of potential diaspora contributions and, more fundamentally, recognize diasporas as key actors in the development arena. As this volume suggests, donors and development processes would benefit from including diaspora associations in development consultations, needs assessments, and priority setting for the purpose not only of disseminating information about donor activities but more essentially to *exchange* information with diasporas to better inform these activities. In this sense, donors may also play a major intermediary role between homeland and host-land governments and diaspora groups.

Diasporas represent important opportunities for more formal development organizations to recruit expertise and solicit information for development programs, and to disseminate information about priorities and programming, potentially reducing duplication and cross-purpose efforts (Brinkerhoff 2004). Diaspora organizations can act as important intermediaries between traditional development actors, and diasporas and local communities, for example, identifying needs and priorities of local communities and communicating those to donor organizations, NGOs, and diaspora members to solicit funding and expertise; and diaspora organizations may demonstrate innovative programs and approaches that can be replicated and/or used to advocate for traditional actor administrative and programmatic reforms (Brinkerhoff 2004). Examples of both can be found in the experience of postconflict reconstruction in Afghanistan (Brinkerhoff 2004) and Liberia (Lubkemann 2004b).

Given the importance of diaspora organizations for mobilizing contributions, donors might also consider building diaspora organizations' capacity. For example, the mission of the Office of Private and Voluntary Cooperation of the US Agency for International Development is the capacity building of the private and voluntary organization (PVO) sector and local NGOs. Its matching grant program requires PVOs to partner with local NGOs for the purpose of capacity building. Donors might consider special training events as well as potential matching/partnering mechanisms for this purpose. Donors can also make significant contributions to diaspora networking. Already, several donors have web-hosted databases with search capabilities to link homeland jobs with diaspora skills.[3]

Further, donors may play a crucial role in assisting developing country governments to think strategically about crafting migration policy strategies and frameworks, notably for engaging their diasporas. The Global Commission on International Migration (2005) highlights three *C*s with respect to migration policy: coherence, capacity, and coordination. The report emphasizes that policy related to migration is uncoordinated and often contradictory, not only at the international level but at the national level as well. In response, donors can assist homeland governments in policy design, in addition to building their implementation capacity. Donors could also use their convening power to initiate networking activities and events and to demonstrate the potential of diaspora contributions. Focusing homeland governments on diasporas and their potential contributions can add additional incentives in terms of leveraging investments in improving homeland democracy and development policy frameworks—since diasporas will often demand such improvements. Incorporating diasporas into development planning can additonally inform country-specific targets of related strategies.

Donors have been making progress in terms of policies and programs related to remittance capture. In addition to funding research (e.g., Pieke, Van Hear, and Lindley 2005; Orozco 2003; Lowell and de la Garza 2000; Özden and Schiff 2005; Van Hear et al. 2004), donors have experimented with interventions (as reviewed by Manuel Orozco, Chapter 10) to enhance the efficiency of remittance transfer (e.g., the Inter-American Development Bank's Multilateral Investment Fund), and have solicited partnerships and proposals from hometown associations (e.g., USAID). In seeking to leverage the impact of remittances, for example, donors have been promoting regulatory reforms (Martin 2001), and brokering relationships to encourage diaspora investment (Gillespie, Sayre, and Riddle 2001).[4]

Unfortunately, some donor initiatives better serve as examples of what not to do—for example, the USAID-sponsored program www. IraqPartnership.org announced at a meeting with the Iraqi American community in Michigan in September 2005. In then administrator Andrew Natsios's own words, the initiative was framed precisely to target the diaspora community: "We view the Iraqi-American community as an important partner. We know that you are eager to assist and in response we have developed a tool that allows you to contribute directly to local development projects in Iraq" (Natsios 2005). Despite these intentions, the Web page makes no effort to link with or reach out to diaspora organizations in its appeal for donations to support community projects. The site is impersonal and US government focused. It offers no opportunities for diaspora members to engage—other than with their dollars—for example, in suggesting project ideas or providing feedback on advertised initiatives. From its announcement in September to the following January, the "Partnership" raised only $1,500. If the partnership in question had truly been made with diasporas, the results might have been less lamentable.[5]

Migration is not likely to diminish, and diasporas are active with or without an intervening role of foreign aid. The challenge forward for the foreign aid community is to (1) respectfully acknowledge the nature of household remittances and support their expansion of household options and choice, (2) recognize diasporas as an active and legitimate actor in the development arena, and (3) develop policies and programs, with diaspora organizations and sending and receiving governments, to better harness and enhance constructive development contributions.

Notes

1. See, for example, regarding Somalia (Brinkerhoff 2006a) and Afghanistan (Brinkerhoff 2004). It was also quoted by a Haitian diaspora member in a discussion concerning "Haiti's Diaspora: Can It Solve Haiti's Enduring Social Conflict?" (Washington, DC, US Institute of Peace, July 25, 2006).
2. For a case study from Nepal, see Brinkerhoff (2005).
3. See, for example, the EU (European Union) and the International Organization of Migration Return of Qualified Afghans Program. Also, the Development Gateway lists available jobs by country and maintains active participation from and links with diaspora organizations from a variety of countries.
4. Pieke, Van Hear, and Lindley (2005) caution donors not to seek to formalize informal money transfer systems, since these systems emerge as adaptive responses to the constraints and opportunities presented to heterogeneous migrant groups. *Hawala* systems, for example, are based on trust and telecommunications and often do not require receipt of the money prior to transfer. They are typically less costly than formal systems. Many migrants find such systems particularly helpful in the early stages of their migration before they have been able to enter the formal banking market in the host country.
5. The poor performance, if not failure, of this initiative was a subject of complaint in one of USAID administrator Andrew Natsios's last interviews before leaving office, wherein he placed the blame on lack of media attention (National Public Radio interview, January 14, 2006).

Part 1

Diasporas' Response to Homeland Conflict

WORLDWIDE, CONFLICTS ABOUND,[1] and OECD (Organization for Economic Cooperation and Development) member countries are spending billions of dollars for postconflict reconstruction and development.[2] These conflicts produce many refugees and are the cause for much migration.[3] Analyses of the role of diasporas in security and conflict have concentrated on their support for insurgencies and their contribution to political instability (see, for example, Byman 2001; King and Melvin 1999/2000; Cohen 1996). Few studies have instead focused on the potential constructive contributions of diasporas to homelands experiencing or emerging from conflict.

The role of diasporas as interest groups in conflict-torn homelands must be acknowledged for any realistic understanding of their potential constructive contributions. Diaspora nationalist movements can influence homeland politics, fostering instability and supporting continuing conflict, as documented, for example, among Sikhs and Hindus in diaspora (Biswas 2004). Sometimes the aim of diaspora identity politics is simply to keep the ethnic identity alive; often this objective combines with more political aims to create and sustain an ethnic homeland. For example, in the 1990s, Kurds in London broadcasted Kurdish-language television throughout Europe and into Turkey at a time when Turkey did not permit Kurdish-language television. The program featured folk dances, children's programming (Marcus 1995; qtd. in Koslowski 2005b), and alternative news reporting, including issues of Kurdish human rights (Verrier 1997).[4] Diaspora members have been known to become more "ethnic" than their ethnic counterparts who remain in the homeland, sometimes even reinventing their identities and histories. This is well documented in the Hindutva (Hindu Nationalist) movement (see Lal 1999; Rai 1995; for the Alevi case, see Sökefeld 2002).

The international community recognizes that sustained peace must account for the interests of nationals who have left their geographic homeland, whether they intend to return or not. Depending on the nature of the conflict and the make-up of refugee and migration waves, diasporas likely reflect the very factions that led to conflict. Reconciliation may necessitate their participation in peacebuilding and reconstruction. For example, diasporas are important constituents for constitutional processes. Hence, significant efforts were made to include the Afghan diaspora, primarily in Germany and North America, in the drafting of the Afghanistan Constitution in 2002; broad participation from the diaspora was also sought for providing feedback on the draft, including through Afghan diaspora online discussion forums (e.g., AfghanistanOnline) (Brinkerhoff 2004). Diasporas as interest groups can additionally assist in reconstituting legitimacy for postconflict governments. For example, campaigning for the 2005

Liberian elections may have been more intense in the United States than in Liberia itself (see Lubkemann, Chapter 3).

The very affinity that may result in supporting conflict also lends itself to reconstruction and development, as the chapters in this volume attest. Janelle Kerlin's review of organizations in the Afghan American diaspora (Chapter 2) suggests that homeland crisis may inspire renewed interest even among later diaspora generations (see also Brinkerhoff 2004). Beyond more general support, this interest may target issues and needs specific to countries emerging from conflict. In fragile and postconflict states, diasporas contribute to governance by supporting effectiveness, legitimacy, and security. For instance, the Afghan diaspora supports development projects, notably rebuilding for education; the Egyptian Copt diaspora holds the government accountable for implementing its own laws vis-à-vis discrimination against Copts; and the Somali digital diaspora discusses issues and prospects for rebuilding Somalia across clan divides, potentially discouraging members from engaging in direct conflict (Brinkerhoff 2007).

Particularly in postconflict scenarios, tapping the diaspora may at once be necessary and unavoidable, given the drive among some diaspora members to insert themselves into the rebuilding process. This introduction to Part 1 reviews diasporas' potential constructive contributions to postconflict peace and development. It concludes with implications for both postconflict homeland governments and the international community.

Diaspora Contributions to Conflict and Postconflict Societies

Diaspora contributions to postconflict reconstruction and development can be significant, and their role may be essential, especially since the track record of donor attention to the long haul of postconflict reconstruction is abysmal. In a study of ten postconflict countries, a pattern emerged wherein official development assistance spiked in the immediate aftermath, gradually declined in the subsequent two years, and then fell "precipitously" (Schwartz, Hahn, and Bannon 2004; qtd. in Blair 2007, 166). The most noticeable and commonly recognized diaspora contributions include: economic remittances, human capital, and political influence, including international advocacy.

Remittances

Despite the attention to remittances generally, less studied and understood are remittance volumes and impacts in countries embroiled in or recovering from conflict. That remittances are essential to sustaining livelihoods during conflict is well known. But their contribution to peacebuilding, reconstruction, and postconflict development requires more research and analysis. By sustaining livelihoods and basic services during conflict, diaspora remittances may represent a foundation upon which peace and development can be expanded (see Fagen and Bump 2006). Importantly, remittances may be the only factor preventing disarmed and demobilized combatants from reengaging in violence, especially when jobs may be scarce in the immediate aftermath of conflict (see Lubkemann, Chapter 3). Since by definition conflict countries have hampered institutions or nonexistent institutions, most financial transfers occur through the informal sector, exacerbating concerns about their application to the conflict itself. These systems are often major conduits for external actors—including businesses and development agencies. As Stephen Lubkemann's review of the Liberian experience (Chapter 3) illustrates, during conflict, diaspora members may not question the need to send remittances; but as the homeland transitions toward peace, they may be more likely to ask for justifications for requests and to evaluate each one accordingly.

Studies of economic remittances to Somalia may be illustrative for other conflict and postconflict countries (see Maimbo 2006). Remittances are estimated to support 40 percent of urban household incomes (Kulaksiz and Purdekova 2006), and have supported education investments throughout Somalia's long conflict (Lindley 2006). Remittances have driven the development of financial service mechanisms and communication technologies (Maimbo et al. 2006), and have expanded trade (Nenova and Harford 2004). Waldo (2006) reports that these financial systems are not as informal as may be assumed. Among other things, they enjoy broad trust from diverse groups based, in part, on some degree of transparency.

Human Capital

Diaspora populations may be one of the most fruitful sources for human capital for reconstruction and development.[5] Human capital contributions may take the form of repatriation or shorter-term philanthropic support. On the latter, for example, the US-based Liberian diaspora is planning to retrain medical staff and rebuild the University of Liberia and Cuttington College (Lubkemann, Chapter 3).

Diaspora human capital is often necessary to staff and restaff government and development programs. For example, in Afghanistan and Iraq, the filling of specific government and development positions was and is solicited from among diaspora members with the requisite expertise; similar recruitment occurred in the former Soviet Union and Eastern Europe (see, for example, King and Melvin 1999–2000; see also Shain 1994–1995). While not often documented or systematically researched, international organizations and their contractors look to diaspora populations to staff their reconstruction projects and programs. Derick Brinkerhoff and Samuel Taddesse's (Chapter 4) review of the Research Triangle Insitute's (RTI International) efforts to recruit from the diaspora to staff the Local Governance Program in Iraq may be the first published documentation to date. Through the private sector, diaspora members bring their entrepreneurism, knowledge, and skills, sometimes as the first to invest in postconflict countries, whether due to perceived ethnic advantage, a more informed risk analysis, or altruism (as discussed in Part 2). Furthermore, diasporas can combine cultural and/or language knowledge and local networks with skills, knowledge, and networks from abroad (as discussed in Part 3) for the purpose of jump-starting reconstruction efforts.

Research has shown for some time, and recent debates on migration have highlighted, that migrants are more likely to return (permanently or temporarily) if they have permanent legal status in the host country. Such status may be more likely in the case of the highly skilled, who receive preferential treatment in the immigration process. But this may not always be the case, particularly for those who may be the best match of skills to needs in the homeland, and particularly in postconflict situations, where residential standing may be based on temporary legal status.

Permanent return may not be necessary or realistic. Migrants may have the motivations to serve the homeland, but at the same time may enjoy a quality of life in an adopted homeland, perhaps with a set career trajectory and children integrated into the host culture, such that permanent return is not desirable. Rather than forgoing their potential knowledge and skills contributions altogether, temporary, virtual, and circular options may be more palatable and even welcomed options. Participating in short-term consultancies through the development industry is one such way to contribute without full repatriation (Brinkerhoff and Taddesse, Chapter 4). Philanthropic opportunities for short-term skills transfers are also organized by diaspora organizations for that purpose—for example, by Afghans4Tomorrow (Brinkerhoff 2004).

Diaspora participation may be essential for the expertise that is needed but may also pose challenges to security and the legitimacy of reconstruction efforts. First, a recent review of postconflict state building confirms that the repatriation of diaspora members can lead to the emergence of a new political elite, which can give rise to new political tensions (Chesterman, Ignatieff, and Thakur 2004). As early as 1976, Armstrong suggested that the privileged position of such repatriated diaspora members would be short lived, since they would continue to be perceived as outsiders and the value of their contributions would diminish with the acquisition of these skills by native elites. For example, the experience of Eastern Europe in drawing from its diaspora to staff key political and governmental positions was short lived because Western diaspora members came to be seen as threats to the local political and economic elites (for the Ukraine experience, see King and Melvin 1999/2000). Diaspora members may have mixed motives for seeking participation in the reconstruction of their homelands. Some may aspire to political power and influence, exacerbating these tensions as well as the other challenges noted below.

A second set of challenges pertains to the diaspora experience itself. Those who have professional skills are often the first to leave and the most likely to successfully integrate into receiving societies, and therefore may be less inclined to return even for short-term service opportunities (see, for example, IOM 2005). Those who do return may face resentment and blatant hostility for having escaped the worst of the conflict (e.g., IOM 2005). Their perceived relationship to the homeland may even inspire a hubris, with inaccurate assumptions about the local culture and systems. Depending on the length of their separation from the homeland, they may be more or less effective at navigating political and cultural systems and reading associated cues. Research on diaspora human capital posits that effective contributions are most likely if the period of absence does not exceed ten to fifteen years (Olesen 2003). In postconflict countries, depending on the length of the conflict, it may be necessary to recruit from among these established diasporas anyway, given the loss of human capital and consequent extreme needs.

Experiences from conflict and postconflict settings confirm these challenges. In discussing diaspora knowledge transfer in the Democratic Republic of Congo, Bernard Lututala Mumpasi, rector of Kinshasa University, confirms that returnees may be out of touch with the needs and relevance of their expertise to their native country. Furthermore, he notes that these returnees may manifest disdain for their local counterparts and systems. Such disdain, whether real or imagined, yields significant resentment on the part of local residents, "who, in extremely difficult conditions, make sacrifices . . . to continue to operate, despite being abandoned by politicians and development actors" (qtd. in Government of Belgium et al. 2006, 231). Return programs in Bosnia and Herzegovina, for whatever purpose, generated substantial resentments on the part of continuous residents when the programs provided subsidies in the form of salaries or housing assistance as incentives for returning, to which local residents had no access (see, for example, Black 2001).

Political Influence

Diaspora communities may be explicitly maintained and mobilized for the purpose of influencing international public opinion and building political support for human rights and political freedoms (see Shain 1994–1995). One of the largest contributions diasporas make to insurgencies is through diplomatic pressures (Byman 2001). Assessing the potential opportunity or risk of diaspora advocacy efforts can be challenging. Sometimes partisan interests are at play under the guise of inclusive and democratic platforms, as noted by a member of the Rwandan diaspora residing in Europe (Mohamoud 2005, 48). For better or for worse, home country governments recognize that even settled diasporas "can still advance state consolidation and national development from abroad" (Levitt 2001; qtd. in Nyberg-Sorensen, Van Hear, and Engberg-Pedersen 2002, 18).

Diaspora advocacy may highlight human rights abuses and seek to engage the US government in negotiations with homeland governments. For example, the US Copts Association participated in strategy sessions with President George W. Bush regarding the case of Dr. Saad Eddin Ibrahim, head of the Ibn Khaldun Center for Development Studies in Cairo. Ibrahim had been imprisoned in Egypt allegedly on corruption charges. His case sparked an international advocacy effort, which argued that he was being harassed due to his work on human rights (Brainard and Brinkerhoff 2006).[6]

Diasporas may also mobilize to advocate for peace. In diaspora, ethnic groups who share a geographically defined homeland may mobilize around a unified diaspora identity in order to promote peace in their homelands. For example, the Sudanese diaspora in the Netherlands mobilized across ethnic lines for a peace tour to demonstrate that peace across ethnic lines and based on an overarching Sudanese identity is possible. Cross-cutting cleavages prevent conflict because "they create multiple loyalties, mutual dependencies, and common interests" (Coser 1956; qtd. in Leatherman et al. 1999, 59). These new identities increase the degree of trust across category boundaries.

Finally, as noted above, diasporas are important political constituents in homeland political processes. As Lubkemann describes (Chapter 3), there are fourteen counties in Liberia, yet it is often said that five more exist in the United States (Providence, Philadelphia, the District of Columbia, Staten Island, and Minneapolis). The diaspora at once financed the presidential campaigns for the 2005 elections and provided many of the candidates, including the president, Ellen Johnson Sirleaf. The Liberian diaspora represents the technocratic class of Liberia and is likely to continue its heavy influence on the politics and development of Liberia (Lubkemann, Chapter 3).

Philanthropy

While diaspora philanthropy is common across most countries, whether in conflict or not, in war-torn societies, the motives may be solely philanthropic or combined with aspirations for peace. For example, Salih Kaki from the Sudan Civil Society Forum explains diaspora philanthropy as progress on a learning curve. She confirms why diasporas remain politically involved in their war-torn homelands and suggests that tactics may be changing as diasporas gain a better understanding of how to meet their ultimate objectives:

> Most of us are victims of the bad politics back home. It is because of this painful experience that we have developed this prevailing tendency of supporting different political groupings at home that wage divisive politics and do not want to compromise. There are now attempts by some of us to break this totalizing tendency and relate to the situation back home in a nonpolitical manner. For example, we want to foster conflict transformation in Sudan through the civil society channels. In this respect, we want to promote peace through development by focusing on other very important non-political issues, such as community self-help projects and socioeconomic developments . . . changing the old attitude will not be easy but it is our realisation now that as diaspora we can be more effective in promoting peace in our homeland if we stop relating to the situation back home mainly through political channels. (Qtd. in Mohamoud 2005, 28)

Challenging conditions in the homeland may foster greater philanthropic interest within the diaspora. In response to traditional humanitarian need, for example, one Pakistani diaspora organization (DO) in Britain raised $25 million for relief in the aftermath of the 2005 Kashmir earthquake (Özerdem 2006). As seen in postconflict societies, homeland crisis may also inspire renewed interest among later diaspora generations. Kerlin (Chapter 2) documents how the end of the Taliban regime in Afghanistan spawned the creation of new DOs to support its reconstruction. This event also mobilized many second-generation Afghan Americans for the first time (Brinkerhoff 2004). Some of this support may derive from small-scale, informal efforts. For example, as Lubkemann describes (Chapter 3), after conflict a proportion of financial remittances may be transitioned to in-kind remittances in order to support humanitarian aims, seed microenterprises, or pursue rebuilding and development projects. Liberia has witnessed such a partial transition as diaspora members have sought to reduce dependencies.

On their part, DOs can provide simple and flexible ways for diasporas to contribute skills and resources to philanthropic efforts. Participation is for the most part not very taxing, since it often concerns financial donations, product purchase, and/or information exchange. As they do more generally, in postconflict societies, DOs represent important opportunities for more formal development organizations to solicit information for reconstruction and humanitarian programs, and to disseminate information about priorities and programming, potentially reducing duplication and cross-purpose efforts (Brinkerhoff 2004). DOs' intermediary role among traditional development actors, diasporas, and local communities may be particularly important in postconflict societies, where information and access may be scarce.

Examples from Afghanistan (Brinkerhoff 2004) and Liberia (Chapter 3) serve to illustrate some of the advantages of diaspora philanthropy in postconflict societies. Afghans4Tomorrow is a "non-political organization dedicated to the reconstruction and development of Afghanistan . . . [that] provides essential services to its people through the expertise, knowledge and dedication of Young Afghan Professionals abroad."[7] A4T is a vehicle for members of the Afghan American diaspora to take leave and vacation time from their jobs in order to go to Afghanistan and make contributions of time, energy, and expertise to the rebuilding effort. A4T is particularly innovative in reducing the costs to labor contributions by framing opportunities for the short term, potentially implemented during vacations from full-time jobs or school in the adopted country. Among the projects A4T has implemented in Afghanistan are Ministry of Finance (MOF) training and staffing support, and support to schools. While development industry actors face security issues on the ground in Afghanistan, particularly outside of Kabul, A4T participants enjoy a comparative advantage of knowing the language and culture and blending in as needed.

In 2004 the Liberian Community Association of Northern California shipped a container worth over $12,000 in medical supplies and contributed $30,000 to rehabilitate three hospitals. Over seven years another Liberian DO supported postsecondary education for more than 2,000 refugees in Ghana, providing and administering an annual budget of $150,000. Lubkemann also describes smaller, ad hoc efforts including "Edward," who provided $800 to rebuild the road and three bridges connecting his home village to Monrovia. He subsequently provided an additional $500 for chainsaws and training to start a lumber business.

Implications

The potential contributions of diasporas to peace, stability, and development in conflict and postconflict societies are varied and significant. Postconflict governments and the international community ignore diasporas at their peril. While diasporas have been a factor in stakeholder and conflict analyses for some time, they have not been a major focus of analyses for rebuilding and development, excepting the repatriation of refugees and political and government leadership. Part 1 emphasizes the potential constructive contributions of diasporas through remittances, human capital, political influence, and philanthropy—in part to counterbalance the prevailing and historical emphasis.

Constructive and significant contributions not only suggest a rationale for support; in some cases it may be prudent for postconflict governments and development actors to more proactively recruit from the diaspora and partner with DOs. DOs can provide important intermediary functions, linking development needs and investment opportunities to qualified and interested diaspora members. DOs' comparative advantages, noted above, may also serve to facilitate the development programming of these more traditional actors.

Diaspora members' security in the adopted homeland or host society informs their decision to constructively contribute to homeland reconstruction. Uncertainty and insecurity can contribute to marginalization—social, economic, political, and even psychological. Such marginalization may lead some vulnerable individuals and populations to recruitment into violent activities (see Brinkerhoff 2008a). In addition, studies show that permanent legal status enhances diasporas' incentives and enables their support to the homeland. Interestingly, Liberian president Ellen Johnson Sirleaf has lobbied the US government to grant permanent residence to the many Liberians residing there, or at least to extend their Temporary Protective Status. If Liberians—or other diaspora members, for that matter—knew that they could come and go with impunity, they might be more inclined to investigate options for return, as well as support from abroad.

The following chapters illustrate in greater detail how diasporas' interest in the homeland may be inspired by postconflict opportunities for hope and rebuilding (Kerlin on the Afghan American diaspora), such that they make a range of philanthropic contributions (Lubkemann on Liberia), including limited-term participation in development industry projects and programs for rebuilding their homelands (Brinkerhoff and Taddesse on Iraq).

—Jennifer M. Brinkerhoff

Notes

1. Since the end of World War II, 231 armed conflicts have been recorded worldwide, with 121 of those occurring since the end of the Cold War alone (Harbom, Högbladh, and Wallensteen 2006).
2. According to the OECD, member countries spent $79.3 billion on fourteen postconflict countries between 1971 and 1994, and by 2004 had spent $200 billion in Iraq alone (Barton 2004).
3. In 2005, conflicts generated 12 million new refugees and asylum seekers and 21 million internally displaced people; worldwide, 7.89 million of the refugees had been warehoused for five years or more (US Committee for Refugees 2006). In the United States alone, between 1980 and 2005, over 2 million refugees arrived and over 21.7 million became legal permanent residents (US Office of Immigration Statistics 2006).
4. MED-TV's broadcast license was revoked by the UK Independent Television Commission in 1999. Turkey lifted the ban on Kurdish radio and television programming, though retained heavy regulation, and several private companies began legally broadcasting in 2006 (*Turkish Daily News* 2006).
5. This section draws from Brinkerhoff 2008c.
6. In December 2002 a retrial was ordered and Dr. Ibrahim was released; he was acquitted of all charges in March 2003.
7. From Afgans4Tomorrow website, http//www.afghans4tomorrow.com.

2

Organizational Responses to Homeland Crisis: The US Afghan Diaspora

Janelle A. Kerlin

The growth of diaspora giving and the increasing recognition of the important role it plays in assistance abroad has begun to attract the attention of the international development community as well as the governments of developing countries (Newland and Patrick 2004; Dichter 2003; Orozco 2000, 2003; Orozco with Lapointe 2004; Lapointe 2004; Geithner, Chen, and Johnson 2005; Ministry of External Affairs [India] 2001). Much of the research on diaspora giving has focused on worker remittances (Ratha 2003; Nyberg-Sorenson 2004a; UNDP 2005) and hometown associations (Orozco 2000, 2003; Orozco with Lapointe 2004; Lapointe 2004). While these ongoing sources of funding are important, largely overlooked are other forms of diaspora organizing that work to mobilize resources for projects throughout the homeland particularly in times of crisis.

This chapter examines Afghan diaspora nonprofit organizations in the United States as a case study with important implications for how diaspora organizations generally in the United States might contribute to their homelands in times of crisis. The study focuses specifically on how the combined crises of drought and war in Afghanistan served as an apparent catalyst for the growth and expansion of Afghan-supported US nonprofits in years 2000–2002. The study finds that rather than family-to-family giving through worker remittances or community-to-community giving through hometown associations, many of these organizations worked nation-to-nation in the sense that they attempted to mobilize the Afghan diaspora across the United States to contribute to projects throughout Afghanistan. Data from the National Center for Charitable Statistics (NCCS) show how the combined Afghan crises appeared to spur on the development of new Afghan-supported US nonprofits, revitalize old organizations, dramatically

29

increase philanthropic giving, promote new collaborations, and help diversify types of funding.

Such national-level organizing appeared to be of profound importance for the ability of the US Afghan community to bring together and coordinate people, funding, and collaboration with outside entities for a larger impact on homeland assistance, reconstruction, and development. The Afghan experience holds major implications for international organizations as well as US and homeland governments that have an interest not only in the large-scale mobilization of diaspora communities but also in diaspora organizations that have a big-picture perspective on reconstruction and development. This research also shows the dramatic change that can occur in diaspora communities when they are confronted with crises in the homeland. While there has been anecdotal reference to increases in contributions in such times (Newland and Patrick 2004), this study provides a systematic before and after picture of changes in the organizational infrastructure of this part of the Afghan diaspora.

A few authors have begun to look at types of diaspora organizing that seek to mobilize and intervene beyond households and specific communities. Brinkerhoff (2004) examines the role of the Afghan digital diaspora in the reconstruction of Afghanistan using case studies of three grassroots organizations, two of which exist only in cyberspace. She concludes that these organizations "represent a wealth of information, human resources, skills and networks that can be mobilized in support of existing donor programmes and for the initiation of new ones" (411). Indeed, many of the organizations in this study have a cyber-presence, which suggests similar opportunities. Also, Johnson (2005) looks at the increasing scale of diaspora giving through traditional philanthropic foundations organized around giving to particular countries and regions as well as hometown associations.[1] Her insights are helpful in understanding the value of the several foundations in this study. Nonetheless there remains a dearth of information on the broad range of organizations outside of hometown associations that are important players in the transmission of "collective remittances." Nyberg-Sorenson states, "Although collective remittances may not be nearly as important as family remittances in economic terms, the extra-economic dimensions of organization and experience that accompany collective remittances represents an under-theorized and underutilized development potential" (2005, 2).

The Afghan diaspora organizations in this study include ethnic affinity groups, religious organizations, professional associations, charitable foundations, federations of associations, grassroots development and humanitarian relief organizations, and schools for the preservation of culture. Examples include the Afghan Elderly Association, the Afghan Community Islamic Center, the Afghanistan America Foundation, the Afghan Sports Federation, Afghanistan Relief, Afghan Health and Development Services, and the Afghan Academy. They range from small volunteer-run nonprofits to organizations receiving hundreds of thousands of dollars in revenue every year. As this study will show, some of these organizations initially existed primarily to serve the Afghan community in the United States, but became involved in assisting Afghanistan during the crisis period. A surprisingly large number were created specifically to address humanitarian, development, and reconstruction needs during and immediately after a homeland crisis.

Following a brief overview of Afghanistan's crises and a discussion of methodology, this chapter will review the findings from an analysis of National Center for Charitable Statistics data with respect to Afghan-oriented nonprofits. Specifically, the chapter reviews changes in activities, revenues and expenses, and overall financial well-being of these nonprofits over the period of crises and postconflict. It concludes with four implications for diaspora giving more generally.

Afghanistan in Crisis

The double crises of drought and war in Afghanistan came after the country had already experienced two decades of war and civil unrest stretching basic resources and infrastructure to the limit. The drought from 1999 to 2002 was one of the worst in thirty years. On July 19, 2000, the Center for International Disaster Information described the situation as follows:

> While the initial impact of the drought has been largely economic, the drought conditions are now beginning to take their toll on the health and nutrition of Afghans. The availability of potable water is also becoming a significant issue in urban and rural areas. Increased costs of limited food stocks in certain areas are forcing people to survive on famine foods. . . . It is predicted that between now and June 2001, at least half of the population of Afghanistan may be affected by drought. Three to four million people may be severely affected with another 8–12 million moderately affected.

The international community through the UN World Food Program and other organizations responded to the drought by providing billions of dollars in relief aid. International humanitarian operations were suspended, however, when all international aid workers were evacuated from Afghanistan following the September 11, 2001, attacks in the United States. In October 2001 the United States led an invasion of Afghanistan targeting Osama bin Laden and the Al-Qaida terrorist network for their role in the attacks. The Taliban government, then in power, was also a target for providing support and safe haven to Al-Qaida. International agencies did not return until December 2001. During this two-and-a-half-month period, food aid operations were carried out by Afghan aid workers and Afghan and Pakistani truckers (Kerlin and Reid 2005).

This series of events left Afghanistan in a critical state. Not only was there continued need for food distribution, there were also the enormous tasks of reconstructing the economy and the medical and educational infrastructures, constructing a democratic government, and relocating thousands of Afghan refugees returning to the country. Though billions of dollars in international aid were promised for the reconstruction of Afghanistan, coordination of the aid within the international community and with local partners presented other challenges (Kerlin and Reid 2005).

Beginning in 2000, NCCS data have indicated that these homeland crises spurred the Afghan diaspora in the United States to organize its own relief and development efforts. Most important, existing Afghan-supported nonprofits mobilized Afghan Americans for fund-raising and other purposes. Among other consequences, Afghan Americans also created many new organizations for the sole purpose of contributing to relief, reconstruction, and development in their home country. The following data provide a before and after picture of the catalyzing effect homeland crises had on Afghan diaspora organizations.

Methodology

The organizations in this study were drawn from a large database of digitized IRS (Internal Revenue Service) Forms 990 that 501(c)(3) charitable organizations filed with the IRS in years 1998–2003. Housed at the Urban Institute, the NCCS database provides access to a wealth of information on nonprofits, including location, revenue, expense, asset, and other financial information. It should be noted that this is a quantitative study relying almost exclusively on this database; therefore, motivations cannot be directly assessed nor can actual impacts be evaluated.

The data set of Afghan diaspora organizations in this study was selected by running a search on the names of organizations in the database that included any form of the word *Afghan*. While this approach likely leaves out many Afghan organizations, conducting a wider search that sifts through the tens of thousands of filings in the database for other Afghan-related organizations was beyond the resources of this study. Correlation of the organizations in this data set with major Afghan population centers (see discussion below), however, indicates that it is likely to be at least somewhat representative of the larger universe of Afghan nonprofits across the time periods in question.

The Afghan data set also comes with a few limitations inherent when using the NCCS digitized database to study nonprofit organizations:

• Only organizations with a 501(c)(3) tax status that file IRS Form 990 are included in the database. Organizations with other tax statuses are not included. Also, organizations with annual revenue below $25,000 and religious organizations are underrepresented because they are exempt from filing according to IRS regulations. Organizations meeting these exemption requirements but who still choose to file are in the database.

• Only organizations filing a Form 990 in the years 1983–2003 are found in the database. Even though organizations may have registered with the IRS and received a "ruling date" and/or filed in previous or subsequent years, if they did not file in the years 1983–2003, they are not in the database.

• Some of the forms in the database are IRS Form 990-EZ, which can be filed by organizations with gross receipts of less than $100,000 and total assets of less than $250,000. These forms do not include a separate line for government grants and thus are left out of analysis that involves such grants.

The selection method described above identified forty-one Afghan-related organizations in the NCCS digitized database. Form 990 filings for these organizations were arranged into two data subsets: filings for circa tax year 1999 and circa tax year 2003.[2] These years roughly represent the before and after period of the Afghan crisis. While there were only seven filings for circa tax year 1999, there were thirty-eight for circa year 2003. Data taken from Form 990 filings were supplemented with information gathered from organizations' websites and phone calls to organizations where needed.

The financial information taken from Form 990 filings for these years focuses on several different types of revenue and expenses as defined here. *Government grants* include all government contributions that enable the recipient "to provide a service to, or maintain a facility for, the direct benefit of the public" (IRS 2001, 18). *Private contributions* are a combination of what are called direct and indirect contributions. *Direct contributions* include gifts, grants, and bequests from individuals; giving by corporations, estates, and foundations; any funds raised by an outside fund-raiser in the name of the organization; and membership dues for which there is no return benefit to the giver (IRS 2001). *Indirect contributions* are those funds received indirectly from the public through solicitation campaigns undertaken by federated fund-raising agencies and similar fund-raising organizations (e.g., United Way). They can also include any money organizations receive from affiliated organizations, such as parent organizations sharing in the fund-raising of local affiliates and vice versa (IRS 2001).

Program service revenue includes those funds collected directly from recipients receiving services from the organizations (e.g., fees for service) or third-party payers (e.g. insurance companies). Aside from typical service charges, this also includes tuition received by a school, funds from admissions to concerts or other events, registration fees for conferences, and other forms of compensation received in exchange for a benefit. Program service revenue can also include income from government contracts for work performed on behalf of or for the government and fees paid for by government funds (such as Medicare or Medicaid coverage for hospital services) (IRS 2001).

Expense categories include program expenses, administrative expenses, and fund-raising expenses. *Program expenses* include the amount spent on activities the organization was created to conduct consistent with its tax exempt status. Program expenses also include the organization's unrelated trade or business activities that are taxable as unrelated business income. *Administrative expenses* are the amount spent on the management of an organization, including time spent directly supervising program activities or fund-raising. They may also include costs for meetings of the board of directors, committee and staff meetings of an administrative nature, general legal services, accounting, general liability insurance, office management, auditing and personnel services, annual reports, and investment expenses. *Fund-raising expenses* include the amount spent on soliciting contributions, gifts, and grants. Specifically this includes the cost of

> (a) publicizing and conducting fundraising campaigns; (b) soliciting bequests and grants from foundations or other organizations, or government grants . . . ; (c) participating in federated fundraising campaigns; (d) preparing and distributing fundraising manuals, instructions, and other materials; and e) conducting special events that generate contributions. (IRS 2001, 21)

Data Findings

Basic Characteristics of Afghan Organizations in the Data Set

Research on the Afghan nonprofits in this study first established them as Afghan diaspora organizations and then identified their basic characteristics. As a prerequisite, only those organizations that were involved with the Afghan diaspora—that is, were operated by Afghan Americans or involved Afghan Americans in their operation and/or support—were included in the final data set of forty-one organizations. Table 2.1 shows that the majority of these organizations were concentrated in states with the largest Afghan populations. Table 2.2 provides an overview of the scope of the work of these organizations, particularly with regard to Afghanistan. Significantly, none were found to be hometown associations.[3] The vast majority (73 percent) also had some type of activity that focused on assistance for the homeland even if an organization's primary purpose was to serve Afghans in the United States. Sixty-three percent were involved in activities to mobilize Afghans beyond their immediate US community for the purpose of assisting the homeland. For

77 percent of these organizations, these activities included a website through which they conducted fund-raising for projects in Afghanistan.

Table 2.3 shows the kinds of program activities in which Afghan organizations were engaged in Afghanistan. Assistance in education led the list and included books and funding for teachers as well as school buildings. Building or renovation of infrastructure included schools, orphanages, and clinics. Economic development included job creation and training, often specifically targeting women. Surprisingly, 44 percent of these organizations worked in collaboration with at least one international or government organization in the funding or implementation of their projects in Afghanistan (Table 2.2). Collaborating organizations included government entities such as the US Department of Health and Human Services and the US Agency for International Development (USAID), as well as large multilateral organizations, including the United Nations High Commissioner for

Table 2.1   Comparison of Top Ten States for Afghan Population and Concentrations of Afghan Nonprofits in This Study

States	Afghan Population[a]	Afghan Nonprofits[b]
California	24,569	12
New York	7,540	7
Virginia	7,101	6
New Jersey	1,823	1
Maryland	1,043	1
Texas	965	1
Colorado	767	—
Illinois	652	2
Pennsylvania	571	—
Washington	532	—

Notes: a. Ancestry data from US Census 2000.
b. Nonprofit data from the National Center for Charitable Statistics, nccs.urban.org; the eleven remaining nonprofits are spread out among states not listed.

Table 2.2   Overview of Scope of Afghan Diaspora Organizations Filing in Years 1998–2003 (by percentage of organizations)

Organization Scope	Yes	No	Unknown
Not a hometown association	100	0	0
Primary focus is Afghanistan	61	32	7
Operates programs in Afghanistan	73	10	17
Mobilizes Afghans across the United States	63	22	15
Collaborates with outside organizations	44	0	56

Note: Organizations could choose more than one response.

Table 2.3   Types of Afghanistan Assistance and Development Projects Operated by Afghan Diaspora Organizations Filing in Years 1998–2003

Type of Assistance	Number
Education	17
Economic development	12
Health	12
Infrastructure (schools, orphanages, clinics)	11
Basic relief	10
Democracy/policymaking	4
Agriculture	1

Source: National Center for Charitable Statistics, nccs.urban.org.
Note: Organizations could choose more than one response.

Refugees and the United Nations Children's Fund. They also worked with large and small international charities such as Rotary International, the International Rescue Committee, the Pax Christi Foundation, and Surgeons of Hope. There was also evidence of collaborations among organizations within the Afghan diaspora, often with professional associations such as the Afghan Medical Association of America.

Activity of Afghan Nonprofits over Time

The data set of Afghan organizations provided information on when organizations had their first contact with the IRS, either by registering or by filing a Form 990, and also any subsequent IRS filings for the years 1998–2003. While contact with the IRS does not necessarily mean an organization is new (though sometimes it does), it does indicate a certain level of formality and activity. Analysis showed there was a jump in the number of new and (re)activated nonprofits over the three years of the double crisis of drought and war. Figure 2.1 shows that in 2000, 2001, and 2002 the number of organizations making first contact with the IRS rose dramatically over the previous years and peaked in 2002, when both the drought situation and the aftermath of the United States–led intervention created the worst period of the crisis. The twenty-four organizations in these three years were either newly created during this period or were small organizations that had been in operation prior to this time but had not yet registered or filed a Form 990 with the IRS. Reasons for the latter likely include: they did not need to register or file because they had not ever before generated revenue exceeding $25,000, or they previously had no need for a 501(c)(3) tax status that would allow them to offer a tax deduction to donors.

**Figure 2.1 Documented First Year of Contact with IRS
for Afghan Organizations Filing, 1986–2003**

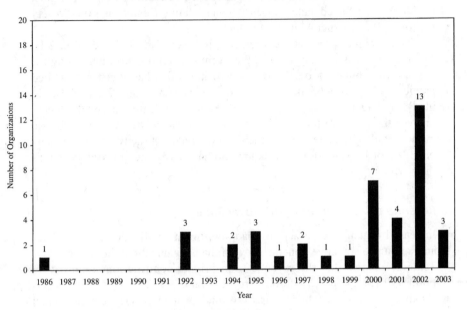

Source: National Center for Charitable Statistics, nccs.urban.org.

Further research is needed to determine whether the peak for first IRS contact in 2002 was also influenced by the more open political situation in Afghanistan after the fall of the Taliban, which could have encouraged the in-country work of new organizations or spurred on older organizations to increased activity. Also needing further investigation is whether or not heightened US government scrutiny of nonprofit financial activity in the post–September 11 period motivated organizations to register or file with the IRS for greater financial transparency. This may have been of particular concern for this set of Afghan organizations because of their dealings in the Middle East. Data suggest this is the case. Almost half of the thirteen organizations whose first IRS contact was in 2002 reported total revenue for that year well below $25,000: Organization for Aid to Afghan War Victims, Afghan Sikh Association of America, Women for Afghan Women (started April 2001), USA Cares for Afghan Children, Partnership for Education of Children in Afghanistan (started approximately 2002), and Global Partnership for Afghanistan (started November 2001).

The number of organizations that filed Form 990 before and immediately following the crisis illustrates the increase in Afghan organizational activity. Only seven organizations filed for circa tax year 1999. These included Afghan Academy, Inc.; Afghan Community Islamic Center, Inc.; Afghan Hindu Association, Inc.; Afghanistan Foundation; Help the Afghan Children, Inc.; Sayed Jamalludeen Afghan Islamic Center; and the Society for Aid to Reconstruct Afghanistan, Inc.

Thirty-eight organizations filed for circa tax year 2003 (see Box 2.1). The increase was due not only to the twenty-seven organizations filing for the first time but also to six older organizations that had registered or filed previously but had a break in filing activity. Data show that five of these six likely filed again owing to increased revenue streams that placed them near or over the $25,000 threshold that requires them to file a Form 990—an event that also indicates new or increased activity. Of the twenty-seven new organizations, twenty-one were known to have assistance to Afghanistan as their primary purpose.[4]

Revenue of Afghan Nonprofits over Time

Increased organizational activity had significant implications for the kind and amount of revenue generated by Afghan organizations in this data set. Table 2.4 shows that the revenue from private contributions reported on Form 990 filings increased 708 percent from 1999 to 2003. Organizations also began to diversify their sources of funding with government grants and program service revenue making up 2 percent and 1 percent, respectively, of overall revenue in 2003. Neither of these revenue sources had been reported in 1999. Private contributions, however, continued to far outpace other forms of income and even increased as a share of total revenue, from 90 to 95 percent, even though other forms of revenue appeared on the scene.

When looking at change across the individual organizational level, the shift from 1999 to 2003 remains significant. In terms of revenue size by individual organization, before the crisis none of the organizations generated more than $500,000 in revenue in a given year. After the crisis two organizations were operating in the $500,000 to $1 million range and one broke over $1 million in revenue. While the largest number of organizations (nineteen) in the circa 2003 file reported revenue of less than $50,000, the next largest number (twelve) reported receiving between $100,000 and $500,000 in revenue. Also, the number of organizations receiving government grants went from none in the circa 1999 file to four in the circa 2003 file in amounts ranging from $14,789 to $56,105.

An in-depth look at the five organizations that filed the more detailed Form 990 both in 1999 and 2003 helps to round out the picture of change (Table 2.5). First, not all organizations experienced an increase in revenue over the crisis period. The Afghan Hindu Association and the Sayed Jamaludeen Afghan Islamic Center both received less in revenue after the crisis than before it. Second, the large revenue increases of a few organiza-

Box 2.1 Afghan Organizations Filing with the IRS, Circa 2003

Continuing Active Organizations from 1998–1999
1. Afghan Academy, Inc.
2. Afghan Community Islamic Center, Inc.
3. Afghan Hindu Association, Inc.
4. Afghanistan America Foundation (formerly Afghanistan Foundation)
5. Help the Afghan Children, Inc.
6. Sayed Jamaludeen Afghan Islamic Center
7. Society for Aid to Reconstruct Afghanistan, Inc.

IRS Registered Organizations Filing Again in 2000–2003
After a Lapse in Filing
8. Afghan Center
9. Afghan Cultural Assistance Foundation
10. Afghan Elderly Association
11. Afghan Physician Association in America
12. Afghan Women's Association International
13. Afghans for Civil Society, Inc.

Organizations with First IRS Contact, 2000–2003
14. Afghan American Association of New Jersey
15. Afghan Coalition
16. Afghan Communicator, Inc.
17. Afghan Health and Development Services
    (Afghan Psychological Association of America)[a]
18. Afghan Relief Fund Inc.
19. Afghan Relief Organization
20. Afghan Sikh Association of America, Inc.
21. Afghan Sports Federation
22. Afghan Women's and Kids' Education and Necessities, Inc.
23. Afghanistan-Delaware Communities Together
24. Afghanistan Relief
25. Afghanistan World Foundation
26. Childlight Foundation for Afghan Children
27. Friends for Afghan Redevelopment
28. Global Partnership for Afghanistan
29. Hope Afghanistan Charity, Inc.
30. Islamic Association of Afghans
31. Islamic Association of Afghan Community
32. Mutli-Ethnic Afghan Schools and Humanitarian Assistance
33. Organization for Aid to Afghan War Victims
34. Organization for the Advancement of Afghan Women
35. Parsa-Physiotherapy and Rehabilitation Support for Afghans
36. Partnership for Education of Children in Afghanistan, Inc.
37. USA Cares for Afghan Children Inc.
    (Women's Alliance for Peace and Human Rights)[a]
38. Women for Afghan Women, Inc.

Source: National Center for Charitable Statistics, nccs.urban.org.
Note: a. Organization is not in the circa 2003 data set because it did not file in 2002 or 2003.

Table 2.4   Main Sources of Revenue for Afghan Organizations, Circa 1999 and 2003 (US dollars)

	Private Contributions	Government Grants	Program Service Revenue	Other Revenue
Circa 1999 filers (n=6)	761,500	0	0	87,110
Circa 2003 filers (n=32)	6,149,521	139,667	2,661[a]	123,118[b]
% change 1999–2003	708	139,667	2,661	41

Source: National Center for Charitable Statistics, nccs.urban.org.
Notes: a. Does not reflect revenue from multiyear, nonprofit, and government contracts totaling $160,870 the Afghan Women's Association International received in 2002.
b. Low number due to loss of $242,094 reported by an organization that lost money on a fund-raising event.

Table 2.5   Panel of Five Afghan Organizations Before and After the Crisis of 1999–2003 (thousands of US dollars)

	Circa Tax Year 1999				Circa Tax Year 2003			
	Private	Government	Other[a]	Total	Private	Government	Other[a]	Total
Afghan Academy	304	—	82	386	283	52	142	477
Afghan Hindu Association	63	—	1	64	49	—	—	49
Afghanistan Foundation	62	—	—	62	92	—	—	92
Help the Afghan Children	262	—	2	264	748	—	1	749
Sayed Jamaludeen Afghan Islamic Center	70	—	—	70	34	—	—	34
Total	761	—	85	846	1,206	52	143	1,401

Source: National Center for Charitable Statistics, nccs.urban.org.
Note: a. The "Other" category includes revenue received from dues and investments.

tions can make it appear that there were substantial increases across many organizations when there were not. In the panel the large increase in revenue experienced by the organization Help the Afghan Children largely carried the overall increase reflected in the total figure of $1,401,000 for circa tax year 2003.[5] Third, further investigation revealed that an organization may indirectly serve as the basis for the collection of informal donations for the homeland that are not reported on Form 990 filings. For example, the Sayed Jamaludeen Afghan Islamic Center, a mosque, though it does raise money on an organizational level, also serves as a gathering place where members individually collect donations and in-kind goods that are then privately transported to Afghanistan by members traveling there.

Expenses of Afghan Nonprofits over Time

Changes in the types of expenses that Afghan nonprofits generated suggest that, as a whole, they became more efficient in their operations. Table 2.6 shows that the large increase in revenue translated into about a thirteenfold increase in program expenses from circa 1999 to circa 2003. Meanwhile, administrative and fund-raising expenses increased 182 percent and 142 percent, respectively. Organizations were able to deliver more assistance with less administrative overhead than was the case previously, as suggested by the much larger increase in program expenses versus other expenses. Indeed, Table 2.7 shows how the percentage of program expenses increased dramatically versus the percentage of administrative expenses, creating a better economy of scale for the assistance and development projects of these Afghan organizations.

Financial Health of Afghan Organizations in Circa 2003

While the growth in number and revenue of Afghan diaspora organizations is encouraging, the question remains whether or not these organizations are

Table 2.6   Main Types of Expenses for Afghan Organizations, Circa 1999 and 2003 (US dollars)

	Program	Administrative	Fund-raising
Circa 1999 filers (n=5)	309,092	194,152	15,667
Circa 2003 filers (n=30)	4,005,761	547,334	237,921
% change 1999–2003	1,196	182	142

Source: National Center for Charitable Statistics, nccs.urban.org.

Table 2.7   Main Types of Expenses for Afghan Organizations as a Percentage of Total Expenses, Circa 1999 and 2003

	Program	Administrative	Fund-raising
Circa 1999 filers (n=5)	60	37	3
Circa 2003 filers (n=30)	84	11	5

Source: National Center for Charitable Statistics, nccs.urban.org.

fiscally strong enough to remain viable partners in assisting their homeland. Analysis of the fiscal health of Afghan organizations in the circa 2003 data set indicates these organizations were generally in good financial health in terms of both income and assets. Table 2.8 shows that about 70 percent of the circa 2003 organizations were operating in the black while about 30 percent were in the red. Research on the nonprofit sector shows that it is not unusual for substantial percentages of nonprofits to be operating in the red at any given time and that this situation is not necessarily cause for concern. Negative balances can often be attributed to cash flow imbalances in revenue and program expenditures that nonprofits show from year to year. Negative balances caused by these imbalances are often reconciled over two or more subsequent years (Reid and Kerlin 2005).

Even if all of the organizations shown to be in the red were operating at a loss, almost all of them have net assets (assets minus liabilities) they can fall back on in times of crisis. Table 2.8 shows that 87 percent of the circa 2003 organizations have assets they can use to counterbalance negative income balances. While average and median net asset balances were on the low side, the vast majority of these Afghan organizations had at least some asset reserve that could be sold or used to guarantee loans when income faltered.

Implications

This chapter analyzed the development of grassroots international development and assistance organizing that the US Afghan diaspora undertook in response to crisis in its homeland. Though further research is needed to test the relevance of this study for other diaspora communities in the United States, four main findings hold important implications for other diasporas as well as their homeland governments and other entities interested in reconstruction and development in foreign countries. First, homeland crises can

Table 2.8 **Percentage of Afghan Organizations with Positive and Negative Balances for Net Income and Net Assets, Circa 2003**

	Nonprofits with Positive Balance	Nonprofits with Negative Balance	Average Net Balance (US dollars)	Median Net Balance (US dollars)
Net income (n=38)	71	29	37,000	6,000
Net assets (n=38)	87	5[a]	125,000	37,000

Source: National Center for Charitable Statistics, nccs.urban.org.
Note: a. Asset information was missing for 8 percent of the data set (3 organizations).

act as a catalyst that dramatically increases private diaspora giving in support of development and reconstruction in the homeland. This study found that the double crisis in Afghanistan appeared to mobilize the Afghan diaspora to increase philanthropic giving thirteenfold toward funds spent on programming.

Second, homeland crises can lead to the creation of new diaspora nonprofits, many of which solely focus on (re)development in the homeland. In the study, twenty-one of the twenty-seven organizations newly filing with the IRS during and immediately following the crisis period (2000–2003) were international development and assistance organizations in their own right, with Afghanistan as their sole focus.

Third, many types of diaspora nonprofits can be involved in supporting the homeland and have agendas that go well beyond assisting their own family members and communities of origin abroad. In this study, community centers, associations, religious groups, and even an academy and sports federation were involved in providing broad support to Afghanistan.

Fourth, homeland crises can inspire new collaborations between diaspora nonprofits and other organizations. Surprisingly, almost half of the organizations in the study showed some type of collaboration with outside entities, ranging from other Afghan diaspora organizations and international charitable institutions to US government and United Nations agencies. Moreover, during the crisis period a small number of organizations began receiving government grants for their work for the first time. This collaborative activity holds promise for the wider engagement of diaspora organizations by the international community as well as homeland governments. Indeed, one potential area for collaboration that was noticeably lacking in this study were efforts by entities in Afghanistan, government or otherwise, to advocate and partner with Afghan diaspora organizations in the United States.

This study also points to the need for further research to determine the effect of new antiterrorist regulations, including Executive Order 13224 and the Patriot Act, on nonprofit organizations involved in international work. Follow-up research is needed to determine the number of organizations in 2002 that filed or registered with the IRS solely owing to the increased scrutiny and threat of new penalties imposed on individuals and entities brought on by antiterrorist legislation. More generally, research is needed on how antiterrorist regulations may discourage or impede the work of US-based nonprofits, especially those operated by people of Middle Eastern descent for the benefit of their homelands. While not numerically significant to make a real case, the fact that the only two revenue-losing nonprofits in the data set were organizations representing Middle Eastern religions raises some questions about whether antiterrorist laws may have discouraged giving to these organizations.

A Final Note on Diaspora Potential

This study has shown that while organizations may be created around a diaspora identity—sometimes with the primary or sole purpose of serving people and communities in the diaspora—these organizations can represent a ready source of capital to be mobilized in times of crisis in the homeland. Though this may not be true for all such organizations, the Afghan experience suggests that the contributions from these organizations to crises in the homeland may be significant. While this study has not investigated the actual effectiveness and impact of diaspora organizations, findings suggest that their mobilization and networking capabilities may make them an invaluable resource for fund-raising, organizing, and collaboration in service to their homelands. These findings hold important implications for homeland governments and participants in the donor industry (donors and NGOs) who may want to strategically target appeals to such organizations for material, in-kind, and human capital contributions to relief and development.

Notes

1. Johnson (2005) cites examples of the American India Foundation, the Brazil Foundation, and the Asian Foundation for Philanthropy.
2. *Circa year* means that filings for the given year were supplemented with filings from the previous year in cases where filings were missing from the given year.
3. This follows Alarcon's definition of *hometown associations* as "organizations . . . formed by migrants from the same locality with the purpose of transferring money and other resources to their communities of origin" (Alarcon 2000, 3).
4. Of the remaining six organizations, three did not have Afghanistan as their primary purpose and three were unknown.
5. Interestingly, Help the Afghan Children was the one Afghan-oriented nonprofit singled out and endorsed by discussants on AfghanistanOnline who were considering how best to help the homeland (Brinkerhoff 2004).

3

Remittance Relief and Not-Just-for-Profit Entrepreneurship: The Case of Liberia

Stephen C. Lubkemann

D ramatic developments in global travel and financial networks and in communications technology over the last quarter century have enabled more and more immigrants to become truly "transnational"—that is, to intensively participate in both their societies of origin and those of new settlements simultaneously (Basch, Glick-Schiller, and Blanc 1994; Levitt 2001b). In response, academics and international policymakers alike have recognized the need to better understand and account for diasporas in a variety of different policy arenas. In particular we have witnessed two surging lines of interest since the turn of the millennium. The first is in the role that diaspora remittances, human capital, and entrepreneurship can, and increasingly do, play in driving the economic development of many migrant-sending countries.[1] Second, there has been growing policy interest—and concern—with the political roles diasporas play in their countries of origin (Koslowski 2005a), and most particularly in the roles that exile groups play in spawning and supporting armed insurgencies.[2]

These two emergent lines of inquiry remain somewhat balkanized, in that studies of "political" and "economic" diaspora influence upon, and involvement in, homelands have demonstrated a tendency to run parallel to, rather than engaging substantively with, one another. Thus, relatively few of the growing number of studies that explore the roles of diasporas in homeland economic development—through remittances or otherwise—have also explored the political implications and effects of diaspora economic participation.[3] The "diaspora-in-economic-development" literature is particularly sparse in addressing war-torn developing countries. At the same time, those studies that have focused on the role of diasporas in conflict-ridden homelands tend to focus almost exclusively on political dynamics while paying very little attention to other forms of involvement, economic and philanthropic, that have garnered the lion's share of analytical attention in the burgeoning "diasporas and development" literature.[4]

This chapter examines some of the potential benefits of explicit cross-fertilization between these hitherto somewhat disparate lines of "diaspora inquiry."[5] More specifically, I explicitly extend the exploration of diaspora influence in a politically volatile context beyond the domain of politics itself, by focusing on diaspora economic activity (e.g., remittances and entrepreneurship) and on philanthropic initiatives that are more typically the focus of attention of diasporas and development studies in nonviolent contexts. This analysis of postconflict Liberia suggests that war-torn countries may constitute a special, though by no means insignificant, subset of the "developing world" in which some of the "conventional wisdom" about the role, relevance, and impact of diasporas in homeland economic development may require critical reevaluation.

This study focuses on likely the largest as well as the most economically and politically influential Liberian diaspora population—those who live in the United States.[6] Following a brief overview of Liberia's civil unrest, I will describe (1) the Liberian diaspora, (2) its economic contributions to the homeland, and (3) its philanthropic activities vis-à-vis Liberia. The chapter concludes with a set of hypotheses for future research. While these build from the analysis of Liberia, they speak to the potential role of diasporas in contributing to postconflict reconstruction and development more generally.

Liberia: Three Decades of Crisis

As a country that was deeply devastated by prolonged civil war that both produced and was influenced by a large diaspora, Liberia provides what is arguably a paradigmatic case for exploring such questions.[7] Liberia's descent into political turmoil began in 1980 with a coup that ended over a century of political dominance of Liberia's Americo-Liberian settler elite and brought a member (Master Sergeant Samuel Doe) of one of the nation's many politically excluded and subordinated indigenous groups to power. Despite an initial commitment to remedying Liberia's long history of social and political exclusion through democratic reform, Doe soon began to exploit ethnic divisions and violence in an effort to consolidate his power. Brutality toward political opponents and the ethnic groups from which they hailed increased dramatically after a failed coup attempt in 1983, as did corruption and misgovernance. On Christmas Eve 1989 a band of some 150 Liberian antigovernment insurgents (Ellis 1999) crossed the border from Côte d'Ivoire into Nimba County and quickly began to gain support from a population that had suffered some of the most severe ethnic repression meted out by the Doe government. Within little more than six months, the insurgency had swollen in size, splintered into rival factions, and succeeded in overthrowing the government and killing Doe.

In the wake of Doe's death and despite regional peacekeeping and international negotiation efforts, Liberia slid into seven years of horrifically brutal civil war, fought among a bewildering number of different factions led by warlords with different ethnic constituents and international backers. A tenuous peace brokered in 1997 brought one of the originators of the 1989 incursion, Charles Taylor, to power. Despite commitments to reconciliation, the Taylor regime continued a policy of brutal repression of political opponents and misgovernance for personal gain while fostering civil wars and political unrest in neighboring countries. Many of the estimated 700,000 refugees who fled Liberia during the 1990–1997 period consequently chose to remain in exile, while a large number of those who returned after the elections once again left the country. This movement accelerated as rival factions again launched armed challenges from neighboring countries against the Liberian government in 2000, sparking even more brutality from Taylor's regime in response. In the face of his deteriorating position as the armed insurgencies successfully advanced, and under considerable international pressure, Taylor went into exile in Nigeria in mid-2003.

A strong level of international commitment and intervention has played an important role in sustaining the peace deal that was brokered among the rival factions and allowed Liberia to fitfully, yet ultimately successfully, navigate a period of political transition that culminated in the election in October 2005 of Ellen Johnson Sirleaf, the African continent's first elected woman head-of-state. Although Liberia continues to confront many daunting challenges, Liberia's tenuous peace appears to be consolidating under the new government.

Characterizing the Liberian Diaspora in the United States

The quarter century of political violence and upheaval suffered by Liberia between 1980 and 2004 generated a global Liberian diaspora comprising several hundreds of thousands of displaced Liberians located in the "near diaspora" in neighboring West African countries (most notably in Sierra Leone, Guinea, Ghana, and Côte d'Ivoire) (Dick 2003), as well as smaller populations numbering in the thousands or tens of thousands that have relocated much farther afield, in the "far diaspora" (most notably in the United States, the United Kingdom, the Netherlands, and Sweden). Liberia's recently elected president herself actually lived for well over a decade in exile working for the United Nations and the International Monetary Fund.

Heterogeneity: Political, Social, Economic

It is important to establish a number of key historical, demographic, sociopolitical, and socioeconomic characteristics of the US-based Liberian diaspora in order to understand their potential contributions and relevance to the postconflict transitional process that Liberia has been undergoing since the end of 2003. Intense two-way migratory flows and spanning social networks between Liberia and North America predate the country's recent turbulence largely because of the unique historical relation that resulted from US involvement in Liberia's founding as a nation in the mid-nineteenth century (Beyan 1991; Sawyer 1992; Moran 2006; Lubkemann 2004a). Throughout the twentieth century the Americo-Liberian settler elite had a long history of sending their children back to the United States to pursue higher education or business interests. From its origins as a transient and socioeconomically privileged population of some few hundred students, diplomats, and businesspeople whose stay in the United States was relatively short-term up to 1980, the Liberian diaspora in the United States has both grown dramatically and changed considerably in composition over the last quarter century such that it is now an ethnically, economically, politically, and socially heterogeneous community.

All factions, ethnicities, and political interests are liberally represented in the US-based diaspora—a fact that also means that many, if indeed not most, of the divisions that have informed Liberia's turbulent conflict are mirrored in the diaspora itself. Whereas many of those who first sought asylum in the United States following the 1980 coup continued to be from the privileged Americo-Liberian segment of society, the several successive periods of Liberian political violence that followed generated waves overwhelmingly dominated by "indigenous" Liberians. These more recent refugee vintages (Kunz 1981) have reconstituted the US-based diaspora so that it includes broad representation from virtually every Liberian county and ethnic group. To the extent that my survey findings from Minneapolis and Massachusetts can be generalized to the whole community of Liberians settled in the United States, it seems likely that the descendants of the American-born settlers are actually a fairly small minority among US-based Liberians, probably representing between 10 to 15 percent of the entire disapora.[8]

The diaspora is also politically heterogeneous. The various vintages that have constituted it over the last quarter century reflect the ebb and flow of political power and the fortunes of various factions in Liberia's long political struggle, and—especially among the political class—the constant flux and realignment of political allegiances and coalitions. Successive waves of violence have brought political rivals to the same shore. Thus, for example, many of the "winners" in 1980, became the "political losers" of the early 1990s who were forced to flee the country. Finally, the diaspora also evidences significant socioeconomic diversity.

The socioeconomic elite was more highly represented in vintages prior to 1990, when the Liberian diaspora in the United States largely comprised those who came on student visas and when the Americo-Liberians were still disproportionately represented. By way of contrast, the most recent arrivals (after the turn of the millennium)—often as the result of their persecution as refugees in West African countries (such as Côte d'Ivoire) where they had previously found asylum—represent a much broader spectrum and, if anything, are socioeconomically skewed in exactly the opposite direction from the earliest migration/refugee waves.

Distribution and Size

One of the characteristics of the Liberian (US-based) diaspora that bears most significantly on its potential impact and relevance to the homeland is its size. This is also, however, perhaps the least well established of its characteristics, with estimates by major international organizations ranging wildly from under 10,000 to over 450,000.[9] Reputable scholars have usually guesstimated somewhere in between.[10] My own research has sought to narrow this range. Although subject to the technical limitations of working with diaspora populations whose parameters are notoriously difficult to define, my provisional estimate, based on a triangulation of the systematic surveys I have conducted and Department of Homeland Security data, significantly narrows that range to an estimate of between 26,000 and 31,500 Liberians (living in 7000–8,500 households).[11]

The distribution of the Liberian diaspora in the United States, although very broad (to date I have personally met or heard of Liberians living in thirty-one states), tends to be concentrated in several well-known urban concentrations. My research certifies populations of a minimum of 1,800 Liberians in Providence, Rhode Island, and 3,700 in Minneapolis/St. Paul. Populations that are likely to fall in a similar range are to be found in the greater metro Washington, D.C., area; Philadelphia; and Staten Island, New York. Other significant concentrations are known to exist in Worcester, Massachusetts; Atlanta, Georgia; northern New Jersey, Detroit; Chicago; and Boston. As Liberians in the United States have increasingly migrated from the East coast to the West, Midwest, and South, new concentrations have reportedly emerged in places as diverse as San Francisco; Lexington, Kentucky; Cincinnati and Cleveland; Miami; Durham, North Carolina; and Houston.

Envisioning a "House with Two Rooms": Transnationality and the Changing Life Strategies of Liberian Diasporans

The dire economic and political conditions that characterized Liberia's chaotic descent into over a decade and a half of war led many Liberians who found refuge abroad, and who initially planned to return to their home-land as soon as possible, to eventually begin to reconsider and recalibrate their life strategies. Although a majority of Liberians living abroad still har-bor a strong desire to reestablish homes in Liberia, their long stays in coun-tries such as the United States have inadvertently generated new social real-ities that have reshaped their social and economic aspirations. Many Liberians have started families and made significant investments in the United States, raising children, and in some cases even grandchildren who have never seen—or barely remember—Liberia.[12] In this sense, most Liberian households in the United States have strong social and economic ties to both their country of origin *and* their country of asylum. While many sincerely want to invest in their homeland and assist in the recovery of their communities and family members who remain in Liberia or are displaced elsewhere throughout West Africa, most remain understandably wary about the future political stability of a country that has witnessed the demise of fourteen previous peace accords in as many years, and are concerned about rampant corruption and the woeful economic and living conditions they would confront if they did return to Liberia. Liberians in the United States are keenly aware of how their war-torn homeland's precarious health and education environment could affect the life chances of their children and families should they return.

At the same time, their experiences in their land of refuge strongly rein-force other motives—such as kinship ties—for remaining involved and invested in a Liberian option. For many, the United States did not turn out to be quite the "promised land" they envisioned. Class, race, and ethnicity conspire to make life in the United States a difficult struggle for many if not most Liberians. Many work multiple shifts at menial jobs, struggling to pay the seemingly endless bills and support family at home, and finding it diffi-cult to conserve the energy or the money that would allow them to pursue the higher education that is so valued in the community. As has been the case for other refugee groups—particularly from Africa (Matsuoka and Sorenson 2001; McSpadden 1999; Abusharaf 2002; Shandy 2006)—many are deeply frustrated by the unwillingness of American employers or institu-tions to accept professional credentials they earned in Liberia or West Africa, forcing them to accept underemployment while they retake courses and degrees they already labored for and feel they have earned.

Moreover, in addition to suffering from the classism and racism that powerfully shape the US socioeconomic landscape, Liberians in the United States more often than not report experiencing further exclusion from the African American community, which sometimes interprets the Liberian dias-pora community's political engagement choices and economic behavior as lacking in commitment to antiracist agendas in the United States, or even as "complicitous" with a system that reproduces racialized structures of dis-crimination. The convergence of these different strands of structural violence plays a significant role in the reproduction of Liberian community identity in the United States, leading even those who were born in the United States and may have never seen Liberia itself to continue to emphasize their "Liberianness" in pointed distinction to other social identities, such as African American, more readily recognized throughout American society.

The experience of this tripartite exclusion of economic struggle, credentialism, and social isolation also plays a significant role in motivating continued involvement and investment back in Liberia itself. To many of those struggling in the diaspora, "Liberia" has become a particular type of narrative cast precisely in contradistinction to the forms of structural violence they experience in the United States itself. Thus, to remain involved and invested in Liberia is to maintain one's marker in an alternative social reality—a different possible world in which one's true social worth is recognized, one's talents fully utilized, and one's social standing acknowledged. An accountant in Washington, D.C., is transformed by such investment and involvement into a potential (and in some cases eventually an actual) assistant bank director in Liberia, a meatpacker in Minneapolis into a potential vice minister in Monrovia, a medical technician in Maryland into a possible provincial health department director, a graduate student in the Carolinas into a potential vice president of the whole country.

Increasingly, diasporan Liberians in the United States choose to think of themselves in new terms, as transnationals. In the context of this chapter, a transnational is a member of a diaspora who finds himself or herself with long-term commitments and responsibilities to both a country of origin and a country of resettlement. Such commitments could include marriage, children, relatives, businesses, school, and work, among others. For transnationals a permanent return to Liberia that would involve simply abandoning their social options or rights to participate in US society is no longer a foregone decision. At the same time, a transnational, unlike a permanent immigrant, is someone who, under the right circumstances, still seeks to invest and establish a home back in their homeland while also retaining a home in the country in which they found asylum. In short, diaspora transnationals are individuals who plot life strategies and see their social, political, and economic future as one that will involve investment and activity in two countries simultaneously.

An increasing number of Liberians in the US-based diaspora seek the opportunity to live the life of "the house with two rooms" (one in the United States and one in Liberia), an expression that has gained growing currency in the parlance of the community over the last decade. Among the 136 Liberian households surveyed in Minneapolis, only 26 percent asserted they had no plans to ever reestablish a residence of their own back in Liberia. Yet equally notable was the fact that 84 percent of those who did plan to reestablish a home in Liberia planned to maintain a residence in the United States as well. Moreover, even among those who did not intend to retain a residence in the United States after establishing a home in Liberia, 61 percent did plan to maintain a savings account or some other form of economic investment in the United States.

Economic Contributions of the
Liberian Diaspora to Their War-Torn Homeland

In the analysis that follows I seek to move beyond what is typically the emphasis on the directly political roles of diaspora elite involvement in war-torn or otherwise politically volatile homelands to explore how the economic and philanthropic contributions of broader diaspora communities may be relevant to the complex socioeconomic and political challenges confronted during postconflict transitions. If diaspora remittances, business investment, and philanthropic contributions are proving to be increasingly important to developing countries and economies as a whole, there are convincing reasons to believe that they are likely to be particularly vital to the economic prospects for countries that have endured prolonged conflict. Most obviously, diaspora remittances may be especially vital in sustaining basic livelihoods in the midst of the economically challenging aftermath of long-term conflicts in which markets have yet to reestablish themselves, employment opportunities are few and far between, and refugees are attempting to return and rebuild homes and reestablish crops or other forms of livelihood-sustaining activities.

The Impact of Remittances

The following data (see Table 3.1) collected from our survey of 136 households in Minneapolis indicate the significant level at which Liberian households in the diaspora reported remitting to relatives in Liberia—or those displaced throughout the West African region—during the years 2002–2004. To summarize some of the more significant findings:

1. Over a three-year period the 136 households surveyed reported remitting a total of just over $1 million ($1,007,718), or an average of just over $335,000 per year) to relatives in Liberia, as well as $631,230 to relatives living in other West African countries (Ghana, Côte d'Ivoire, Guinea, Nigeria, Sierra Leone).

2. Just over 72 percent of all Liberian households reported remitting during this time period.

3. The average amount remitted to relatives in Liberia per household per year ranged between $2,500 and $3,000 per year for all households in the three years 2002, 2003, 2004. If only the households that actually remitted are counted, then the average per remitting household ranges between $3,700 and $4,150 per year in 2002–2004.

Table 3.1   Remittance Behavior of Liberian Households in Minneapolis, Minnesota, 2002–2004

Remittances per Year, per Household (US dollars)	2002 (n=136)	2003 (n=136)	2004 (n=136)	3-Year Totals
>$10,000/year	7	2	6	
$5,000–$9,999/year	20	25	16	
$2,500–$4,999/year	24	20	21	
$1,000–$2,499/year	23	24	29	
$1–$999/year	15	15	14	
$0/year	38	37	37	
No response	9	14	14	
Total $/year to Liberia	368,261	326,566	312,891	1,007,718
Average all	2,900	2,655	2,585	
Average payees	4,138	3,797	3,725	
Total $/year to other West African countries	176,580	175,315	279,275	631,230

If the levels of remitting reported in these Minneapolis households are taken as reasonably representative of the Liberian diaspora in the United States as a whole, and if we extrapolate from the estimated total number of Liberian households in the United States (7,000–8,500), an aggregate picture of these remittances and their potential significance begins to take shape. Thus, by my estimations, the Liberian diaspora was remitting roughly between $19 million and $23 million in cash directly to family members living in Liberia in 2004, the first full year of transitional peace in postconflict Liberia—with an additional $10 million to $13 million going to the significant number of Liberians living in exile throughout the country's immediate West African region. The fact that Liberia's 2002 national gross domestic product (GDP) was calculated at $562 million ($168 per capita), while the projected 2006 annual budget for the government of Liberia (probably the largest employer in the country's formal economy) was merely $80 million (Richards et al. 2005), casts some useful perspective on the potential significance of these remittances for Liberia.

Valuing the "Consumptive Functions" of Remittances in Postconflict Contexts

It has become a cliché in the migration and development literature that the broader "developmental" impacts of remittances tend to be limited by the fact that these flows are mediated at the household level. Much recent policy debate has consequently focused on how to devise mechanisms by which to redirect at least some portion of remittance flows away from what is regarded as "developmentally unproductive" household consumption and toward other more "economically generative" activities (business or capital investment, savings, and so on) that supposedly will have a longer-term and more cumulative impact on local and/or national growth.[13] While the bias against the "consumptive functions" of remittances may merit some reconsideration vis-à-vis developing economies as a whole, I argue it should most certainly be seriously questioned in postconflict and other "quasi-emergency" contexts in which basic subsistence and survival itself is often at stake for the vast majority of the population. In such contexts, remittances may well play a role akin to that of humanitarian aid, and may be as or more important to the mere survival of warscape populations and refugees than the assistance provided by the formal international humanitarian system.

Thus, in just over half of the 129 household life-history interviews conducted in this project (through March 2005), the reconstruction of destroyed habitation was identified as one of the most important reasons for sending remittances to relatives. Arguably, in a country in which in 2005 over 80 percent of housing stock was estimated to have been destroyed (Richards et al. 2005), the role of remittances in facilitating the reestablishment of the most basic conditions for household subsistence and social reproduction should probably not be dismissed as "unproductive household consumption."

Almost one-third (32 percent) of all remitting households (n=84) reported that their remittances provided the primary form of support to over twenty individuals back in Liberia. Another 27 percent reported that their remittances represented the primary source of support to between eleven and twenty individuals, while 18 percent reported between six and ten individuals, and 23 percent reported between one and five individuals. Remittances are also likely to play an important role in enabling eventual refugee return from throughout the broader West African region. In 2001 the US Committee for Refugees estimated that over 200,000 Liberians had been dispersed throughout the West African region, including particularly large concentrations in Ghana, Sierra Leone, Guinea, and Côte d'Ivoire (qtd. in Dick 2003). My survey (in which households reported sending an average of just over $1,400 per year in 2002 and 2003 to relatives living in the West African region *outside* of Liberia) dovetails with the findings of other studies that have identified the crucial role remittances have played in the survival of many regionally displaced Liberians (see, e.g., Dick 2002).

Qualitative interviews in one site of regional Liberian displacement in West Africa (Buduburam, Ghana) in 2004 seemed to indicate that a significant proportion of refugees were requesting greater amounts of support from relatives in the United States than they had in previous years in order to prepare to return to Liberia, since the peace seemed to be consolidating. The survey conducted with Liberians in Minneapolis suggests that the diaspora in the United States responded to such appeals: on average the 136 households in the study indicated an increase of over 60 percent from 2003 to 2004 in the amount of money they sent (just over $2,300 per year) to relatives living in exile throughout the neighboring West African region. The tendency for the refugees both to visit former homelands before returning and to secure the quality of their eventual return by ensuring that they have the means (and often actual goods) necessary to rebuild and sustain themselves when they do repatriate has been extensively documented in the refugee studies literature (for reviews of this literature, see Allen and Morsink 1994; Koser and Black 1999). Analysts have yet to give much consideration, however, to how relationships and remittance flow among different segments of displacement diasporas (in the Liberian case, "far" and "near," respectively, from the United States– and European-based diaspora, and those dispersed throughout West Africa) may play out in postconflict repatriation processes.

The consumptive functions of remittances may also be particularly important—indeed central—to the process of consolidating and securing Liberia's hair-trigger peace in a context in which demobilized soldiers and unemployed youth still have very few economic prospects, and in which 75 percent of the population as a whole is estimated to survive on less than $1 per day (Richards et al. 2005). Lack of employment and a dearth of socioeconomic opportunity in Liberia and throughout the West African region are well documented as the fuel of social grievance that has often rendered the "economy of the gun" a least-unattractive option, particularly among the young (Richards 1996; Richards et al. 2005). As the following comments from a Liberian living in Philadelphia demonstrate, those in the diaspora are often keenly aware of how their remittances can matter in this respect:

> I am the oldest of eight (six brothers and two sisters). . . . Of the five that survive I am the only one who is in America. Four of the brothers have all been soldiers but on different sides. . . . One is killed in battle and one we do not know of . . . but the other two now stay together with one of our mothers. As long as they have some money in their pocket then they will be thinking about the future. . . . But if their pockets are empty then what is their solution? I am always sending a little money today . . . a little money next week . . . whenever I can I send something. . . . This small hope will keep them away from the gun.[14]

International aid organizations are often limited by their mandates or other forms of conditionality in providing assistance to particular warscape populations (such as returning refugees or internally displaced persons) and in giving less, or even none, to others (for example, "stayees"). Remittances—at least in the Liberian case—are far more likely to extend benefits across that country's warscape population as a whole, and thus may potentially mitigate some of the forms of social antagonism and conflict that repatriation and other forms of targeted humanitarian assistance have frequently been documented to generate (Anderson 1999; Koser and Black 1999; Minear 2002; Lubkemann 2004c, 2007). In short, the broader migration and development literature lamenting the "loss" of remittances to household consumption may grossly underestimate the broader social dividends of consumption itself—particularly for peace—in politically volatile and economically challenging postconflict contexts.

Recognizing the "Developmental Imperative" in Remitting

The Liberian case provides intriguing evidence that diasporans may be at least as concerned as international experts with seeing their remittances accomplish more than merely temporarily sustain relatives. In dozens of qualitative interviews conducted over the last two years, I have noticed a pattern of concern among Liberians living in the United States for seeing their family members "do something" with the money that they remit rather than simply "eat it." This objective has become more important as the possibility of lasting peace in Liberia has become more believable: "When there was the fighting no one could do anything. It was a real hand to mouth existence. But now with democracy arrived no one should just be sitting and waiting for Western Union" ("Marshall," Providence, RI, November 2005).

This shift in perspective has begun to reshape the social dynamics and organization of diaspora remitting behavior. Thus, whereas many Liberians in the United States used to remit on a regular basis during the conflict—often either monthly or during a particular holiday season—some have decided to purposely respond to the requests of relatives only on a per request basis, evaluating each request on its merits. Many are mindful in each case of what it is the money sent will actually (or at least purportedly) accomplish. As one young Liberian living in Providence, Rhode Island, explained to me:

> Sometimes my relatives will call me twenty times in a single day and it is always the same story: send money, send money, send money. [It seems as if] when I am sleeping this is all I hear in my dreams—send money, send money. . . . Because there are the two of us [he and his wife are both Liberian and have family in West Africa] the pressure is even greater. I can say there are more than fifty [relatives] who will sometimes call in one month. . . . Before we were sending $250 dollars every month. . . . When the money ran out then we would say that is all we have for the month. Now it is a little different. So, we will still send some barrels during July but now when they call we are first asking what the money is for. . . . If it is for an emergency like an illness we may try to send something [although] if they need the medicine we will prefer to buy it for them here and send it direct. . . . Sometimes it is because the medicines are not available [there], but sometimes we will send it even if it is less expensive there so that we know that it is really for the illness rather than to "eat the

money." When my sister called and needed school fees for the children I sent some money . . . and when she needed money to start some small fish trading business I also sent some cash . . . [but] when she called because she wanted to buy some relish [food] I asked her: "Where is your husband? Why are you still staying with that man when he is not even looking for work to feed his family? Am I supposed to be feeding him too?" ("Ben," Providence, January 2006)

Such accounts reveal that Liberians in the United States are increasingly interested in seeing the money they send home be used for what development analysts might term "generative" purposes, that is, to build human capital and start small enterprises that—small and ad hoc as they may seem—ultimately aim at job creation that will produce self-sustaining streams of income in the "homeland" (Liberia) itself.

This concern is further reflected in the growing preference for remitting in kind (rather than primarily in cash) reported by many of those Liberians in the United States interviewed in the course of ethnographic interviews conducted in 2005 and 2006. Whereas insecurity and corruption have long served as inhibitors for sending goods (as opposed to cash) back to relatives in Liberia, improving security conditions have made this an increasingly popular way to support those relatives. Although this form of remitting did not emerge as significant in the interviews conducted in preparing the 2004 survey, many respondents to ethnographic interviews in 2005 and 2006 (in preparation for a much broader survey) claimed that the value of what they were currently sending to Liberia (primarily in barrels) actually was greater than the amount they remitted in cash. Many respondents emphasized that one of the primary benefits of remitting in kind was that it enabled relatives to initiate small trading ventures:

If we send them shoes, clothes, books . . . anything they are telling us they can sell in the market—this is how we can set them up in their trading ventures. . . . If they are successful they will not be calling so often [to ask for money]. All pockets have a bottom. . . . This is why we need to think strategically. ("Michael," Washington, D.C., February 2006)

This objective of "weaning relatives from remittances" factors prominently in many of the qualitative interviews I conducted in 2005 and 2006. Ongoing and planned future surveys in Rhode Island and Philadelphia will hopefully provide an opportunity to document the generalizability of these ethnographic findings. At the very least, the ethnographic interviews conducted to date strongly suggest the following hypothesis: through their forms of remitting, Liberian diasporans are attempting to do much more than simply provide vital support for relatives. They are also actively engaged in trying to strengthen the economic capacity of relatives to sustain themselves through Liberia-based economic activity.[15]

Beyond Remittances: Not Only for Profit Investment

A very similar sensibility seems to be playing a significant role in other forms of diaspora involvement and investment in Liberia. In our 2005 survey of Liberians living in Minneapolis, 31 percent of household heads reported that at least one person living in their household planned to establish a business back in Liberia. Many had been setting the groundwork for some time. Thus, for example, in mid-2004 I encountered a Liberian businessman who had established a very successful computer training and Internet center on the outskirts of the Liberian refugee settlement in Buduburam, Ghana. Over seventy computers were in use twenty hours a day for a fee that was nominal enough to ensure a long wait for a terminal at peak hours, yet profitable enough to encourage the founder's pursuit of plans for a network of such centers in Liberia itself. Similarly, in 2005 a Community Credit Union was on the verge of being chartered in Philadelphia. The vision of its Liberian founders was to finance both small and large investments by Liberians—some in the United States, some in Liberia, and some that would finance import-export ventures between the two.

While many of those in the Liberian diaspora who described their ongoing entrepreneurial activities or future plans expressed an interest in eventually profiting from these investments, profit was not necessarily their primary motivation for starting a business in Liberia. Many expressed an even greater interest in a variety of potential social returns on these investments, often explicitly emphasizing these as the more immediate priority and expressing a willingness to wait much longer for, and even tolerate a great deal of uncertainty regarding, any eventual financial returns.

Thus, one Liberian professional in Rhode Island explained his plans to open a small trading and transportation business based in Liberia's capital, Monrovia, with branches in the two counties in which he retained kinship networks, Bong and Lofa. As he explained it, the most important and immediate purpose of this investment would be to provide family members in these three areas with employment. Although he envisioned eventually expanding the business and making a profit, profit—and even the business's survival in the long term—were not his foremost concern. He planned to start and support the operations of the business with income from two rental properties that he had acquired in North Providence, Rhode Island. These provided a "safety net" that allowed him to support himself and this venture; "even if that venture fails I will be able to build an 'operation' that will [eventually] locate other opportunities that will profit all of those relatives."

Another Liberian living in Providence (a part-time minister), explained how once he had obtained his permanent US residency status, allowing him to leave and return to the United States at will, he changed his job so that he could take two seasonal jobs (in construction and as a part-time security officer); this would allow him to work intensively for the part of the year he would spend in the United States and return to Liberia for the remaining months. The money he earned, he explained, was used to support a small business venture in which his goal was to employ as many of his relatives as possible; the reason he would regularly return to the United States was that he knew he was employing too many people (in Liberia) to allow him to actually make a profit. He foresaw that this would be the pattern for the foreseeable future, but eventually he would be able to support several young relatives in their own "start-up ventures." He believed they would "remember [me] as the basis of their success."

As with diaspora remittances, many of the business investments that Liberians in the United States are making or planning to make are driven by a complex mix of motivations and objectives that cannot be reduced to either an interest in profit alone, any more than they can be described as gestures of purely altruistic philanthropy. Although further systematic research is warranted, my initial ethnographic investigations suggest that while financial profit is of interest to many diasporan Liberian entrepreneurs, other forms of social return are often of equal, sometimes even greater, and quite frequently more immediate, concern than profit per se. By providing employment opportunities for relatives—even if this involves sustaining financial losses—some diasporan entrepreneurs are, like remitters, hoping to reduce the degree to which relatives make financial demands on their US-based kin.

Diasporans are also investing in social capital. In demonstrating concern for the welfare of relatives (by prioritizing their employment over immediate profits), some diasporan entrepreneurs are reconstituting social relations that have atrophied or otherwise been damaged during the war. By creating opportunities for relatives, diasporans can allay some of the suspicions and resentment that often characterize how those who stayed and endured the hardships of war view those who fled and (at least in relative terms) prospered economically as a result. Through their entrepreneurship, Liberian diasporans are thus renegotiating their position in kinship and community relations. In establishing social status and expanding social networks, they are investing in social capital that may also eventually prove vital in ensuring the financial success of other future entrepreneurial ventures.

Diaspora Philanthropy:
A Neglected "Third Humanitarian Space"?

There is also a considerable amount of diaspora philanthropy that is motivated by a similarly complicated mix of motives. Dozens of diaspora humanitarian organizations and initiatives have sprouted up over the last few years throughout the United States in an effort to provide assistance back home. Some of these initiatives are not insignificant in scale. Thus, in 2004 the Liberian Community Association of Northern California sent a container with over $120,000 of much-needed medical supplies and contributed $30,000 to the rehabilitation of three rural hospitals in Liberia. Over the last seven years, another US-based diaspora organization created and supplied funding for an education program that has successfully provided postsecondary education to over 2,000 Liberian refugees in Ghana, raising and administering a budget of over $150,000 per year. In 2005 the program graduated its first class of 200 teachers with associate degrees accredited by the nearby University of Legon. An expansion of this program into Liberia is in development. Major efforts are afoot among professionals in the diaspora to contribute to the retraining of medical staff and the rebuilding of the University of Liberia (UL) and Cuttington College. A major conference with this objective was organized by UL's director in 2005 at his former place of employment, the University of Pennsylvania in Philadelphia.

In contrast to the aforementioned initiatives, the overwhelming majority of diasporan humanitarian efforts are much smaller in scale and scope. They are often ad hoc efforts, undertaken by one or another of the literally dozens of local chapters of local Liberian community, alumni, or county associations, or by Liberian church congregations throughout the United States, that decide to send a few containers of food, medicine, textbooks, or school chairs, in response to a specific need. Frequently these initiatives are organized by and around the efforts of a specific individual who has recently visited Liberia, seen a specific need in his or her "home community," and become personally vested in seeing that need met. Such individuals may even contribute substantial amounts of their own resources to helping satisfy these needs, contributing cash and traveling back several times to ensure that the money is used appropriately.

In one such case, recounted at a local county association's 2006 annual convention, an individual (I will call him Edward), who worked three different jobs as a waiter in the Washington, D.C., area, described his remarkable contribution over the last two years to the remote village in which he had been born. His first visit to find relatives had required several days of journey by car, by boat, and by foot because bridges and roads had been destroyed by the war. During his visit it became clear that the greatest needs of the village stemmed from its problems with lack of outside access, primarily because the old road had been mined and three small bridges destroyed. With a contribution of $800, Edward provided the villagers with tools and resources they required to clear a new road and build three rudimentary bridges over streams that would allow a four-wheel vehicle to reach the community, if not during the entire year, at least during the dry season. Indeed, when Edward visited the following year, he was able to hire a car that took him all the way to the village itself in considerably less time than his first trip had taken.

On this second trip, community leaders asked for Edward's assistance in establishing a small-scale lumber extraction business. Above all they needed a chainsaw and funds to pay for a truck to take their first shipment of lumber to the nearest market. On his return to the United States, Edward purchased a chainsaw and sent it back through relatives in Ghana. When the villages communicated back to him that the chainsaw was breaking down, he paid for a Ghanaian operator to go and instruct the villagers in the chainsaw's use and to repair the machine. Once he was notified that the first load of lumber was ready to be sent to market, Edward had a relative in Monrovia hire an independent truck driver to go to the village. By his account a total investment of $1,500 had provided the village with the means to now run a self-sustaining, small-scale lumber extraction and milling business.

Largely unnoticed by the international aid community, such diaspora efforts cumulatively constitute a hitherto unexamined and unaccounted-for "third humanitarian space" (Lubkemann 2005a) that may be structurally different in significant ways from the international "postconflict apparatus" spearheaded by the UN agencies and well-known international NGOs. Elsewhere (Lubkemann 2005a) I have proposed the need for a deeper and more systematic investigation of diaspora humanitarians whose activities may offer new alternatives as well as challenges to policymakers seeking solutions to the daunting challenges of kick-starting war-decimated economies and pursuing postconflict reconstruction and development.

Questions for Future Comparative Research

Policymakers who do not account for the growing and increasingly complex economic role of diasporas in the postconflict transitions of war-torn countries such as Liberia do so at their own peril. To do so ignores a key and often confounding piece of the political and economic puzzle as well as an important potential resource. As an interim study in a much more comprehensive and still ongoing examination of the relevance of Liberia's US-based diaspora to that country's postconflict transition, I offer as a conclusion the following hypotheses as worthy of more in-depth, systematic, and comparative research. While these build from the Liberian case described above, they imply important considerations for diaspora involvement and postconflict rebuilding generally.

First, the initiatives of diasporan humanitarians and investors are likely to benefit from far more nuanced forms of local knowledge than typically evidenced by international organizations. It is well documented that humanitarian organizations consistently fail to adequately account for and address the social, cultural, and historical differences of the varied contexts in which they work (Anderson 1999; Smillie 2001; Minear 2002). Humanitarian organizations at almost all levels remain mired in a cookie-cutter mode of operation, transplanting programs and personnel largely whole cloth from one theater of crisis to the next. It has not been uncommon for the best-intentioned international relief efforts to prove not only ineffective but even harmful to their recipients because international humanitarian actors did not account for specific cultural norms, had little understanding of capacities that were already locally available, or did not understand local social, economic, or political dynamics.

By way of contrast with foreign technical assistants, diasporans are far more likely to be conversant in one or several local languages, be knowledgeable of the local and national history, and understand local social conventions. Such forms of "cultural capital" may enable diaspora organizations to identify problems in need of solutions in terms that more closely reflect the interests of aid recipients (rather than donors), and to pursue solutions that are more locally appropriate. By way of example, the bridges that Edward was able to fund for his hometown would likely be regarded as thoroughly inadequate by an international NGO or their donors. Yet they were built with local materials and know-how that ensure that for the foreseeable future, they can be easily repaired and maintained by the community itself without additional external inputs. Indeed, the scale of Edward's initiative was so small (in terms of financial outlay) that it would be highly unlikely to ever make sense as a viable project for an international NGO; yet it was arguably far more effective in identifying and responding to local economic needs than much larger and financially cumbersome international initiatives might prove to be.

Second, local social connections, when combined with local knowledge, are likely to enable diasporan humanitarians and investors to more accurately gauge and effectively respond to the nuances of postconflict market conditions, which are often both volatile and threateningly opaque to outside organizations. Liberia is representative of an increasingly common form of "fragmented war" (Lubkemann 2005b) in which many local social tensions that are unrelated to the struggle for state power play a significant role in scripting wartime violence. Knowledge of these subplots and access to those who can assess their dynamics are vital for assessing risk. Thus, for example, the aforementioned entrepreneur who ran an Internet and computer training center for his compatriot refugees in Ghana explained how he was drawing up his business development plan for Liberia not only by monitoring national political developments but also by monitoring locally specific political conditions in several areas where he envisioned establishing centers. This monitoring is based on information he receives from those who continuously circulate back and forth between the refugee camp in Ghana and those areas in Liberia. Similarly, Edward explained how his knowledge of a long-standing dispute between rival claimants to a form of traditional village office allowed him to successfully locate the bridge he helped the villagers to build so that the responsibility for its maintenance would not become entangled in that particular dispute.

Third, inasmuch as social connections play a significant role in determining where within war-torn societies diasporan philanthropists and investors choose to pursue their initiatives (and where remittances are sent), diasporic forms of aid are likely to have relatively greater social reach and potentially provide more comprehensive coverage than those offered by international actors. International investors are particularly unlikely to pursue opportunities in high-risk or inaccessible and logistically challenging areas that may still attract the attention of diasporans such as Edward, who are drawn to such locations despite such obstacles because of their social ties.[16] Moreover, even though humanitarian agencies are officially in the business of identifying and mitigating need and suffering, the de facto practice of the enterprise ultimately has a tendency to respond first and foremost to other taskmasters, such as the political proclivities of donors, staff safety considerations, and marketplace competition, which implicitly skew organizations to more readily consider shouldering the doable than that which may most need to be done. Thus, not unlike most postconflict contexts, any comparison of a "map of need" with a "map of aid provided" would evidence significant disparities, with humanitarian organizations more heavily concentrated in areas of more easy access (such as the national capital or a handful of other urban concentrations).

While in the Liberian case my own survey research indicates that the US-based diaspora is broadly representative of different ethnic groups, political factions, and regions, it should be noted that the capillary potential of diaspora aid in all postconflict contexts is heavily dependent on the correspondence between the social composition of the diaspora and the homeland population. Thus, the extent to which diasporas are themselves overrepresented by people from particular regions, ethnic groups, political factions, or socioeconomic classes is likely to influence both the coverage of diaspora aid and the political impact of philanthropic and economic postconflict contributions.

Fourth, an incentive structure that is responsive to kinship ties and membership in the society being assisted will differentiate diaspora initiatives from international efforts in several other important ways. I have already posited that an interest in social returns may be as or more important than financial returns to many diasporan investors in postconflict contexts. Some other important differentiating implications of this motivation structure include the following:

• The possibility that diaspora organizations will operate within longer-term horizons (than international organizations) that are delimited by the need of relatives and home communities rather than by the funding whims of bilateral donors that so often shape international humanitarian action.

• Both diaspora humanitarian aid and investment may have a higher risk threshold than international counterparts having no personal social ties to the communities they assist are willing to tolerate.

• Diasporan investors and humanitarians may be more willing to persist in the face of apparent losses and/or reversals, much as in the case of the part-time Liberian minister in Providence who actually structured an expectation of nonprofitability into his own privately financed short- and medium-term home investment/assistance strategy.

Fifth, the vast majority of diaspora aid and investment initiatives in Liberia (and probably in most other postconflict contexts) are very small in scale, which may lead some analysts to question their potential importance or effectiveness in contributing to postconflict socioeconomic regeneration. The potential benefits of microscaling, however, especially in postconflict contexts, may deserve more careful consideration and empirical research. Thus, for example, several Liberian diasporan church leaders emphasized the importance of remaining modest in their assistance efforts in order to more effectively navigate the rampant corruption and criminality that prevailed in Liberia during the early transitional period. As one church leader explained to me: "It is far better to send a dozen barrels now and another dozen barrels in six months, and then again after the holidays. Or maybe just one container at a time. . . . But if you get too ambitious and send a dozen containers at once then you will be noticed by those who have 'interests.' Big gestures make big targets." Such nuanced assessments of local realities cast some critical light on the international community's default interest in always seeking ways to scale up and may in fact suggest the potential merits of actually scaling down.

Conclusion

As we march into the twenty-first century, the unfortunate reality is that much of the developing world is also the war-torn world. In some postconflict settings, diasporan economic activity may be an innovative part of the solution for achieving and securing sustainable peace, human security, and development in war-torn societies. Yet diasporas may also undermine these same objectives in other ways, such as through predatory economic activity or by accentuating socioeconomic differentiation. In most cases, it is likely that diasporan economic activity will have many different—and sometimes contradictory—effects on postconflict development.

In conclusion, three things seem certain. First, policymakers in war-torn nations such as Liberia cannot neglect the diaspora factor if they seek durable peacebuilding and development solutions. Second, a great deal more systematic empirical research on the economic activity of diasporas in war-torn contexts is sorely needed. Third, scholars and policy analysts must consider whether the specific structural conditions in war-torn developing nations require a different set of assumptions and questions than those that frame the study of diasporas and development in nonviolent settings.

Notes

1. See Freedman (2005), Lowell and Findley (2002), Levitt (2001b), Meyer (2001), Hunger (2002), Orozco (2003), Newland and Patrick (2004), Nyberg-Sorenson (2004c), Orozco et al. (2005), Özden and Schiff (2005), Burgess (2006), Brinkerhoff (2006a).

2. See Shain (2002, 1999, 1993), Weiner (1993), Cohen (1996), Tölölyan (1996), Van Hear (1998), Pottier (1999), Collier and Hoeffler (2001), Sheffer (2003), Lyons (2004, 2006), Ostergaard-Nielsen (2006), Ögelman (2005), Lyon and Uçarer (2005).

3. But exceptionally, see Levitt (2001b), Glick-Schiller and Fouron (2001), Smith (2005).

4. But exceptionally, see Brinkerhoff (2004), Lindley (2006a), and Shandy (2006).

5. This discussion is an excerpt from a larger and still evolving project on the Liberian diaspora and its role in their war-torn homeland.

6. The broader and still ongoing research project from which this interim study is drawn involves several different lines and methods of investigation, which to date include over 120 life-history surveys completed primarily in the Rhode Island and Washington, D.C., area; extensive ethnographic interviews and participation in a variety of community meetings and events since 2002; and household surveys conducted in Rhode Island, Minneapolis, and Massachusetts, as well as Ghana. While this discussion draws on all these sources, it draws in particular on data collected through a survey conducted in 2004 in Minneapolis, some of the results of which are published here for the first time. This survey of 136 Liberian households represents one of the first attempts to generate survey data through a systematic sampling process that can deliver reasonably representative data. The sampling strategy involved the recruitment of households from the most broadly representative social institution in the diaspora (congregations of worship), sixteen of which participated in this survey in Minneapolis. Several polls in other forms of voluntary association (local community associations, professional associations, county associations) suggested that over 84 percent of all Liberian households have at least one member who regularly participates in a congregation of worship.

7. For more detailed information on Liberia's recent history, see Sawyer (1992), Huband (1998), Adebajo (2002), Levitt (2005), Richards et al. (2005), Moran (2006).

8. In my Minneapolis survey of 136 households, only 4 percent of all respondents claimed Americo-Liberian or Congo status. Another possible 7 percent claimed to be "Liberian"—an answer that is as likely to be a political statement rejecting the "ethnic divisions" that since the early 1980s have come to play such a

prominent role in the country's conflict, as it is to signal settler descent. Even inclusion of these respondents produces a total of no more than 11 percent. An earlier pilot survey of thirty-one households in Massachusetts produced a very similar result (with 7 percent claiming Americo-Liberian or Congo status and another possible 10 percent claiming to be simply Liberian).

9. The US Committee for Refugees estimated that between 1987 and 2004 a total of 9,143 Liberians had been admitted to the United States as refugees (http://www.refugees.org/world/article/nationality_rr00_12.cfm); while the head of the UN Mission in Liberia, in an interview in 2005, claimed that 450,000 Liberians lived in the United States (http://www.un.org/webcast/worldchron/trans924.pdf). The Union of Liberian Associations in the Americas frequently has floated the figure of 300,000.

10. For example, Moran (2005) recently cited 100,000.

11. To the extent that the Minneapolis survey is more broadly representative of the US-based diaspora as a whole, it is possible to make a rough estimate of approximately 26,000 Liberians living in 7,000 households. I review the methodology in greater detail elsewhere (Lubkemann 2007). Ongoing surveys in Rhode Island and Philadelphia will test the validity of the assumptions about the representativeness of the Minneapolis diaspora population. As rough as these estimates may be, they nevertheless represent a systematic and transparent effort that significantly narrows the range of numbers that have circulated in public and official discourse.

12. In my Minneapolis survey, 58 percent of households have US-born children.

13. A particularly insightful critique of this literature is provided by Iskander, Chapter 8 of this volume.

14. While most Liberians in the United States have some form of legal status, that is not necessarily the case for all members of the community. In order to safeguard interview subjects (as required by the human subjects protocol approved for this research project) and encourage frank and forthright discussion, all of my interviews with Liberians in the United States have been conducted on the condition that interviewees remain anonymous. Accordingly, in certain cases I have chosen to provide pseudonyms (no real names are provided in this chapter) and more specific locations and dates for individuals I quote, while in other cases I have deemed it more appropriate to refer to individuals and the location of our interviews in more general terms. All interviews for this study were conducted between January 2003 and June 2006.

15. This hypothesis was tested in a more comprehensive survey round in 2007.

16. Here I am referring to legal rather than illicit forms of international enterprises. It is of course well documented that a whole other cadre of international actors have avidly pursued illicit forms of trade in Liberia and neighboring West African countries, which have often depended precisely on exploiting factors such as remoteness and relative inaccessibility, contributing to the actors' ability to conceal their activities and avoid the scrutiny of the state and international authorities (Reno 1996; Richards 1996; Ellis 1999; Adebajo 2002; Richards et al. 2005; Moran 2006).

4

Recruiting from the Diaspora: The Local Governance Program in Iraq

Derick W. Brinkerhoff and Samuel Taddesse

As noted in "The Potential of Diasporas and Development" in this volume, diasporas are recognized as significant actors in international relations. Diasporas on occasion seek to influence the foreign policy of their host country regarding their homeland (Shain 1994–1995) and, in some cases, have been instrumental in publicizing human rights issues and in mobilizing international public opinion in favor of regime change. Scholars have focused on the potential of diaspora groups not only to advocate for changes in their home states but also, as a result of their efforts to intervene, to contribute to insecurity and instability there as well (see King and Melvin 1999–2000). Such concerns surface strongly in fragile and/or failing states. A Rand Corporation study identified nineteen countries with insurgencies that had important support from diasporas (Byman et al. 2001). Collier and Hoeffler (2001), for example, note that poor postconflict countries with diasporas face a sixfold increase in the probability of the reemergence of violent conflict.

A perspective on the role of diasporas in foreign policy, state fragility, and societal conflict that targets only their negative contributions, however, is incomplete. Emerging experience and analysis, including this volume, have identified positive roles that diasporas can play. Specific to postconflict states, Nyberg-Sorenson, Van Hear, and Engberg-Pedersen (2002, 34) stress that diasporas and their resources can and should be mobilized for "reconstruction as part of wider international peace-building, reconciliation and reconstruction efforts, with special emphasis on avoiding the generation of new tensions that might lead to new rounds of conflict and displacement."

There is wide interest in such mobilization. For example, among diaspora members themselves, Internet-based organizations have emerged to mobilize the diaspora to support reconstruction in Afghanistan (Brinkerhoff

2004). Donor organizations and postconflict governments seek to engage diasporas as well. For example, in Iraq the Iraqis Rebuilding Iraq program was founded in 2005 as a joint initiative of the Ministry of Planning and Development Cooperation (MOPDC), the International Office for Migration, and the United Nations Development Programme.[1] The program selects diaspora members to work in Iraqi government ministries and agencies for assignments ranging from three months to a year. The IOM initiated a similar program for Afghanistan.

This chapter examines one of the ways that diaspora members can contribute to development and reconstruction of their home country—through participation in donor-funded projects and programs. The case of the Local Governance Program (LGP) in Iraq, funded by the US Agency for International Development, is reviewed. The chapter argues that the recruitment and posting of diaspora members can help to address three of the challenges facing postconflict reconstruction efforts: (1) the need for technical expertise; (2) the need for language skills, context-specific knowledge, and cultural understanding; and (3) the need for speed. This chapter contributes to two streams of analysis. The first is our thinking on the positive role of diasporas in development, specifically postconflict reconstruction. The second concerns analysis of effective program interventions to promote capacity building and institutional reform.

The LGP (Phase 1 and 2), implemented by RTI International, recruited and hired a number of diaspora Iraqi professionals (DIPs) for assignments in Iraq. In total, LGP1 hired twelve DIPs, of which 40 percent continued to work with the successor program, LGP2 (2005–2008). At its peak staffing level in January/February 2004, the LGP had hired and fielded more than 230 expatriate professionals of which 5 percent were DIPs. At the outset of LGP2 there were approximately thirty-two expatriate professional staff. This analysis focuses on DIP staff during LGP1.

After a note on methodology, the chapter describes briefly the context in Iraq and provides an overview of a few key points regarding the Iraqi diaspora. It next introduces the LGP, its components, and accomplishments. The next section presents how and where the DIPs contributed to the successful implementation of LGP activities and to the achievement of its objectives. The analysis examines why these DIPs were more or less successful in their areas of responsibility. In the conclusion, we offer some lessons learned.

Methodology

The findings presented in this chapter are based on personal field observations and experience working with some of the DIPs, interviews with RTI recruiters and managers, and responses to a survey questionnaire completed by DIP staff of the LGP.[2] These interviews and surveys sought data on RTI's motivations for seeking to hire Iraqi professionals from the diaspora, DIPs' motivations to join LGP and return to Iraq, effectiveness and ineffectiveness of the DIPs in performing their assigned responsibilities, and other value-added that DIPs brought to the program. A difficulty in conducting this research is that US labor laws prohibit the collection of data on ethnic background, and its use in hiring decisions. As a result, the authors relied upon their personal knowledge and informal connections to identify diaspora members to survey.[3] The sample size is relatively small (twelve strategically placed diaspora professionals), and the discussion covers a single case. Thus, the analysis and findings should be seen as suggestive.

Iraq and the Diaspora

Under the Saddam Hussein regime, the highly centralized Iraqi state combined authoritarianism, "clientelism," and ethnic politics to rule from Baghdad through a hierarchy of provincial, municipal, and neighborhood structures. The Baath Party's elaborate patronage and social control system, fueled by oil revenues and consolidated under Saddam Hussein, created a "shadow" state, where, behind the formal institutions of government, the members of the ruling party elite operated. The regime suppressed or destroyed social relations other than those integral to the Baathist system of state domination; ethnic divisions were exploited, and traditional tribal groups were enlisted for purposes of social control.

Many Iraqis fled the oppressive regime of Saddam Hussein over the years. The Iran-Iraq War of 1980–1988 stimulated a major exodus, with an estimated 300,000 Iraqis of Iranian descent expelled. Another wave of migration took place in the wake of the first Gulf War in 1991. Accurate data on the Iraqi diaspora are not available. The UN High Commissioner for Refugees estimates that around 1 million Iraqis live in the countries immediately surrounding Iraq, and an additional 350,000 live in countries outside of the region. The Independent Electoral Commission of Iraq came to a slightly higher estimate of 4 million expatriate Iraqi voters. Some country-specific figures exist. The 2000 US census identifies 90,000 Iraqis living in the United States, and estimates in the UK are in the range of 250,000.

The role of the Iraqi diaspora in the prewar planning and postwar political maneuvering has been well documented. Iraqi diaspora members contributed their country knowledge and expertise to the Future of Iraq project, which provided background analysis and planning for the postwar period. The Department of Defense largely ignored this information, relying instead on the optimistic scenarios put forward by a small group of Iraqi exiles led by Ahmed Chalabi.[4] Following the cessation of major combat operations, returned Iraqi exiles took up positions in the interim government's Iraqi Governing Council. While we recognize that Iraqi diaspora members have been, and continue to be, important actors in the politics of Iraq's postwar reconstruction and in private sector activities, our research focus is on the role of diaspora members as technical assistance providers in donor-funded reconstruction projects.

The Local Governance Program

The LGP's immediate objective concentrated on the restoration of basic public services and support to local administrations with service delivery responsibility. The longer-term objective was to establish subnational government structures and procedures that would assure responsive and transparent local services, while putting in place democratic governance mechanisms—elected councils at neighborhood, city, and provincial levels—that would support the empowerment of local authorities and citizens. LGP1 activities included strengthening of administrative and budgeting systems for service delivery, training and capacity building in modern municipal-management tools and approaches, establishment of democratic councils, capacity building for civil-society organizations (CSOs), coordination with central authorities on local governance issues, and civic education and democracy training. The project also had a grants component to provide rapid assistance for small-scale infrastructure investments.[5]

LGP1 worked toward its objectives, despite a challenging security environment in Iraq, a situation that subsequently worsened in intensity. LGP1 facilitated the formation of 437 neighborhood councils, 195 city/sub-district councils, 96 district councils, and 16 provincial councils. Over 20,000 council members were trained. The program helped to restore access to basic public services for a significant number of Iraqis, and strengthened the capacity of local civil authorities to provide basic public services effectively and efficiently. In the political and governance area, the LGP enhanced the leadership skills of local government officials and facilitated access of citizens to local government through council participation. It facilitated the development of CSOs, to help citizens cooperate and strengthen their capacity for advocacy. For example, the supported women's associations, together with others, succeeded in defeating Resolution 137, concerning the imposition of Islamic law or *sharia* and helped establish a 25 percent quota for the representation of women in the Transitional National Assembly. To raise the political awareness of citizens and strengthen citizen participation in the political and economic development of Iraq, a total of 22,000 Civic Dialogue Program/Democracy Dialogue Activity events were held throughout Iraq, with more than 750,000 Iraqis participating. More detailed descriptions of these program areas follow.

Restoring Basic Services

For much of Year 1, the LGP was the main USAID project dedicated to working with local government service providers to restore access to essential public services. Small-scale repair projects and small infrastructure improvements were carried out with technical assistance from LGP staff with experience in public utility operations and city management. Rapid-response grants (RRGs) were provided for the refurbishment of facilities, small repairs, the purchase of spare parts and small tools, including such equipment as water quality monitoring and testing equipment.[6]

Increasing Service-Delivery Efficiency and Effectiveness

Throughout Years 1 and 2, the LGP teams worked to improve the efficiency and effectiveness of local government service departments through rehabilitation and refurbishment of office facilities, through the restoration of operations, and through workshops, on-the-job training, formal seminars, study tours, and individual day-to-day interactions. These efforts focused on bringing contemporary city management tools and techniques to Iraqi technical personnel, who were generally well trained in their technical and professional specialties, but had little exposure to modern public-sector management methods. Such personnel were also unaccustomed to notions of customer satisfaction and public accountability.

The LGP provided technical assistance to local government departments to build and enhance their capacity to plan, budget, implement, and manage service-delivery programs. More than 5,000 department heads and managers were trained (May 2003–January 2005) in expenditure forecasting, current expenditure budgeting, capital budgeting, performance measurement, and customer satisfaction surveys. Historically, budgets had been set at the central level and simply handed to local department heads. In addition, the LGP provided technical assistance, training, and RRGs for development, installation, and use of computerized accounting and financial management systems. The LGP's service-delivery and capacity-building initiatives were informed by a local department assessment survey that was first piloted in Al-Basrah in July 2003 and later extended to cover key institutions in all governorates, excluding the Kurdish governorates of Arbil, Dahuk, and As Suleimaniya.

Creating an Enabling Environment for Good Governance

Recognizing that local governments were operating without an enabling legal framework, and in an effort to resolve the funding bottlenecks created by central government ministries in Baghdad, the LGP also addressed the issue of decentralization. In February 2004 the LGP collaborated with the Ministry of Municipalities and Public Works (MMPW) and USAID's Economic Governance Program to organize a national conference on fiscal and administrative decentralization. The conference was chaired by the minister of municipalities and public works, Nasreen Barwari, with Iraqi and international speakers presenting. More than 200 people from the governorates and central ministries attended. As follow-up, a series of regional conferences was held in Al-Basrah, Arbil, and Al Hillah. In Year 2 the LGP worked with the MMPW to set up a pilot decentralization program at selected localities. Simultaneously the LGP organized regional conferences to raise awareness and galvanize local government officials to join together to create local government associations to advocate for an enabling legal and regulatory framework. The LGP and the Ministry of State and Provincial Affairs hosted these events jointly. As a result of the conferences, local governments began to form associations.

Transparent and Accountable Local Governance

By March 2004 the LGP had facilitated the formation of, or worked with, 437 neighborhood (*hayy*), 195 subdistrict (*nahiya*), 96 district (*qada*), and 16 governorate councils. By the LGP's second year, more than 20,000 council members had been trained on council roles and responsibilities, council oversight of executive departments, and citizen outreach. In some governorates, councils were also trained on participatory planning and budgeting. The January 30, 2005, election, however, resulted in the almost complete turnover of governorate councils. Elections for *qada'* and *nahiya* councils were also postponed. During this interim period, the LGP produced council-training materials and provided training to members of newly elected provincial councils. In total, the LGP trained approximately 507 newly elected governorate council members from all across Iraq, of which 136 were women. LGP council-training material was prepared in English, Arabic, and Kurdish, and distributed to all government council members via CD-ROMs.[7] Continued intensive training of council members under LGP2 has contributed to the inclusion of councils as a legitimate governmental entity within the new Iraq constitution.

Strengthening Civil Society

During Year 1 the LGP focused on fostering a context for civil society by both improving the ability of subnational institutions to deliver services to the people and by forming or strengthening CSOs. The LGP helped individuals to identify others with common interests and to form associations for professionals, youth, women, veterans with disabilities, and other interest groups. LGP assistance to these groups mainly focused on how the groups could monitor the actions of, articulate the needs of, and assist local government as partners to achieve common goals. Among the most successful were the women's associations that the LGP supported, as noted above.

During Year 2 the focus on civil-society development shifted to a political awareness campaign for citizens in response to the Coalition Provisional Authority's (CPA's) decision to advance the timetable for Iraqi sovereignty. The campaign first focused on familiarizing citizens with the elements of the CPA's Transitional Administrative Law and, subsequently, worked toward creating an informed citizenry to participate in national and local political processes. USAID (2005) credits the campaign with contributing to the large voter turnout for the January 30, 2005, election.

Economic Revitalization

Important to postconflict reconstruction is the reestablishment of economic activity and employment creation. LGP activities focused on five broad areas of public resource management and decisionmaking to facilitate and sustain economic activity in Iraq: improving the institutional environment for economic growth, developing human resources, exploiting key economic opportunities, investing in strategic infrastructure, and involving stakeholders.

With regard to improving the institutional framework for economic development, for example, in Arbil the LGP provided technical assistance to strengthen the Kurdish Regional Government's capacity to identify, program, and implement actions to augment the local economy, and assisted with the preparation of a regional development strategy. In At Ta'mim the LGP provided assistance to the Kirkuk Business Center (KBC) to stimulate business expansion and employment. In Ninawa the LGP facilitated the establishment of the Ninawa Business Center, which included a small-business incubator. In Kirkuk, Al-Basrah and Babil, chambers of commerce were supported to promote public-private partnerships, expand economic opportunities, and participate in public affairs.

With regard to human resources development, for example, the LGP assisted the Kirkuk City Council in establishing an Employment Services Center to foster merit-based, transparent hiring in the public and private sectors. The Center developed mechanisms to register unemployed applicants, match their qualifications to available jobs, and facilitate their hiring. Since opening in August 2003, it has processed and placed more than 28,000 workers. The LGP also supported the Kirkuk Vocational Training Center, which equips trainees with skills in high demand in the labor market (e.g., air-conditioning repairs, automobile repairs and mechanics, carpentry, welding, electronics, sewing, and basic computer skills).

The LGP worked to exploit key economic sector opportunities and rehabilitate and renovate commercial structures and facilities. For instance, LGP funded the computerization of the Kurdistan Bureau of Tourism, training of the staff, and the development of an online tourism travel guide. The program funded a conference on the renovation of the Arbil Citadel, which the city hoped to promote as a tourist and cultural attraction. LGP assisted the As Samawah City Council and Municipal Directorate in renovating an open-air market to provide a clean and safe area for local vendors and consumers and to generate revenue for the city. In Dhi Qar, LGP provided support to the Dhi Qar Directorate of Municipalities and the Provincial Council in renovating a commercial market and office building complex to reactivate business and local economic development. In Al-Basrah, LGP supported the rehabilitation of a slaughterhouse that previously dumped environmentally hazardous waste into local waterways. In Al Hillah, the Sewing Association building was rehabilitated and equipped with sewing machines to help generate income for 800 women.

The LGP promoted stakeholder participation, including involving women in economic planning. For example, in the preparation of the Arbil Economic Development Strategy, LGP collaborated with the Kurdistan Regional Government and Salahaddin University to host a forum on critical themes relating to economic growth. The attendees included representatives from relevant ministries, provinces, and districts; from the private sector and the business community; from women's groups, neighborhood community organizations, and the NGO community; and from the media and representatives of the general public. As a result of this forum, a long-range local economic development plan was developed. In addition, the LGP sponsored training workshops that addressed cultural issues that deny women business opportunities. It also provided individualized training sessions covering specific skill sets such as "marketing your business," "how to access microfinance," and "how to network for success." Hosted in Arbil, As Suleimaniya, and Dahuk, the workshops provided 150 women with encouragement and increased skills in small-business development. Similar workshops were conducted in Tikrit and Baghdad.

Finally, the LGP itself contributed to employment generation and the economy. It hired more than 3,000 Iraqi professional and project support staff. As of the end of June 2004, it had approximately 2,700 Iraqis on its payroll and had paid out approximately $8.5 million to its Iraqi staff in the form of salaries and wages. Furthermore, the LGP's use of Iraqi consultants and subcontractors injected about $11.6 million into the local economy. An additional $5.8 million was expended within Iraq for the purchase of various types of goods and material.

A Caveat on Accomplishments

LGP1's major focus was on enhancing the effectiveness of subnational service delivery and the administrative institutions of representative local government. The above discussion offers highlights of the accomplishments of the LGP, which was but one small element in the nation-building exercise launched by the United States–led invasion and subsequent reconstruction. The initial gains in administrative efficiency and local responsiveness to citizens that LGP has supported, however, are at grave risk as of this writing. In Iraq in the 2000s, regional autonomy, decentralization, socioethnic power sharing, and the role of Islam remain contested issues that are highly political. Only an internally led political solution can ultimately address the problems facing the country, and eventually diminish violence, contribute to basic security, and achieve some measure of societal consensus. At the time of this writing, Iraq's prospects for stability and recovery appear dim, since sectarian violence shows no signs of diminishing and the current elected government is largely ineffectual (see, for example, ICG 2006).

DIP Contributions to LGP Accomplishments

The diaspora Iraqi professionals made significant contributions to the accomplishments of the LGP reviewed above. Of the twelve DIPs, seven were hired as civil-society specialists; two were engineers working on public service delivery, including irrigation, and water and sewerage infrastructures; one continued under LGP2 to work as a public administration specialist and trainer; one was hired as an urban planner but worked as a civil-society specialist; and one continued in LGP2 to serve as the national information technology director for the LGP. Collectively, the inventory of knowledge and skills brought by the DIPs included

- Urban planning.
- Civil and structural engineering.
- Computer and electronic engineering.
- Irrigation and agricultural engineering.
- Public administration, accounting, and financial management.
- Anthropology and social science.
- Information and communications technology.
- International relations and conflict resolution.
- Language and cultural skills.

Almost all the DIPs surveyed agreed that their language and cultural skills were valuable and increased their job effectiveness. They were able to reach into Iraqi communities quickly to organize neighborhood, subdistrict and district, and provincial councils and to initiate other LGP activities. They were effective at mobilizing the community to work together to solve community problems. Sharing a common language with the target population greatly simplified both formal and informal communication. It eliminated the need for translator-interpreters who, unless well qualified and trained, could easily subvert or distort the information being transmitted and the work at hand. Moreover, as information "gatekeepers," translator-interpreters can have significant power over local Iraqis and can easily manipulate information and resources to their own advantage. Besides language and cultural knowledge, knowing the social fabric of the Iraqi communities and being known by the community generated trust and quick acceptance for RTI program activities, which facilitated rapid start-up of activities.

About 40 percent of the DIPs had links to former colleagues in Iraqi government institutions and family ties to those in national government and the Interim Governing Council. The DIPs' knowledge and relationships with former colleagues and their family and ethnic affiliation with some of the national Iraqi policymakers paved the way for the LGP's interaction with central government ministries. These connections were used to expand the LGP's national-level policy reform activities. For example, one of the DIPs introduced a senior LGP staff member to the minister of Municipalities and Public Works, Barwari, while she was visiting Kirkuk in early August 2003, thus establishing a continuing relationship. The MMPW was among the first central government entities willing to experiment with decentralized governance by delegating the administration of selected urban services in targeted pilot localities. In addition, a DIP introduced LGP senior staff to the governor of Al-Basrah Governorate, who later became the minister of state and provincial affairs. This introduction facilitated work with this ministry, which cohosted a series of conferences on federalism and decentralization and local government associations. As a result, several local government associations formed in the central and southern regions of Iraq to share ideas and assets.

Beyond personal relationships, through their contacts and knowledge of the local communities, DIPs were able to solicit the cooperation of key individuals and involve them in LGP activities. For example, in Babil, Karbala, and Wassit, the DIPs were instrumental in orchestrating contacts with, and enlisting tribal leaders to participate in, LGP activities. They also served as conduits for contacts with community leaders and local-government officials.

The DIPs were able to transmit knowledge of international best practices, relate them to the situation in Iraq, and engage their counterparts in discussions about application to Iraq. They could get into the heart of sensitive issues such as ethical codes, corruption, and transparency that would be difficult for others to do without bruising Iraqi pride. In general, the DIPs understood and appreciated the misery and deprivation that Iraqis had experienced for over fifty years and were, therefore, tolerant, patient, and willing to build capacity of Iraqis without judging, labeling, or condescending to them. The DIPs also served as role models to local Iraqis, who could identify with them. This was especially important when the program called for shifts in attitudes, values, and behaviors.

The DIPs felt that speaking and understanding the language, while a plus, was not the same as being from that country. Being from Iraq provided an immediate bond, and helped to establish trust, mutual respect, and commitment. It also helped in understanding the meaning and subtleties of hand gestures, facial expressions, and other body movements, which form part of the spoken language, but for which there are no equivalent Arabic words. This enhanced DIPs' effectiveness as trainers of a local Iraqi cadre. For example, the DIP-provided training to local Iraqi staff hired for the Civic Dialogue Program was passionate, animated, and effective. The DIPs were able to convey the purpose of the program and content of the message in precise terms, using relevant examples relating to Iraq's past. Consequently, the trainees were galvanized to carry the initiative forward sometimes at great personal risk. As indicated above, they held 22,000 events reaching more than 750,000 people all across Iraq, over a ten-month period, with minimum supervision.

The following three more-detailed descriptions of diaspora contributions illustrate these and other advantages of hiring DIPs to staff donor-funded development contracts.

Establishing the Baghdad City Council

In May 2003, after dismissing the Saddam Hussein–era Baghdad City Council, Ambassador Paul Bremer, the US civilian administrator of Iraq, announced that his priority was to establish a new city council in Baghdad by July 2003. A female Iraqi American senior civil-society specialist, Dr. Amal Rassam, was asked to fly to Baghdad to assist with preparations for the establishment of a new representative Baghdad City Council. Dr. Rassam had worked in Iraq for many years as an anthropologist. She came from a prominent Baghdad family, and she and her family enjoyed a good reputation in the Baghdad community. At the time of her work on LGP1, one of her sisters was a resident of Baghdad teaching at the University of Baghdad and another sister worked for the CPA media office.

Before Dr. Rassam's arrival in Baghdad, little background reference material was available on how the city functioned prior to the occupation and what the roles and responsibilities of the city council were. The LGP and the USAID–Department of State (DOS) team had learned that the previous city council consisted of about two-thirds central government department heads (directors general), and the remaining third had been selected by national Baath Party officials. The LGP sought to develop a council that would represent the population, not the central government. Several Iraqi municipal staff were instrumental in providing information that enabled the design process to move forward.

From a spatial-planning point of view, Baghdad was organized along detailed grids. The city was divided into nine districts, and within these nine, eighty-eight neighborhoods were initially identified; later another six were added to accommodate the densely populated Sadr City. At least initially the LGP and the USAID-DOS team determined to work within these spatial boundaries once it was established that neighborhoods generally were ethnically and culturally homogeneous. The LGP worked with the military, CPA, and Baghdad City municipal department heads to design a council system for the Baghdad metropolitan area. The group's efforts led to a design with three initial levels of councils: neighborhood advisory councils, district advisory councils, and an interim city council. Once the city council was formed, the Baghdad regional council and the Baghdad provincial council were added.

Given the months that it would have taken to determine voting roles, establish an electoral process, and hold citywide elections, the planning team decided to build up the city council by holding town-meeting-type gatherings in each neighborhood. The challenge was to ensure, especially at the outset, that the city council would be as representative of the population as possible. The council formation team consisted of Dr. Rassam from the LGP, one US Army colonel assigned to the CPA with previous experience in the Middle East, and nine members (one per district) of the Iraqi Reconstruction and Development Council (IRDC) (the IRDC was made up of members of the US Iraqi diaspora, hired by the US Department of Defense). The team relied initially upon coalition forces to assemble Iraqi citizens for meetings regarding councils.

The first caucus meeting took place in the district of Al Kindi, just outside the International Zone, in a local restaurant. Twenty-five men and three women attended. Dr. Rassam introduced the plan for setting up councils, and the Iraqis peppered her with inquiries about the role of the councils, their legal and budgetary status, how members would be selected, and so on. Since many of the issues had yet to be resolved, answers were not available; and at times discussions became tense and arguments broke out. After explaining what was at stake, Dr. Rassam instructed her audience about the particulars of the nomination and selection process, and invited the attendees to pass the message to others in the neighborhood, consider who would be suitable candidates for nomination, and mobilize people to attend subsequent meetings. At the second meeting about fifty citizens gathered, more discussion occurred, and several people nominated themselves and said a few words about why they wanted to be on the council. Fifty-five people attended the third meeting, and the selection process yielded twelve council members.

Thus began the Baghdad council formation process. By July 2003 the deadline set by the CPA, eighty-eight neighborhood advisory councils, nine district advisory councils, and the Baghdad City Council were formed. The provincial and local council leadership training provided by the DIPs in Baghdad was a highly sought-out training event. Council members risked assassination to attend these training events. The seminars were provided in Arabic, using culturally relevant examples that the Iraqis could relate to. (LGP2 continued and expanded the training program for council members, using locally hired staff.)

The successful and timely council formation is largely attributable to the effective work done by the DIPs. As indicated above, as with much of the postconflict planning in Iraq, the council development process was hampered by gaps in knowledge of the institutions and prevailing conditions prior to the occupation. For example, councils have existed in Iraq since the 1960s, but they were instruments of central government control rather than representative of citizens at the local level. Intervening in local neighborhoods required trust and cultural sensitivity. Iraqi Americans,[8] led by Dr. Rassam, spoke the language, understood the culture, and shared Iraqi concerns with rebuilding their capital and their country. LGP relied on DIPs and Iraqi local staff with in-depth experience in, and knowledge of, the Middle East and Iraq.

Economic Development in the Kurdish Governorates

Establishing a functioning market economy in Iraq was an important target of US foreign policy objectives in Iraq. The challenge facing the CPA and the coalition forces was how to restore basic services and establish a political structure and policy environment that would lead to the creation of a vigorous free market economy. In postconflict Iraq, people have little experience with an open market economy. The legacy of decades of a heavily controlled state-run economy included limited private initiative, citizen dependency on the state, and an economic infrastructure in shambles. The LGP responded with its Local Economic Development (LED) initiative. The LGP's experience confirmed that local governments that have strong institutional mechanisms for stakeholder input are successful in attracting investment and generating employment, and local governments that invest strategically in developing people's skills to meet current and future labor demand have a greater potential for creating income and employment opportunities. LGP success in the At Ta'mim and Kurdish governorates was facilitated by a DIP who had close ties with officials in the Kurdish Regional Government.

Cameron Berkuti, a Kurdish American public administration and training specialist, provided management training, facilitated the establishment of the Joint Committee on Economic Development, and helped to establish and strengthen the Project Coordination Center to give the local government legitimacy through inclusion and empowerment. The Project Coordination Center constitutes a model approach to participatory integrated development planning that maximizes the use of civilian and military resources in a postconflict environment. Professional knowledge, his Kurdish ethnic affiliation and networks, and his motivation to help and build the economy of his country were key to this DIP's effectiveness in carrying out his assignment.

The At Ta'mim LED initiative helped create conditions that led to the generation of 12,000 jobs. The Kirkuk Business Center played a critical role in assisting Kirkuk contractors to obtain subcontracts and employ local workers in the first and largest public infrastructure project implemented in Kirkuk, the Iraqi Army Base Project. The KBC was recognized for its role in promoting economic development during a visit to the KBC by US ambassador John Negroponte in August 2004. More significantly, At Ta'mim local government authorities took ownership of the LED initiative and promoted the approach in a regional conference in Kirkuk in November 2004. The purpose of the conference was to share best practices and lessons learned on LED planning with local government officials from around the country.

Strengthening Civil Society in Ninawa

The Saddam Hussein regime had maintained party and state control over what in other countries are independent civic groups. The Baath Party established unions representing every occupation—for example, the Lawyers' Association, the Iraqi Nurses' Association, the Iraqi Engineering Union, the Iraqi Teachers' Union, Iraqi Women Federation, and so on. These organizations functioned as extensions of the party, mainly to gather information about people in their communities, and were largely detested and feared by ordinary citizens. In other words, true civil-society groups were absent or operated underground.

The transition in Iraq was so sudden and abrupt that civic groups had almost no time or space in which to develop gradually. In most country transition situations, the opening of space takes place over an extended period of time, as a regime's grip weakens, which allows civil-society groups to learn to play a public role as they evolve. Following the overthrow of the Iraqi regime, a number of informal groups interested in public issues—for example, human rights and women's rights—began to emerge at the local level. The LGP worked with these groups throughout the country.

When the LGP deployed in Mosul, the capital of Ninawa province, in June 2003, the project team encountered many nascent civic groups, eager to see what civic activism could do in the suddenly freer atmosphere. Most of them were very loosely organized and had little or no prior experience with collective action. Typically they consisted of a few courageous men or women who had decided to try to do something positive for their communities.

Hind Haider, an Iraqi American civil-society specialist, had left Iraq as a small child. She was deployed in Iraq in June 2003 as the leader of the LGP civil-society team in Ninawa. Haider was able to quickly mobilize and begin to establish and strengthen civil-society organizations. She recruited, hired, and trained local Iraqi staff to assist her in the CSO-strengthening initiative. One of the first tasks of her team was to undertake a survey to determine the number and kinds of CSOs that existed in the governorate, if any. Conducted through the University of Mosul, the survey identified seventy-six civil-society organizations. The majority of those CSOs, however, were the remnants of the Saddam Hussein–era unions, syndicates, and federations. The second-largest group consisted of ethnic- and religious-based humanitarian organizations. The smallest category comprised newly formed human rights groups and one women's organization.

Despite the difficult security situation that had gripped Mosul beginning in late 2003, the LGP civil-society team assisted fourteen CSOs. The team developed and provided rapid-response grants, training, and technical assistance. One-on-one consultation sessions were held with the fourteen CSOs that came to the LGP office for assistance. Technical assistance and training included review of the organizations' bylaws, work plans, program ideas, and proposal writing. Basic nuts-and-bolts operational assistance covered skills such as how to run meetings, how to set agendas, how to agree on assignment of tasks, and how to keep minutes of meetings and record decisions. Haider and her team researched, developed, and distributed a concise booklet translated into Arabic and Kurdish, which covered essential topics for new CSOs. These included the definition of a CSO, how to write a mission statement, how to develop objectives and goals, how to create institutional bylaws, how to write a proposal, and how to fund-raise. Over the course of the first year, the team also produced three more comprehensive manuals for CSO capacity building. These covered human resources management, outreach and membership development, and financial management.

The team's support to the Women's Social and Cultural Society of Mosul enabled its president to achieve sufficient stature to be elected to serve on the Ninawa provincial council. As of this writing, Mosul is a socially conservative city with many pockets of violent insurgency. In the face of great adversity and danger, this CSO stands out for its courage and determination to build a brighter future for women in Iraq. Haider developed a special connection with this CSO that gave the women courage to stand and fight for their human rights. She became a role model for young Iraqi women in Mosul.

Local LGP staff played a vital role in ensuring the success of the program. These motivated and capable staff interacted effectively with a wide range of CSOs, built trust and confidence, and tailored the technical assistance tools and approaches to the Iraqi context. When Haider was evacuated to Dahok in November 2003 because of security threats, the local staff continued to provide technical assistance and training to those targeted CSOs. In addition, when the Democracy Dialogue Program was launched in January 2004, the LGP local staff was able to introduce the program in Mosul. It organized and facilitated Democracy Dialogue events throughout Ninawa until the program's end in November 2004.

Overview of the Local Governance Program's Diaspora Iraqi Professionals

Of the twelve Iraqi professionals, one-third were women. Only one of these women continued to work with LGP2. Of the twelve, 40 percent continued their employment with LGP2. All of these Iraqis were first-generation diaspora members residing in the United States and had left Iraq during Saddam Hussein's Baathist regime. More than 60 percent had completed a bachelor's degree or other higher education before leaving Iraq; and 25 percent had completed up to high school. With the exception of one individual, most of them had acquired a significant part of their education in the United States. They were all exposed to Western culture, values, and lifestyles. Almost 95 percent were adults at the time they left Iraq. The DIPs had varied ethnic and religious backgrounds: Arabs (90%), Kurds (10%), Christians (25%), Shia (42%), and Sunni (33%). Some were allied to groups that opposed the Baathist regime, while some were sympathetic; still others were nonpolitical.

Motivations for Joining the Local Governance Program

The DIPs' strongest reason for returning to Iraq was their desire to build a democratic Iraq where human rights are respected. Their second reason was to expand their professional experience and advance their career development. These DIPs worked actively to modernize Iraqi institutions and management systems including planning, budgeting, and monitoring and evaluation in service delivery, and at the same time acquired new management and leadership skills working side-by-side with experienced and seasoned non-Iraqi international professional staff. For 80 percent of these DIPs, their LGP assignments were their first international professional consulting experience.

With the deterioration in the security situation, DIPs who initially considered reestablishing themselves in Iraq changed their minds. For those who left at the end of LGP1, not surprisingly, security reasons were frequently cited, as well as family commitments.

Recruitment and Hiring of the Diaspora Iraqi Professionals

The RTI team recruited these DIPs through various means, including word of mouth, referrals by friends and colleagues, and newspaper and Internet advertising. RTI was conscious of the need to recruit qualified professionals who were not security risks. For that reason it was deemed important to use one of the DIPs to review the applicants. A female DIP who had been hired at the start of the LGP played the role of screening and approving applicants. It was later discovered, however, that this individual was perhaps too much of a gatekeeper. Overall she approved only 15 percent of the applicants presented to her. It was alleged that she approved only individuals known to her through her network of friends.

Some Difficulties in the Use of Diaspora Iraqi Professionals

More than 60 percent of the DIPs had preference for assignment in their ethnic area, where their family line was known and respected. While this presented some advantages, as noted above, it also had some negative side effects. First, when RTI did not assign them to the province of their choice, some DIPs showed resentment. Second, those who were assigned closer to their original communities and were put in leadership positions tended to prefer hiring and mentoring individuals from only their own ethnic group, a practice that RTI did not approve. The LGP sought actively to hire local staff for as many functions as possible, and several of the surveyed DIPs suggested that to some degree a few of the DIPs abused their discretionary hiring power to establish small but effective "fiefdoms." In fact some had a small army of drivers and bodyguards, partly as protection and partly as a demonstration of status and power.

On occasion, there were also some signs of rivalry and division among the DIPs. Some made it clear that they would not work with specific individuals. In many cases the fractures were across ethnic lines, though occasionally religious affiliation was the divider. In one case the DIP purposefully avoided associating with the other DIPs because this person did not want to disclose the identity of her family. The gatekeeper issue in recruitment mentioned above is another example of the impact of factions among DIPs. In hindsight, independent due diligence combined with use of multiple DIPs to help in recruiting and screening applicants from the Iraqi diaspora for the LGP might have led to more applicants being employed by the program. Reliance on one individual may have limited the diversity and number of individuals hired by the LGP. The difficulties identified here are minor, however, compared with the significant contributions the DIPs made to the LGP.

Diaspora Iraqi Professionals and the Challenges of Postconflict Reconstruction Projects

As the above discussion illustrates, LGP1 benefited importantly from the services of the DIPs, and LGP2 continued to do so. Personnel and project reviews determined that more than 75 percent of these DIPs were effective both on their originally assigned jobs and in extending LGP activities to different communities. Most served at great personal risk, since many were accused by fellow Iraqis as being traitors and collaborators with the foreign powers that controlled Iraq. Although the number of diaspora members engaged was few, their efforts and impacts were significant regarding the successes achieved by the LGP. The authors' research confirmed the roles the DIPs played in addressing the three challenges identified in the introduction.

Technical Expertise

All of the DIPs recruited, as noted above, had technical skills appropriate to their assigned LGP responsibilities. The DIPs working on council formation, civil-society strengthening, and Democracy Dialogue used their skills to teach, facilitate, and mobilize the Iraqis they collaborated with. This "doing with," rather than "doing for," has long been recognized as associated with effective technical cooperation (see Berg 1993). Further, this facilitating approach helped to build Iraqi ownership for the changes the LGP sought to put in place, another factor identified with successful reform (Brinkerhoff 1996). It should be noted that a facilitative approach to technical cooperation and an ownership-building strategy characterized all the technical assistance providers in the LGP, not just the DIPs, though the DIPs' language and cultural understanding may have enhanced their speed and ability to build trust and establish mutual understanding.

Language, Contextual and Cultural Knowledge

Successful implementation of postconflict reconstruction templates depends upon the translation of program designs into strategies and interventions that will work in the country. This translation depends critically upon the ability to communicate with country actors; to understand the context, in terms of history, culture, politics, administrative systems, and so on; and to apply that understanding for fine-tuning plans in ways that lead to desired outcomes. Because of their ability to speak the languages used in Iraq, their deep understanding of the underlying social fabric and power relations at all levels of Iraqi society, and the rapport they were able to establish with local actors, the DIPs were instrumental in helping the LGP to devise approaches that led to results. In postconflict situations, external interveners often have limited local knowledge and become dependent upon individuals who speak Western European languages and are familiar with donor procedures and needs. While many of these individuals are well meaning and are sincerely interested in assisting in reconstruction, others seek to influence reconstruction efforts to advance their own interests.[9] For the LGP the DIPs helped program decisionmakers to interpret what they were told by Iraqi counterparts and identify hidden and/or conflicting agendas.

Speed

In postconflict situations, speed can be critical in addressing reconstruction needs. The LGP and all the Iraq postinvasion projects were under intense pressure from the CPA to launch in-country operations and to reach scale quickly. Getting programs up and running as well as meeting immediate needs while avoiding the inadvertent creation of problems for the longer term are critical to success. For the LGP the DIPs were instrumental in the rapid start-up of the council creation process, the early identification of CSOs worthy of support, the targeting of rapid-response grants, and the ramp-up of the Democracy Dialogue sessions around the country. The DIPs' language and context skills, and their cultural understanding, coupled with their technical expertise, helped greatly in contributing to a speedy program launch. Further, in several cases, their personal networks and connections facilitated building relationships with key local actors who helped the LGP to initiate activities in the field quickly.

Conclusion

This research confirms that diaspora members can bring value-added to postconflict reconstruction and development projects. Successful technical assistance depends upon appropriate technical expertise, a facilitative and collaborative approach to working with in-country counterparts, and relevant language and sociocultural contextual knowledge. Diaspora professionals can be an excellent source of these skills and attributes, and in many cases have the additional advantage of being able to tap into personal and family networks of expertise and influence. They also bring a set of values from their adopted country that is an asset to the kinds of democratizing reforms that accompany postconflict reconstruction. These potential advantages and the experience of the LGP suggest that while all technical assistance personnel should be technically qualified, DIPs' lack of previous experience in the international development industry should not alone dissuade recruiters from hiring them (80 percent of those studied here lacked such experience).

A caveat in the use of diaspora professionals in reconstruction and development is that they may import aspects of societal divisiveness into the reconstruction effort in ways that may or may not be readily apparent to expatriate staff. Employers of diaspora members may be limited in their ability to identify such potential problems prior to posting DIPs to their project assignments in the home country, and to address the problems due to pressures from funders for speed and implementation of particular policies, for example, maximizing local hires.

One commonly noted source of friction regarding diaspora returnees working on international development projects is resentment on the part of those who remained in the country, and endured the conflict and its hardships, toward those who left and then returned, often with higher salaries and other benefits. Anecdotal evidence suggests, for example, that this has been a problem in Afghanistan. Such frictions were not reported in the LGP case, however.

The LPG case highlights the contributions of diaspora members in the context of donor-funded reconstruction programs. These programs are only one of the avenues through which diaspora members can help to address the needs of their homelands following societal conflict. Additional studies are needed to examine and evaluate the full range of options for accessing the technical expertise and the cultural backgrounds that diaspora members bring to postconflict reconstruction.

Notes

1. See the website at http://www.iraq-iri.org/.
2. Derick Brinkerhoff was a member of an LGP policy advisory group, and made short-term visits to Iraq. Samuel Taddesse was posted to Iraq long-term, first as regional team leader in northern Iraq covering the governorates of Arbil, At Ta'mim, and Ninawa between April and September 2003, and later as the LGP's National Program and Policy Information director between September 2003 and August 2004. The views expressed in this chapter are solely those of the authors and should not be attributed to either RTI International or USAID.
3. Participation in the survey was strictly voluntary, and a few LGP DIPs declined to respond.
4. There are numerous sources that analyze and criticize the United States–led

invasion and postwar reconstruction in Iraq. Just a few examples include Barakat (2005), Jabar (2004), and Phillips (2005).

5. LGP2 continued activities intended to improve the efficiency and effectiveness of local government, support subnational governance reforms, and create a supportive policy environment for decentralization.

6. By March 30, 2005, LGP received 224 RRG proposals—with a total value of $15.7 million for Year 1 and $1.6 million for Year 2 of the LGP. Of these totals, 213 were approved in Year 1 and the remainder in Year 2. Of the total number of approved grants, 196 were successfully completed, 6 remained incomplete, and 22 were canceled due to the security situation. RRGs were used to "jump-start" local civil administrations' ability to restore essential services by rehabilitating and refurbishing offices so that these civil administrations could resume operations and provide adequate, functional workspace for their staff. Additionally, the use of RRGs facilitated citizen participation in local political processes by providing local councils with rehabilitated and furnished work and meeting places, and strengthening the capacities of CSOs.

7. The LGP's Council Training Modules cover the following topics: local council authorities, meeting procedures, code of conduct, governorate councils and executive duties, transparency and team work, council procedures and functions, citizen participation, legislative oversight, budgeting, and decentralization.

8. The LGP worked closely with members of the IRDC, particularly in the early days of Baghdad's council formation when few project staff were deployed to Iraq. These were members of the US Iraqi diaspora recruited by the DOD to assist the CPA in reconstruction. They were mostly Chaldean and Assyrian Christians and Shia Muslims. The CPA tried to match up IRDC individuals with districts (they worked mainly at the district-advisory-council level), that is, placing a Shia in a predominantly Shia district, for example. In the early days the LGP depended upon IRDC members assigned to Baghdad's nine districts to help mobilize citizens to come to neighborhood and district council selection meetings.

9. For the LGP, this dynamic arose in the area of decentralization. CPA advisers based in Baghdad relied upon Iraqi counterparts with vested interests in retaining power at the center; consequently, some CPA officials did not support the LGP's efforts to support subnational administrations (Brinkerhoff and Mayfield 2005).

Part 2

Mobilizing Diaspora Homeland Investment

GLOBALIZATION HAS REDUCED barriers to trade and investment around the world, dramatically increasing the integration of the world economy. Goods, services, and capital move increasingly faster and more readily across national borders. Simultaneously, globalization has given rise to accessible global communication and transportation technologies, global media, and transnational political, commercial, and cultural organizations, which link emigrants and their descendants to their ancestral homes both physically and psychologically. As discussed in the introduction to this volume, "The Potential of Diasporas and Development," these linkages can foster a transnational, diasporic identity—a sense of homeland belongingness and responsibility despite the fact that the individuals are embedded within the political, economic, and social fabric of their country of residence. Beyond contributions through household remittances and political influence, diasporic identity—coupled with increased ease of international trade and investment—has given many twenty-first-century emigrants and their descendants increased motivation and ability to participate in the economic development of their homeland.

It is not uncommon to hear of an immigrant sending money home to support a family business, buying stock in a homeland company, or even establishing a business in the homeland. Diaspora community members also support homeland private-sector development in indirect ways, through purchasing homeland goods and services (see Orozco, Chapter 10); donating in-kind goods, such as computers and production equipment to homeland businesses; providing technical and market expertise to homeland entrepreneurs; and encouraging their employers in their country of residence to establish relationships with businesses in their homeland.

Scholarly inquiry examining the role that diasporas play in developing the private sector in diasporans' homelands is an interdisciplinary stream of research, currently being forged in the disciplines of anthropology, economics, international business, public administration, and sociology. Yet much of the extant work in this area is in its infancy. The chapters in this section move this body of work forward by focusing on two critical issues: (1) which diaspora communities are likely to invest in their homeland's private sector, and (2) what institutional mechanisms can be leveraged to encourage and facilitate this investment.

This introduction to Part 2 provides an overview of existing work related to diaspora involvement in the development of the private sector in diasporans' homelands. It then discusses how each of the included chapters contributes to this growing research stream.

Diaspora Contributions to Private Sector Development

The interdisciplinary literature examining the involvement of diaspora community members in homeland private-sector development most often focuses on the supply of capital—financial, human, and social—transferred from the diaspora to private sector actors, such as firms, managers, and entrepreneurs, in the homeland (see Table 1).

Financial Capital Transfers

The bulk of the literature regarding diaspora involvement in homeland economies focuses on diaspora remittances. Research contributions in this

Table 1   Diaspora Involvement in Homeland Private-Sector Development

Type of Capital Transfer	Transfers → Recipients in Homeland Economy	Example Citations
Financial	Remittances → households	Russell and Teitelbaum (1992); Massey, Goldring, and Durand (1994); Taylor et al. (1996a); Taylor et al. (1996b); Orozco with Lapointe (2004); Cohen (2005)
	Financial donations → communities	Barkan, McNulty, and Ayeni (1991); Orozco with Lapointe (2004); Torres and Kuznetsov (2006)
	Capital investment → real estate, firms via portfolio investment, VC funds, foreign direct investment	Gillespie et al. (1999); Gillespie, Sayre, and Riddle (2001); Ramamurti (2004)
	Nostalgia product/service consumption → firms	Milman, Reichel, and Pizam (1990); Chapin (1992); King and Gamage (1994); Parameswaran and Pisharodi (2002); Ogden, Ogden, and Schau (2004); Palumbo and Teich (2004); Mundra (2005)
Human	Know-how, skills, technology transfer → governments, firms, NGOs	Saxenian (1999); Saxenian (2002b); Meyer and Brown (1999); Hunger (2004); Hall (2005); Stark (2004); Carr, Inkson, and Thorn (2005); Seguin, State, and Singer (2006); Pandey et al. (2006); Kuznetsov, Nemirovsky, and Yoguel (2006)
Social	Transnational production and supply-chain networks → firms	Minoglou, Pepelasis, and Louri (1997); Kyle (1999); Saxenian (1999); Kapur (2001); Uduku (2002); Chang (2004); Cheung (2004)

area primarily emanate from the fields of economics, finance, and sociology (e.g., Russell and Teitelbaum 1992; Massey, Goldring, and Durand 1994; Orozco with Lapointe 2004). Cohen (2005) divides this literature stream into two categories: research that focuses on national-level outcomes owing to remittances (e.g., Taylor et al. 1996a) and work that examines the local effects of remittance practices (e.g., Massey, Goldring, and Durand 1994; Taylor et al. 1996b).

Much of the work in this stream focuses on the impacts of family remittances. By increasing the level of household disposable income, family remittances contribute to homeland private-sector growth by increasing the amount of local goods and services households are able to purchase. Others note that family remittances can be used to start up a business or infuse an existing family-owned business with much-needed capital.

As mentioned above, a growing body of research explores the role of money that is remitted back to communities through institutions such as hometown or community associations (e.g., Barkan, McNulty, and Ayeni 1991; Orozco with Lapointe 2004). Empirical findings from this area of inquiry reveal that such associational remittances are often used to provide infrastructure and other services that the state cannot or will not provide. In some cases, communal remittances are used to improve the local infrastructure (e.g., paving roads or providing electrification and other utilities) or human capital (e.g., enhancing the quality and quantity of medical services or education available in the community), which can create a more enabling environment for business development in the homeland. In other cases, communal remittances are invested in homeland companies by purchasing shares of stock in these firms (Torres and Kuznetsov 2006).

Research in the field of international business examines the capital investments that diaspora community members make in homeland real estate and firms via portfolio and direct investment. For example, Gillespie et al. (1999, 2001) found that diasporans' homeland investment interest was characterized by a dual investment motivation: they felt compelled to invest in their homeland economies both for altruistic and pecuniary reasons. These studies also uncovered diasporans' belief in an "ethnic advantage" that would enable them to be more successful in a homeland business relative to the typical, nondiasporan investor. In a recent review of the foreign investment literature, Ramamurti (2004) noted that the role of the diaspora in homeland investment should be a key area of future research.

A substantial amount of work in the area of marketing, international trade, and tourism explores the motivations for and impact of the consumption of products and services from homeland companies by the diaspora. Research in marketing explores the impact of acculturation/assimilation on product purchase decisions and response to marketing promotion campaigns (e.g., Ogden, Ogden, and Schau 2004). Contributions in this area also examine how an individual's diasporic identity might impact the way he/she feels about the country of origin of particular products or services, particularly those associated with his/her home country (e.g., Parameswaran and Pisharodi 2002). Differences in the diaspora mind-set and responses to marketing strategy led Palumbo and Teich (2004) and others to argue that companies should consider consumer levels of acculturation when segmenting the market. Contributions in international trade build upon this literature and examine the role that immigration plays in affecting international trade patterns (e.g., Mundra 2005).

Most of the work on diaspora consumption of homeland services focuses on diaspora tourism to the homeland. This work recognizes and attempts to quantify the economic impact of such tourism (e.g., King and Gamage 1994). It also explores the impact of this tourism on the strength of ethnic attitudes (e.g., Milman, Reichel, and Pizam 1990) and how such tourism motivates diaspora community members to increase their homeland participation (e.g., Chapin 1992).

Human Capital Transfers

As noted in this book's introduction, until the early part of the twenty-first century, much of the work on immigration and human capital focused on "brain drain" effects, how the loss of talent and know-how negatively affected homeland economies. Subsequently, discourse regarding the impact of migration on homeland human capital shifted to a discussion of "brain gain" owing to the return of expatriates to their homeland or homeland human-capital training efforts of the diaspora (e.g., Saxenian 1999; Stark 2004). Work in this area chronicles the economic development potential of brain gains (e.g., Hunger 2004; Seguin, State, and Singer 2006); the causes, consequences, and policies promoting brain gains (e.g., Hall 2005; Pandey et al. 2006; Kuznetsov, Nemirovsky, and Yoguel 2006; Wescott and Brinkerhoff 2006); and the role of homeland repatriation in career development (Carr, Inkson, and Thorn 2005).

Of central interest to much of this work is the issue of the diffusion of technology and production know-how from the diaspora to the homeland. Meyer and Brown's (1999) study of diaspora-homeland knowledge networks identified forty-one such networks attached to thirty countries. Each network linked highly skilled diaspora members with homeland individuals in various ways. Such knowledge networks are cited as a driving force behind industry-specific growth in several contexts, such as the Indian software industry (Saxenian 2002b).

Social Capital Transfers

The large body of work on ethnic entrepreneurship in the fields of sociology and economics primarily focuses on social capital advantages of the immigrant in the host country. Several historical accounts of transnational trade networks exist in the literature (e.g., Minoglou, Pepelasis, and Louri 1997; Chang 2004). In the late 1990s and early 2000s studies of contemporary transnational trade networks began emerging (e.g., Kyle 1999; Uduku 2002; Cheung 2004) that explored how individuals and firms in the home country benefit from co-ethnic social contacts in the diaspora. This research chronicles how diaspora ties can provide information to homeland entrepreneurs and firms, such as import and operational regulations, consumer demand, and competitive intelligence. It also explores how diaspora members serve as intermediaries helping home-country nationals identify financial resource contacts and distribution partners in the diasporans' country of residence. Diasporas also help decrease informal trade and investment barriers for homeland firms by enhancing the country-of-origin reputation of these firms (Saxenian 1999; Kapur 2001).

Encouraging and Facilitating Diaspora Involvement in Homeland Private-Sector Development

The growing body of knowledge about diaspora economic involvement in the homeland begs the question, How can the economic potential of the diaspora be effectively targeted and developed by the homeland? The three chapters in Part 2 seek answers to this question.

In the first chapter, "The Factors Conducive to Diaspora Investment: Comparing China, Armenia, and Ireland," Milton Esman develops a conceptual framework for understanding why certain diaspora communities are more successful at making homeland economic contributions than others. Drawing on the case studies of the overseas Chinese, Armenian, and Irish Catholic American diaspora communities, Esman identifies three critical factors that determine the degree and nature of diaspora homeland economic involvement. First is the investment climate in the country of origin. Governments bear the burden of transforming diasporas' economic interests into investment action by creating an enabling environment for business development. Second is the investment capability of the diaspora community. Esman observes that not all diasporas are equal when it comes to entrepreneurial know-how, experience, and resources. Third is the diaspora's inclination to invest. Often these inclinations are linked to the push and pull factors that generated the diaspora's emigration in the first place.

The two remaining chapters in this section explore organizational mechanisms for translating diaspora homeland economic interest into actual private sector development outcomes. Kate Gillespie and Anna Andriasova's chapter, "Supporting Business Development: Armenia's Experience," examines the institutional environment that gave rise to and affected the activities of three different diaspora business support (DBS) programs in Armenia: the

Armenian Business Corporation, the Lincy Foundation Loan Programs, and the Izmirlian Foundation Loan Programs. In each case, the authors analyze the institutional input, output, and control sets of these programs to derive propositions about the institutional conditions that enhance and discourage diaspora support for homeland businesses.

Gillespie and Andriasova generate several propositions regarding factors that facilitate successful DBS. These factors include homeland government institutional stability and the dedicated "staying power" of diaspora social entrepreneurs. These propositions also point to the importance of agents in the homeland, those responsible for the selection of client firms and the disbursement of funds to those firms. The authors posit that agents most likely to be successful in private sector development activities are those (1) with experience in small- and medium-size enterprise support, creation, and management; (2) who adhere to strong industry-specific governing principles; and (3) who possess strong governance cultures. The nature and scope of organizational activity also contributes to DBS success; organizations targeting specific client objectives and needs, offering an integrated service portfolio beyond mere financial support, and proactively participating in and working with other organizations to influence the macroenvironment are associated with more successful private-sector development initiatives. Finally, the authors highlight several factors that hinder DBS. For example, they observe that interference by homeland and country-of-residence governments may render private sector development initiatives ineffective, and they note that host governments lacking the necessary experience and political will often make poor diaspora business support agents.

The final chapter of Part 2, "Homeland Export and Investment Promotion Agencies: The Case of Afghanistan," by Liesl Riddle and Valentina Marano, argues that national export-promotion organizations and investment-promotion agencies can be leveraged by homeland governments to encourage and facilitate diaspora homeland private-sector development. These organizations play an active role in economic development by promoting homeland goods and services abroad and attracting foreign investment to the homeland. Drawing on the case study of Afghanistan, the authors demonstrate the opportunities and challenges that homeland EPOs and IPAs face when targeting their diaspora communities. Although diasporans may have strong interest in contributing to the economic development of their homeland, they may not be willing or able to return to their homeland to directly participate in private sector development activities. Riddle and Marano suggest that homeland EPOs and IPAs can bridge the gap between diaspora capital potential (financial, social, and human capital) and the needs of homeland economic actors (entrepreneurs, managers, and firms). The authors note that EPOs and IPAs must adapt their existing activity set in order to effectively market homeland economies to diaspora community members.

Necessary adaptations include modifications to their target marketing strategies and their knowledge-provision, networking, and advocacy services to meet specific diaspora needs, experiences, and skill sets.

Conclusion

Globalization has facilitated both the economic means and psychological motivations for emigrant communities and their descendants to actively participate in the economic development of their homelands. Understanding the various ways diaspora communities contribute to homeland private-sector development through financial, social, and human capital is the central focus of the growing body of interdisciplinary work in this area. The contributions in this volume impel this research agenda by probing the ways in which diaspora interest in homeland economic development can be encouraged, facilitated, and amplified to yield the greatest impact on homeland private-sector development.

—Liesl Riddle

5

The Factors Conducive to Diaspora Investment: Comparing China, Armenia, and Ireland

Milton J. Esman

This chapter addresses the effects of diaspora communities on the economic development of their former homelands through direct investment in productive enterprise. I also examine the conditions within the diaspora that facilitate such transactions, and the effects of the policies and behavior of homeland governments on investment incentives. The cases I have selected are overseas Chinese in East and Southeast Asia, Irish Catholics in the United States, and Armenians in France and California. Following a brief review of diaspora identity and characteristics, I present the three cases and, through a comparative analysis, I identify factors most conducive to diaspora homeland investment.

Characteristics of Diasporas

Diasporas are intergenerational phenomena. They encompass not only the first, migrating generation but also their progeny as well. Individuals belong to a diaspora as long as they identify with that ethnic community. Members of diasporas hold multiple identities, reflecting their occupational, political, ideological, and cultural backgrounds, interests, and loyalties. While ethnic identities tend to be long-lasting, circumstances encountered in the host country may evoke other identities that compete with ethnic solidarity for their time and attention.

In some countries, such as France, there have been powerful incentives and pressures for individuals to integrate—culturally, by using the mainstream language and adopting its way of life; and socially, by participating in mainstream institutions and eventually intermarrying.[1] As social integration occurs and individuals move to the mainstream, attachments to their ethnic community and to diaspora institutions tend to wither; for some, they cease entirely. As noted in earlier chapters, others, having adopted the mainstream culture and way of life, nevertheless maintain attachments to their ethnic community out of a sense of pride in their ethnic identity, of obligation, or of nostalgia for their "roots" and their grandparents' culture.

In other countries, cultural and especially social integration are not encouraged, neither by the indigenous society nor by the diaspora community. Such is the case in some of the plural societies of Southeast Asia, Malaysia, for example, where the Chinese and Indian minorities cling to their inherited cultures and collective identities, while the Malay Muslim majority denies them the status of *bumiputera* (native sons), relegating them to second-class citizenship. Successive generations of such diasporas are likely to maintain their separate collective identities and lead separate existences, even as they share occupational and other associations with members of the indigenous majority and make expedient adjustments to their laws and customs, such as fluency in the national language.

The homeland to which they maintain a sentimental attachment is likely to be the country from which the first generation migrated, the repository of their ethnic origins and the burial grounds of their ancestors. In a few cases, however, the "homeland" may be geographically removed from their actual country of origin. The recent ancestors of North American Jews did not migrate from Israel, nor did most diaspora Armenians migrate from the Caucasus. Their loyalties are to the land that the current generation of fellow ethnics, owing to historical circumstances, now regard as their legitimate homeland.

Roughly speaking, there are two classes of diasporas. *Labor diasporas* consist mainly of unskilled individuals with little formal education and no business experience. Like North Africans in France, Turks in Germany, and Mexicans in the United States, they join the lower rungs of the employment hierarchy in their host country. *Entrepreneurial diasporas,* by contrast, include substantial numbers of people with business experience and skills. They are on the lookout for opportunities to start their own businesses in their adopted country. Like Jews in the United States and Chinese in Indonesia, they may find it necessary to begin in low-skilled occupations, but through education or enterprise, members of the first and certainly of the second generation soon emerge as professionals and businesspeople, some becoming very wealthy. These capabilities, along with government policies in their former homeland, affect their ability to contribute to the economic progress of the country they have left behind.

Members of all diasporas remit funds to their families. The purpose of most transnational migrations that produce diasporas is to improve economic opportunities; living frugally, their earnings provide the modest surpluses that enable migrants to send money back to their needy families. As has been mentioned, in the aggregate, these small remittances add up to important macroeconomic resources for the home country, as foreign exchange earnings.[2] Since the bulk of these remittances are used for family consumption, and improving living standards, and relatively little is devoted to investment, they have only marginal effects on their country's economic development. While the volume of remittances decreases as succeeding generations adapt and integrate into their adopted country, some family remittances continue as charity, while governments in the home country extend themselves to encourage, facilitate, and maintain the flow of these useful funds.

A Tale of Three Diasporas

Following is an overview of three countries and their diasporas and their economic relationships vis-à-vis their homelands.

Overseas Chinese

After the demise of Mao Zedong in 1976 and the subsequent defeat of the Gang of Four, Deng Xiaoping emerged as the paramount leader of the People's Republic. He reversed the Maoist policy of autarchy and economic isolation and proclaimed the Four Modernizations, which required China to open its doors to foreign scientific, intellectual, and economic influences. Foreign private investments in industry and infrastructure were welcomed. The external response was immediate and massive, launching China's transformative process of rapid economic modernization and economic growth that has been sustained to this writing. What have attracted foreign investors are China's low-cost, disciplined labor force, abundant raw materials, enormous domestic market, and generous tax incentives.

Japan and the United States have been the sources of important investments, but during the first two decades of the Four Modernizations, no less than 75 percent of investments originated from the Chinese diaspora in Hong Kong, Taiwan, and Southeast Asia, including Chinese multinational firms headquartered in Singapore, Malaysia, and Indonesia (Li and Li 1999). These family-owned and -operated firms dominate the economies of all the Southeast Asian states. Their owners and managers have been reared in societies that behave according to Chinese cultural norms, including fluency in Mandarin and in the dialects of coastal South China. Beyond their extended families, their business methods function through informal networks of trust, avoiding as much as possible involvement with legal procedures, government regulations, and bureaucratic and judicial institutions.

These networks (*guanxi*) can incorporate government and Communist Party officials whose approval is needed to secure licenses, permits, and other requisites for efficient operations, often in return for profit sharing and expedient side payments. These methods enable overseas Chinese businesspeople to capitalize on their familiarity with Chinese culture and their language skills to circumvent legal and bureaucratic obstacles to business operations. For this reason, Western and Japanese firms often seek them out to participate in joint investment ventures, especially in the Special Economic Zones in the southeastern coastal provinces. Because of family control, these firms are able to seize opportunities, take greater risks, and make faster decisions than Western corporations.

As capitalists, overseas Chinese investors expect to make money from their operations on the mainland, most of which are relatively small compared with Western and Japanese ventures, and are export oriented, labor intensive, and relatively low technology. Many of these investors, however, are also motivated by sentimental, noneconomic incentives, among them the desire to help the communities that had been the homes and burial places of their forebearers.[3] Moreover, they harbor the expectation that as China once again becomes a power to be reckoned with and gains in international prestige, its successes will reflect favorably on China's sons and daughters overseas. This is similar to the attitude of many wealthy American Jews who promote private business ventures in Israel and buy State of Israel bonds less for business reasons than as acts of charity and determination to help Israel succeed.

Overseas Chinese include persons from all walks of life: laborers, mechanics, clerks, professionals, and shopkeepers. Some have demonstrated outstanding business acumen, achieving wealth and economic power. They possess the means and the sentiments that motivate direct investments in the mainland economy. The People's Republic of China (PRC) government since 1978 has adopted and implemented policies that welcome foreign private investment that enables their participation in the economic revival of their erstwhile homeland. This is the conjunction of demand and supply that facilitates diaspora participation in the economic development of their ancestral homeland.

Knowledgeable students of China's political economy predict with confidence that "the dominance of overseas Chinese in China's foreign direct investment is unlikely to change in the near future" (Li and Li 1999, 239).

Irish Catholics in the United States

In the century from 1820 to 1920, millions of men and women emigrated from Ireland, the population of the Emerald Isle dropping by half, from 16 to 8 million. About 5 million came to the United States, two-thirds of them

Catholic. Among persons of Irish descent in the United States, about half are Protestant—Presbyterian, Methodist, Baptist, and Episcopalian. They became a component of the American Anglo-Protestant mainstream. Irish Catholics, on the other hand, became a distinctive ethnic and religious minority, their progeny now numbering about 25 million.[4] They came in large numbers in the wake of the great famine of the mid- and late 1840s, a labor diaspora, comprising predominantly poor, uneducated, unskilled peasants. The men gravitated to construction sites, railways, mines, and factories, performing much of the heavy, unskilled labor for the expanding US economy. Many of the women found work in household service. The more talented and ambitious joined the clergy of the Roman Catholic Church, building and operating the extensive networks of religious, educational, and charitable institutions of American Catholicism. Others practiced their skills at political organization, constructing and managing the Democratic Party political machines in every major city of the Northeast and Midwest. They encountered hostility, sometimes violent, plus social contempt and economic and social discrimination and exclusion that persisted until the end of World War II.

Yet this diaspora remained in the United States, fewer than 10 percent returning to Ireland. They maintained their interest in the *Auld Sod,* remitting funds to their families and following with sympathy the struggle in their erstwhile homeland for home rule and independence from the hated British colonial establishment. A minority attempted to participate actively in the struggle, sending money and arms to the Irish Republican Army. As early as 1866 a band of "Fenians" using surplus Civil War rifles and ammunition launched a failed invasion of British North America (Canada) that was repudiated by the US government in Washington.

Irish nationalism is a "deeply revered tradition" among Irish Americans (Duff 1971, 65). But after Ireland achieved de facto independence in 1921 (except for the six northern counties), their interest in Irish politics gradually waned, succeeded by a sentimental nostalgia for the old country marked by visits to relatives and tourist sites. Their main effort, aside from the struggle to support their families, focused on earning the credentials that would gain them entry into the US middle class and on achieving respect and acceptance for their community and its institutions. Irish Americans participated with distinction in all of the United States' wars, earning a reputation as among the most patriotic of their compatriots. Yet, until World War II, very few Irish Catholics possessed the wealth or corporate resources that would have enabled them to make significant investments in Ireland's economic development.

World War II was the watershed in the United States that swept away the barriers of discrimination against unpopular European minorities, Irish, Italian, Jewish.[5] This enabled large numbers of Irish Catholics gradually to enter the ranks of corporate management. Succeeding decades witnessed the emergence of Irish Catholics with the necessary wealth and influence to steer investments to Ireland's economic modernization. Perhaps the best known of American Irish Catholic plutocrats was Joseph P. Kennedy, the patriarch of the Kennedy clan. By the 1970s, in terms of educational achievement and per capita income, Irish Catholics ranked as the second most "privileged" of the United States' ethnic communities (Greeley 1977). Though the means were there, investments to the homeland did not follow.

During the nineteenth and twentieth centuries, prior to the mid-1980s, Ireland's economy stagnated. Except for industrial enclaves in the Belfast area of Northern Ireland, the economy remained mostly agricultural. The British ruling power had little interest in Ireland's economic modernization, and for the first half-century of independence after 1921, Ireland's governments fumbled with laissez-faire and protectionist policies that yielded low growth, high unemployment, and continued out-migration. "Ireland's growth rate in the 70 years prior to 1985 was below that of every European country, except Britain" (Sweeney 1996, 39). When in 1973 Ireland joined the European Economic Community (EEC), it was one of the poorest and economically most backward countries in Europe.

In the mid-1980s, prodded by the EEC, its government initiated a new strategy for economic development and modernization. It would attempt to attract foreign direct investment by emphasizing its low rate of corporate taxation, its improved physical infrastructure (thanks to projects sponsored by the EEC), and its educated, English-speaking labor force. Together it was hoped that these would provide an attractive manufacturing platform for exports to the European common market. The response was immediate, spectacular, and transformative. Foreign investment capital poured into Ireland. From 1987 to 2005, no fewer than 1,100 firms set up operations in Ireland, including 450 US companies that invested $252 billion, mostly in information system components, pharmaceuticals, and chemicals. In the decade from 1987 to 1996, economic growth averaged 5.4 percent annually, increasing to 8 percent from 1995 to 2002. New jobs averaged 1,000 a week; unemployment, though still high, declined; emigration ceased; and in the decade following 1995, Ireland's population actually increased by 12.5 percent (Finfacts 2005).[6] By 2003, having surpassed Britain, Ireland could boast the second highest per capita GDP in the European Union.[7] To accompany its economic modernization, Ireland became socially secularized as its conservative church hierarchy retreated to its pastoral functions.

Ireland's economic takeoff is one of the great success stories of recent times, for which, however, the Irish American diaspora can claim little credit. During the four decades preceding the takeoff, the policy environment did not provide incentives that would invite foreign investment. Though there were wealthy members of the diaspora with the means and the ability to steer investments to the Irish economy, they declined to do so. Nor did they exert pressure on the government to improve the investment climate, even though many sustained their interest in their ancestral country, as demonstrated by the flow of North American tourists on Aer Lingus, the ethnic Irish airline. After 1986 the US corporate response to investment opportunities was so buoyant that wealthy Irish Catholic Americans felt little need to make special efforts on behalf of Ireland's economic development.

This is an example of a diaspora that retained an abiding affection and affinity for the ancestral homeland, a number of whose members possessed the means to contribute to its economic development, but found it unnecessary to do so even when changes in government policy made their participation possible.

The Armenian Diaspora

Armenians are an ancient people united by a distinctive language, a turbulent history, and a proud 1,700-year Christian experience embodied in the Apostolic Armenian Orthodox Church. Collective memory of the genocide committed during World War I against the Armenian minority in Anatolia is an important element in the cohesion and militancy among contemporary Armenians everywhere. Among its 10 million members, about a third—3.2 million—inhabit the Republic of Armenia, a landlocked, resource-poor, mountainous area in the Caucasus. The majority comprise the diaspora, scattered throughout the world. While 2.5 million live in Russia, the most affluent and influential Armenian communities are in France and the United States. About half of the 800,000 American Armenians are located in the Los Angeles area.

During the five centuries of Islamic Ottoman rule, the Christian Armenians, as a "people of the book," were tolerated as a self-governing community under the direction of their religious leaders. Like Greeks and Jews, they served as economic middlemen between the ruling Ottoman warriors and administrators and the mass of the peasantry. The same was true in Eastern Europe under the Tsars. Moreover, Armenians were receptive to American Protestant missionaries who established schools, medical clinics, and institutions of higher learning for the benefit of their Armenian protégés.[8] Thus, Armenians possessed a long-standing entrepreneurial experience and American-sponsored higher education that enabled them in the diaspora to prosper in commercial, financial, business, and professional roles. During the seventy-year Soviet occupation of their homeland, the diaspora was split into highly organized, contending political factions based in large part on their attitudes toward the Soviet regime. Some became associated with widespread violence directed at Turkish targets, including Turkish diplomats (Gunter 1970, 19–24). After the disastrous earthquake in 1988, they united in raising funds and providing relief and logistical assistance for the hundreds of thousands of victims, especially in the capital city, Yerevan, and its vicinity.

Armenia was a constituent republic of the Soviet Union. With its dissolution, Armenia gained independence in 1991, was admitted to the United Nations, and shortly thereafter affiliated with the World Bank and the International Monetary Fund. Its economy, however, collapsed because its inefficient Soviet-era industries lost their protected markets. As a dual consequence of the earthquake and the economic collapse, per capita income fell by 75 percent, with two-thirds of the people subsisting at or near the poverty line. Thirty-five percent of total household income came from diaspora charitable remittances. During the ensuing decade, an estimated 1 million men and women emigrated, half to nearby Russia, the other half to France and the United States.

From 1992 to 1994 the newly independent republic fought a war against neighboring Azerbaijan over the enclave of Nagorno-Karabakh (Karabakh), which lies within the internationally recognized borders of Azerbaijan but contains an Armenian majority. The impoverished Republic of Armenia waged and won this war, resulting in the ethnic cleansing of several hundred thousand Azeri from Armenia and Karabakh and an equivalent number of Armenians from Azerbaijan. The Armenian army established and maintains a narrow corridor through Azerbaijan, linking Armenia with Karabakh. A cease-fire negotiated by the United Nations took effect in 1995. Azerbaijan and Turkey inflicted additional pain on Armenia by blockading its commerce until such time as Armenia withdraws its forces from Karabakh. Nevertheless, by 2005, the World Bank estimated that Armenia's per capita GDP had recovered to the preindependence level as the result primarily of growth in agricultural production, which continues to employ 45 percent of the labor force.

The Armenian diaspora has rallied to the support of independent Armenia. Annual remittances to Armenian households are variously estimated to run anywhere from $300 to $900 million, constituting as much as 30 percent of gross national product (GNP). For many households benefiting directly from remittances, these are estimated to constitute as much as 80 percent of family income. Most of these funds are spent on consumption items, but some are invested in home improvements, education, and small businesses (Roberts 2004).

Among the more active diaspora contributors to independent Armenia is the venerable Armenian General Benevolent Union established in 1906, with headquarters now in New York and chapters throughout the world. Its annual budget ranges from $30 to $35 million. It supports educational, cultural, and charitable activities both in Armenia and the diaspora, including the American University in Yerevan, health centers, soup kitchens, and orphanages.

The largest diaspora contributor is the Lincy Foundation of Beverly Hills, California (discussed in greater detail in Chapter 6), founded by the Armenian American billionaire financier Kirk Kerkorian. From 2001 to 2009 its programmed expenditures total $150 million, of which the largest component is devoted to road construction and repair, a critical infrastructural need for a landlocked country that must depend for its economic expansion on foreign trade. Among the foundation's projects was the construction of a modern highway connecting the Republic with Karabakh. Lincy also provides loans for small businesses, repairs for housing damaged by the 1988 earthquake, and restoration of such cultural institutions as museums and theaters.

Second and third generations of the wealthy and influential Armenian diaspora in the United States are thoroughly Americanized (see Bakalian 1993, 393–444). They have acculturated to the English language and participate in the educational, cultural, economic, political, and voluntary institutions of the mainstream. A significant number marry outside the ranks of the diaspora. Nevertheless, Armenian American organizations exert unremitting pressure on the US government to deny economic assistance to Turkey until such time as the Turkish government acknowledges and apologizes for the genocide of 1915–1916.[9] They also lobby Congress to provide generous foreign aid to Armenia. In 2004 the US Agency for International Development programmed $75 million for Armenia—in per capita terms one of USAID's largest development assistance programs—for a variety of activities in water management, health services, small business, and democratization. Since independence, the World Bank has programmed $270 million for Armenia, for a wide spectrum of projects, mainly in agriculture, health and sanitation, and public administration.

More than two-thirds of the world's Armenians live in the diaspora and are committed to the survival of their collective identity, their church, and the welfare of their newly independent ancestral homeland. Elements of the diaspora, especially in France and the United States, are economically well situated to contribute to the Republic's economic development. Because of its tiny domestic market, industrial and service investments, if they are to be viable, must be oriented largely to exports. The investment climate, however, remains unfavorable. Though a generous set of incentives have been legislated, the commercial blockade imposed by its neighbors impedes prospects for exports and this will probably continue, since Armenia is unlikely to relinquish its de facto annexation of Karabakh. Diaspora expenditures have thus been concentrated on raising living standards and the quality of life for the nation's 3.2 million inhabitants, strengthening its institutions, and improving the physical infrastructure. Meanwhile, discouraged by the poor investment climate, prevailing corruption in government, and uncertainties concerning contract enforcement, the diaspora "is now more willing to send funds for charity than for investment" (USAID, Armenia 2004, 14).

Three Propositions

These three cases suggest three variable factors that affect a diaspora's ability and inclination to contribute to the economic development of their ancestral homeland. The first is the *investment climate* in the country of origin. Where its government welcomes foreign direct investment, protects private property, enforces contracts, permits the remittance of profits, and provides either a large internal market or opportunities for exporting, these constitute incentives for members of the diaspora to commit funds to the economic development of their former homeland. Where such incentives are absent, investment even from a faithful diaspora will not occur.

The second variable is the *capability of members of the diaspora.* Members of a labor diaspora are unlikely for several generations to command the wealth that would enable them to invest their surpluses abroad. They might dutifully remit funds to help relatives and contribute to charitable, religious, and cultural institutions, but these are likely to be used primarily for consumption. By contrast, diasporas that include a cohort of entrepreneurs can respond differently. Some of these businesspeople, having achieved economic success and even great wealth within one or two generations after emigrating, possess the means that enable investment in their former homeland.

The third variable is the *diaspora's inclination.* They may have no interest in helping a former homeland where they were oppressed and treated as second-class persons. For example, the long-standing Greek diaspora from Anatolia, having been summarily deported during the 1920s, has no inclination to contribute to Turkey's economic development, nor do Jews who fled Tsarist persecution or Communist efforts to suppress their collective identity and culture have any desire to contribute to Russia's progress. Members of a diaspora may be so firmly integrated into their host country that they no longer identify with their ancestral land of origin and thus have lost the will to provide assistance. On the other hand, diaspora individuals who are culturally and socially well integrated into their host country may nonetheless share a continuing sense of obligation to their country of origin and a willingness to provide substantial assistance.

Table 5.1 summarizes this analysis as it applies over time to the three

Table 5.1   Diaspora and Homeland Characteristics and Inclination to Contribute

Diaspora	Capability	Investment Climate	Diaspora Inclination
Chinese	Positive	1949–1978 Negative 1978–2006 Positive	Positive
Armenians	Positive	Negative	Positive
Irish Americans	1820–1945 Negative 1945–2005 Positive	1820–1986 Negative 1986–2006 Positive	1820–1986 Positive 1986–2006 Uncertain

variable factors treated in this article. A number of overseas Chinese, having achieved economic success, possessed the means to invest substantially in their ancestral country. During the Maoist era, foreign private investment was unwelcome, but this policy was reversed after 1978. Expatriate Chinese maintained a strong attachment to their culture, their collective identity, and the belief that, should China successfully modernize and regain the world's respect, its new-found prestige would reflect favorably on them. Thus, the investment response was positive.

Armenians, especially in France and the United States, have achieved professional and economic success. While most are well integrated into the institutions and way of life of their adopted country, they maintain strong feelings of collective identity and responsibility for the welfare of their fellow ethnics. This has been reinforced by undying memories of the genocide during World War I. This defining experience, coupled with the 1988 earthquake, confirms Kerlin's findings from Chapter 2, that perceived needs and related tragedies in the homeland can spark or strengthen diaspora inclination. The Armenian diaspora has the requisite means and inclination, but the investment climate in Armenia has been so negative as to preclude serious private investment. They have contented themselves, instead, primarily with generous charitable donations.

After 1945, when discrimination against Irish Catholics in the United States mostly ceased, a number of Irish Americans achieved wealth and prominence in corporate America. But the investment climate in Ireland, with its small domestic market, was unattractive. After Ireland joined the EEC, and especially after its government adopted investment-friendly policies in the mid-1980s, the investment climate changed for the better and Ireland took off into a spectacular burst of economic growth. The investment response from US corporations was so pronounced that Irish Catholic business leaders, notwithstanding their continuing affection for the old country, saw no need to make a special effort on its behalf.

Conclusion

There are many ways that members of ethnic diasporas can manifest their affection and support for the homeland and society that they and their fore-bearers have left behind. These include financial remittances to families, personal visits, charitable contributions to institutions and communities, and pressure on their own government to implement policies, such as generous foreign aid, that benefit their former homeland. But if they are to promote its economic development, as this chapter demonstrates, three conditions must prevail: members of the diaspora must possess the requisite means; they must be favorably inclined to assist their former homeland; and its government must implement policies that welcome foreign direct investment.

Notes

1. The rejection, often violent, of French culture by many North African Muslim immigrants and their children, and their unwillingness to integrate into the national mainstream—in effect their unwillingness to become Frenchmen and -women—confronts France (and other European countries) with an unprecedented social, moral, and political crisis.

2. For example, remittances from Mexican emigrants working in the United States totaled $16 billion in 2005. This is the world's largest flow of family remittances and is growing at a rapid rate. Remittances will soon exceed Mexico's earnings from petroleum exports. While the bulk of these funds are used for family consumption, some help to finance microenterprises. The Mexican government provides special facilities to maintain and enhance the flow of these funds (data from the El Paso branch of the Federal Reserve Bank of Dallas).

3. For a good summary of the cultural dimensions of overseas Chinese participation in the mainland economy, see Wang (2001, 154–159). During the Maoist era when private enterprise was proscribed, overseas Chinese were limited to remitting funds to assist their relatives and their native communities.

4. Prior to the 1840s the majority of Irish arrivals in the United States were Protestant.

5. Irish Catholics had been suspected of owing primary loyalty to a foreign potentate, the pope, rather than to US democratic institutions. They were accused of undercutting labor standards, offering to work for less than prevailing wage rates.

6. In 2005, for example, net in-migration amounted to 53,400. Only 4,300 came from the US diaspora, and 13,800 from the diaspora in the UK. The remaining two-thirds came from the European Union and the rest of the world (Republic of Ireland, Central Statistics Office 2005).

7. There are vulnerabilities in Ireland's recent economic performance, including a very high rate of foreign ownership of its economic assets, very little research and development activity, and persistent poverty of a third of the population.

8. Christian missionaries were not allowed to proselytize among Muslims.

9. To illustrate the intensity of Armenian sentiment on this subject: the *New York Times* recently carried a story under the headline "Armenian Furor over PBS

Plan for Debate" (Archibold 2006). In April 2006, the Public Broadcasting System had scheduled an hourlong documentary about the 1915–1916 genocide titled "The Armenian Genocide." While satisfied that the documentary confirms the charge of genocide, spokespersons for the Armenian American community protested the plan for a subsequent discussion, in which two of the participants would deny that these events constituted genocide. The Armenian position is that the genocide is a proven historical fact and that denying it constitutes an affront to the memory of its victims.

6

Supporting Business Development: Armenia's Experience

Kate Gillespie and Anna Andriasova

Diasporas are increasingly targeted for assistance to business development in developing countries where difficult business environments often discourage investment from Western multinational corporations (Gillespie et al. 1999; Ramamurti 2004). Such strategies appear reasonable, since Gillespie et al. (1999) have shown that interest in homeland investment can be significant across diaspora communities. Furthermore, notable homeland investment has been observed in a number of countries. Egypt's economic liberalization in the late 1970s increasingly relied on investment from overseas Egyptians when investment from US, European, and Japanese multinational corporations failed to meet government expectations (Gillespie 1984). China followed a similar pattern during its early years of market liberalization when diaspora Chinese established more projects than did investors from the United States, from Japan, or from any single European country (Bolt 1996).

Interest in homeland investment can be triggered by general business concerns such as market opportunities in the homeland or emerging business difficulties in the adopted country. For example, a number of Egyptian businesses fled Egypt in the 1960s during the increasingly socialistic administration of President Gamal Abdul Nasser and set up operations in Lebanon. However, Egypt's subsequent economic liberalization under President Anwar Sadat coincided with Lebanon's civil war, thus promoting the return of some of those businesses to Egypt. Interest in homeland investment may also be triggered by perceived limitations to the advancement of diaspora members in their adopted countries. Diaspora investment in India's high-tech industry has been attributed in part to the perception of many expatriate Indians working in the United

States that they were passed over for management positions in the United States (Gillespie 2007).

As noted in the introduction to Part 2, Gillespie et al. (1999) also identified two factors that increased the likelihood that an Armenian, Cuban, Iranian, or Palestinian diasporan resident in the United States would be interested in homeland investment. The first was ethnic advantage. When diaspora members believed they knew the homeland and its business environment better than the average US person, they were more likely to be interested in homeland investment. The second was more altruistic. When respondents agreed with the statement "I believe that diaspora members in the United States should invest in businesses in the homeland and not just donate to homeland charities," they were more likely to be interested in homeland investment.

In cases where homeland markets are limited in size, where political risk is high, and/or where operational obstacles are very challenging, the importance of altruism in homeland investment becomes all the more salient. In such cases, homeland governments look to their diasporas not only as a potential source of investment but as a potential source of social entrepreneurs as well, in both the profit and not-for-profit sectors. Social entrepreneurship in the not-for-profit category can entail enacting new nonprofits or NGOs (Mort, Weerawardena, and Carnegie 2003; Fowler 2000), introducing innovation within NGOs (Thompson, Alvy, and Lees 2000), or engaging in for-profit businesses in order to support charitable programs (Davis 1997; Fowler 2000). Social entrepreneurs involved in the for-profit category are credited with augmenting their concern for the generation of wealth for business owners with a consideration for the well-being of workers and the benefit of the larger community in which the business is embedded (Cook, Dodds, and Mitchell 2003). As such, their vision of wealth creation encompasses a broader group of beneficiaries and a more extended timeline (Sfeir-Younis 2002; Wallace 1999). It is hoped that diasporas, especially those from homelands with more problematic business environments, will bring that extra commitment and motivation that extend beyond entrepreneurship for mere profit.

Despite a relatively high interest in homeland investment exhibited by many diasporas, difficulties arise in turning interest into actual investment. Many diaspora members may wish to invest in the homeland but are unable or unwilling to participate directly in business ventures. Even finding social entrepreneurs who have the ability to leave their adopted countries and return to the homeland is very challenging. Diasporans who are very committed to their homeland may not envisage a career there. Furthermore, many diaspora members who are concerned with the economic development of their homelands are not themselves entrepreneurs. This has led to calls to channel diaspora money to existing businesses or new ventures in the homeland in ways that do not require investors to become actively involved in the on-site management of these ventures (Gillespie, Sayre, and Riddle 2001; Gevorkyan and Grigorian 2003).

The experience of Armenia offers lessons for homeland governments and diaspora members who are concerned with homeland private-sector development. Armenia has sought to mobilize such diaspora business support (DBS) in the homeland since the early 1990s. This chapter reviews DBS during the first fifteen years of Armenian independence. The DBS was channeled through different paradigms of social entrepreneurship by three philanthropic organizations—the Armenian Business Forum (ABF), the Lincy Foundation, and the Izmirlian Foundation. Each of these organizations began business-support projects with the same vision: to assist Armenia by supporting small- and medium-sized enterprises (SMEs), which in turn were expected to create jobs and help the Armenian economy. Each pursued a different model, and the projects undertaken by these organizations include both for-profit and not-for-profit ventures. ABF raised funds from diaspora businesspeople who first loaned to and then invested in Armenian SMEs via the Armenian Business Corporation (ABC). The Lincy and Izmirlian foundations supplied funds to loan to Armenian businesses but utilized agents to administer these loans. These agents comprised the government of Armenia (GOA), Armenian banks, a United States–based development NGO, and an international bank.

Following is a description of the Armenian context and the methodology we employed in our study. We then examine the business support experiences of ABF, the Lincy Foundation, and the Izmirlian Foundation and present a series of propositions for improving the effectiveness of DBS.

Armenia and Its Diaspora

Present-day Armenia is a small, landlocked country located in the trans-Caucasus region between Turkey, Georgia, Azerbaijan, and Iran. Formerly the smallest republic in the Soviet Union, as reviewed in Chapter 5, Armenia emerged as an independent state after the collapse of the Soviet Union in 1991. Under the Soviet central planning system, Armenia had developed a modern industrial sector, supplying manufactured goods to other Soviet republics in exchange for raw materials and energy. The country's economy was badly undermined once these relationships collapsed subsequent to the dissolution of the Soviet Union.

Despite attempts to liberalize key sectors of its economy and reform its trade and foreign exchange regimes, Armenia's transition from a planned economy to a market economy proved problematic (Gelbard 2005). Massive privatization occurred quickly and without adequate transparency. Similar to Russia's experience with privatization, state assets were sold at low prices and transferred rapidly into the hands of a few private parties (Hakobyan 2003). A proliferation of new banks resulted in several bank crises and the collapse of dozens of weak and mismanaged banks (Safdari, Scannell, and Ohanian 2005). Armenia's economic transition was further hampered by the aftermath of the severe 1988 earthquake as well as disputes with neighboring countries, including the war with Azerbaijan over its Armenian enclave of Nagorno-Karabakh (Paul 2000). Within only a few years, Armenia faced massive unemployment and emigration.

Not surprisingly, Armenia looked to its relatively large diaspora for support. Out of 9 million Armenians in the world, only 3.5 million currently reside in Armenia. Large diaspora communities can be found in Europe, the United States, South America, the Middle East, and Russia.

The Armenia diaspora traditionally focused on the Armenian church and the collective memory of the Armenian holocaust (Paul 2000). In response to Armenia's economic crisis, however, the diaspora mobilized on an unprecedented scale to send financial and material aid to the homeland (Panossian 1998). In ten years ending in late 1999, fourteen diaspora organizations donated an estimated $630 million (Anonymous 1999). While philanthropic transfers helped Armenia to survive during its early and difficult years of independence, more than humanitarian assistance would be necessary for Armenia to achieve even the level of prosperity it had enjoyed under the Soviet system.

Foreign direct investment in the nation's economy was generally viewed as a panacea that would create much-needed jobs, develop export industries, and foster trade and business ties with other countries. Two Armenian presidents, Levon Ter-Petrosyan and Robert Kocharyan, personally appealed to the diaspora to invest in the homeland and help develop the nation's economy. A few Armenian investors from the United States, Europe, Iran, and Russia established businesses in the homeland, but this investment fell far short of what was envisaged both in overall scale and size of projects. As foreign direct investment from the diaspora foundered, diaspora philanthropic organizations sought new paradigms for supporting local business development in Armenia.

Methodology and Framework for Analysis

In the preliminary stage of our research, we sought to identify the full population of organizations involved in DBS in Armenia. We began by investigating institutions and organizations established by diaspora Armenians to help the country during its economic transition. Most of those organizations were involved in humanitarian assistance. To qualify for analysis in the scope of this study, however, a project had to be organized by or with funds of diaspora Armenians for the purpose of supporting the development of business enterprises operating in Armenia. By searching secondary sources, asking respondents with knowledge of the area, and confirming our findings during the resultant interview process described below, we identified three diaspora organizations actively operating in the area of business development: the ABC, the Lincy Foundation, and the Izmirlian Foundation. A second part of the preliminary stage of research involved collecting secondary information on regulations and institutions that could influence DBS, as well as information on the three organizations we were researching. Main sources of the secondary information were local and international newspapers and magazines. We searched publications in three languages—Armenian, Russian, and English.

Of special interest were the interviews given to local and international media by the representatives of the three organizations under investigation. Though each of these organizations had been operating in Armenia for several years, there was little published information about them in the national and international press. The only exception was the Lincy Foundation, which inspired many newspaper articles. But most of these concerned the philanthropic activities of the foundation, not their business support programs. Nonetheless, it was possible to locate seven interviews with representatives of the three organizations, which we used to supplement our own interviews as well as to establish additional historical perspective.[1] These interviews were supplemented by press releases of the organizations and several commentaries written about them.

Given the exploratory nature of our research, we then undertook a series of in-depth interviews with key representatives from the Armenian Business Corporation (three key respondents), the Izmirlian and Eurasian foundations (four key respondents), and the Lincy Foundation (two key respondents), as well as other respondents who were chosen based on their knowledge of diaspora investment in Armenia. Respondents within each organization were chosen based on their current status and/or their personal history with the organization. We then asked these respondents for the names of other appropriate respondents.

Potential respondents were contacted via an e-mail in which objectives of the research and appropriate human-subject guidelines were described. Fifteen in-depth phone interviews were then conducted. After analyzing the interviews, follow-up questions were explored via e-mail or telephone for purposes of elaboration, clarification, and reaching consensus when discrepancies arose among respondents. An extensive description of the organization's experience based on multiple primary sources as well as secondary sources was compiled and sent to at least one key respondent within each organization for comment on and confirmation of the facts presented.

In order to compare and contrast the different paradigms of DBS in Armenia, we examine how organizations are influenced by their institutional landscape. Lammers and Hickson (1979) separate an organization's institutional landscape into three components: the organization's control set, input set, and output set. According to Lammers and Hickson, these sets determine the domain, scope, and nature of an organization's activity and consequently affect organizational performance. A control set includes entities with the power to decide if and under what conditions the organization can function. Control sets are usually associated with governments that regulate organizations. These sets may also include political players, such as political parties or lobbies. Entities that provide the means by which the organization is able to operate constitute the organization's input set. For example, input sets for organizations supporting SMEs may include philanthropic organizations, financing institutions, government agencies, and/or international development organizations. An organization's output set encompasses clients, customers, and other entities or individuals that utilize the organization's service. Output sets reflect an organization's control and input sets. Nonetheless, they can change over time, even within the same organization. In our analysis we apply this institutional framework in order to generate performance propositions concerning DBS in Armenia.

Diaspora Business Support in Armenia

To facilitate cross-case comparison (Eisenhardt 1989) of the experiences of the projects established by the three above-named organizations, a brief overview of each is presented below.

Armenian Business Corporation

In 1991 the GOA invited approximately 600 well-known diaspora Armenians to establish a new organization, the Armenian Business Forum. This organization used its influential members to mobilize charitable funds for Armenia among its diaspora and to seek out potential foreign investors. In the words of one ABF member:

> We were working with the local . . . government knowing that 20 percent [of the humanitarian assistance] was reaching the people. ABF tried to bring investors, factory owners, big and small business people to invest. . . . I personally took 50 businessmen from [the] US. None of them succeeded. They all lost their shirts and returned because [of] strong Mafia thief organizations.[2]

By 1994 the Armenian economy had deteriorated even further, and the president of the country called upon the diaspora to invest in the weakened economy. The ABF responded by establishing the Armenian Business Corporation. After creating ABC, the ABF became operationally inactive. The new company was registered as a for-profit, ordinary, joint-stock company with a total capitalization of US$320,000. Original participants were all members of the ABF and included businesspeople from seventeen countries. According to ABC's 2001 Shareholder's Packet, ABC was "aimed at unifying the efforts of [the Armenian diaspora] to assist the development of private business in Armenia and thus improve the social climate in the country."[3]

Originally, ABC primarily made loans to local businesses based on the advice of an influential government official. Unfortunately, many of the companies who received loans from ABC went bankrupt, resulting in a high number of bad loans. From 1997 to 1999, ABC had essentially maintained a full-fledged office simply to take care of court cases resulting from bad loans. In 1999 the acting president and his two predecessors wanted to liquidate the company.

Instead, a restructuring of the company took place. Original shareholders were given the opportunity to withdraw their investment at a value slightly less than the face value of the shares, and a large number of the founders decided to exit at that time. Outstanding shares fell from 31,179 to 821. One of the key figures promoting the restructuring, Hovsep Seferian, was chosen as the new ABC president. Seferian, a Lebanese-born citizen of Brazil, was president or managing director of ten companies, eight of which were located in Armenia. Under its new management, ABC undertook to increase the base of its shareholders. The company decreased the nominal value of each share, attempting to make them more widely available while still targeting the Armenian diaspora. In a press conference in 2000, Seferian remarked: "ABC shares will have eternal value. . . . Most importantly, independent of the financial profit to the shareholder, an ABC share will give the owner the spiritual satisfaction of helping and serving the Motherland, because it is key to the creation of new job opportunities and new success stories."[4]

The business model also changed. ABC shifted from supporting firms seeking loan financing to businesses that were willing to undertake an equity joint-venture in which ABC was the majority partner. A major ABC shareholder commented on the change: "After long years of losses (time and funds) we found that [this new model] was the only way to . . . help businessmen in Armenia because they participate in their business. If they want to steal, they steal their [own] funds."[5] Day-to-day business was left to the minority partner. The minority partner understood, however, that

ABC had the legal power to change a company's management and would do so in the event of managerial dishonesty or if the company operated with losses attributed to its management.

By 2004, ABC had ten employees and listed 251 owners. Its assets exceeded its capitalization, and the company was finalizing its application to issue new shares and debenture notes to be sold in Armenia and the diaspora. ABC was actively involved in seven joint ventures, including fruit and vegetable processing, gas stations, potato production, stone mining, and a law office. An eighth venture, a fishery, was legally registered, but the land upon which the fishery ponds were to be established was illegally occupied. ABC was involved in time-consuming legal procedures to try to secure the land for their project. Although listed on the Armenian Stock Exchange since 2001, ABC had yet to pay a cash dividend. Like most other Armenian stocks (Khachaturyan 2004), ABC stock was rarely traded.

The Izmirlian Foundation Loan Programs

In 1991 a family of wealthy diaspora Armenians established the Izmirlian Foundation. Headquartered in Geneva, the foundation was charged with the mission of improving the lives of Armenians throughout the world. In 1999 the Izmirlian Foundation committed up to US$3 million (dependent upon loan approvals) to augment the Eurasia Foundation Small Business Loan Program, operating in Armenia since 1995. The Eurasia Foundation, which implemented small business loan programs in both Armenia and Ukraine, was established by the US government (USG) in 1993 and was primarily funded by the US Agency for International Development. Headquartered in Washington, D.C., it was an independently managed grant and loan organization with field offices in the twelve newly independent states of the former Soviet Union. Its small business loan program was developed to assist Armenia in fostering entrepreneurial activity. By the time of the Izmirlian donation, the loan program had disbursed US$3.8 million to 133 small- and medium-sized businesses and was credited with creating more than 900 new jobs.

The Izmirlian Foundation had been considering a loan program when a mutual acquaintance brought the two foundations together. At the signing of the grant agreement, Dikran Izmirlian, the president of the Izmirlian Foundation remarked, "We have been looking for a concrete way to help Armenians build their country. Without a strong banking sector and small businesses empowered to create new jobs, the economy will not reach its full potential."[6] The contribution from the Izmirlian Foundation represented the largest grant the Eurasia Foundation had received outside the USG and more than doubled the funds available through its existing Small Business Loan Program in Armenia. In recognition of this grant, Eurasia's loan program in Armenian was renamed the Izmirlian-Eurasia Small Business Loan Program.

While the Izmirlian Foundation supplied partial funding to the new joint program, the Eurasia Foundation managed it. In the news release reporting the Izmirlian contribution, the goals of Eurasia's program were described as twofold: (1) to provide long-term working capital and capital expenditure financing to new and existing Armenian businesses, and (2) to "foster the development of small business lending capacity in Armenian banks by introducing a proven lending methodology that can support small businesses and offer low loan loss ratios."[7] Loans for up to two years and US$125,000 were made available to Armenian SMEs. Prospective borrowers were required to submit an application that was jointly evaluated by Eurasia and a participating bank, and successful applicants were subject to monitoring, either monthly or quarterly. According to one Izmirlian representative in Armenia, no advice of "a systematic nature" was proffered to clients. Still, by year-end 2003, the program experienced less than 1 percent of loans past due and less than 5 percent of loans had been written off, calculated before the full sale of collateral. For example, over a five-year period (both before and after the Izmirlian contribution), the program provided almost $0.5 million dollars in loans to five companies involved in egg production, helping to transform Armenia from an egg importer to a net exporter of eggs. In addition, the increased production resulted in lower egg prices in Armenia.

In 2003 the Izmirlian and Eurasia foundations were projecting changes in their loan program. Beginning in 2004 the two foundations planned to establish a finance company of which each would own 50 percent. This finance company was designed to continue the work of the loan program but bypass the Armenian banks. A director at Eurasia's Armenian office remarked, "At some point banks have to go on their own and make their own loans and not use our money."[8] The pursuant joint venture, however, was short lived. In 2006 Eurasia decided to sell their interest to the Izmirlian Foundation. Overall, the partnership between the two organizations had provided about eighty loans, seventy of which remained active.

At about the same time, the Izmirlian Foundation entered into a second venture to provide loans to small- and medium-sized businesses in Armenia, this time with the Black Sea Trade and Development Bank (BSTDB). Eleven countries participated in this regional bank, which was established in 1998 and began operations the following year. Financing of SMEs was a bank priority, since small- and medium-sized companies were an important segment of the domestic private sector in most member countries.

The Izmirlian Foundation and the BSTDB each contributed US$2 million to launch a joint finance facility for the purpose of financing Armenian SMEs. A February 2003 press release stated that the BSTDB–Izmirlian

Foundation joint finance facility would provide loans in US dollars or in euros for capital expenditures and working-capital requirements of SMEs in amounts ranging from US$125,000 up to US$500,000. Expected financial returns to the Izmirlian Foundation from this enterprise were to be used to support philanthropic activities in Armenia.

The December 2002 online newsletter of the bank's parent organization, the Black Sea Economic Cooperation, noted that the program would be strengthened by the participation of the Netherlands Management Cooperation Programme (NMCP), which would be responsible for auditing client companies as well as offering them "technical assistance of high expertise . . . and sharing best operational practices."[9] The NMCP, originally a public-private partnership between the Dutch government and two industry organizations, had evolved to become an independent organization that assigned volunteers as advisers to projects in developing countries and Central and Eastern Europe.

After three years in operation, the participating organizations terminated the program. The reason given was a disagreement between BSTDB and the Izmirlian Foundation. BSTDB wanted to increase profitability by increasing the interest rates charged to clients, and the Izmirlian Foundation wished to keep interest rates low.

The Lincy Foundation Loan Programs

The Lincy Foundation was established by Kirk Kerkorian, an Armenian American billionaire and philanthropist. In 1998 a loan program to assist small- and medium-sized companies was signed by the GOA, the Central Bank of Armenia, and the Lincy Foundation. The foundation agreed to loan the GOA US$100 million without interest for a six-year period. The GOA was to loan money to Armenian banks at no more than 3 percent per annum. In turn, the banks would provide qualified businesses with loans in amounts between US$100,000 and $1 million for an annual interest rate not to exceed 15 percent. To qualify, applicant firms were required to be majority-owned by Armenian citizens.

The GOA created a project implementation office to oversee the loan program and a special commission to approve loans. No Lincy Foundation employees were directly attached to the program. When, however, the commission approved any loan, the loan request would then be presented to the Lincy Foundation to assure that proposed projects met criteria set out by the US Internal Revenue Service. Under these criteria the Lincy Foundation was not allowed to provide money to finance certain operations such as the production of arms or hazardous material. Projects were also required to follow certain environmentally safe production practices.

Within two years the GOA approached the Lincy Foundation, requesting that funds be diverted from the SME loan program to infrastructure projects. In response, the Lincy Foundation agreed to provide the GOA with a US$95 million direct grant for infrastructure programs, and the SME loan program was scaled back to US$45 million. In addition, another $30 million was allocated to a program that could provide either loans to or equity investment in projects in Armenia that were majority foreign-owned. For this new program, Armenian banks were bypassed and the GOA was put in charge of lending this money directly to projects. The new program was implemented in May 2001 with a November 2003 termination date.

By July 2001, only US$20 million of the funds allocated to Armenian SMEs had been distributed. At that time, the GOA requested that the program be discontinued, with the remaining US$25 million to be allocated to infrastructure programs. The Lincy Foundation complied, and loans ceased in 2002. By July 2002 the foreign investment loan project had received thirty-five to forty business plans but only around four of them had been approved by the GOA. The GOA requested that this program too be discontinued, and the Lincy Foundation agreed. No loans or equity investments were ever made under this program, and the US$30 million was reallocated to infrastructure projects.

Comparing the Three Paradigms

Table 6.1 illustrates the different control, input, and output sets of the projects described above. Following is a discussion and associated propositions about how performance may be impacted by a project's institutional landscape.

Control Sets

As noted above, control sets determine under what conditions an organization can function. The Armenian case study suggests that the performance of DBS projects can be affected by both homeland and adopted-country governments.

Homeland governments. All projects operating within Armenia were required to abide by the laws and regulations established by the GOA, which in many cases were being developed just as these projects were being implemented. The Armenian Business Corporation, for example, discovered that its plans to resell stock acquired from founding investors who decided to sell out in 1999 were suddenly halted by a securities commission established in 2000 to enforce Armenia's new securities regulations, passed in that same year. Similarly, ABC's early experience, involving an office dedicated full-time to trying to collect collateral on bad loans, can be credited to

Table 6.1 Institutional Environment of Diaspora SME Support in Armenia

Project	Control Set	Input Set	Output Set
Armenian Business Corporation			
Pre-1999	GOA	Armenian Business Forum Diaspora investors	Small–medium Armenian businesses Larger diaspora investors
Post-1999	GOA	Diaspora investors	Small–medium Armenian businesses Larger/smaller diaspora investors
Izmirlian Foundation			
Izmirlian–Eurasia small business loan program	GOA USG	Izmirlian Foundation Eurasia Foundation Armenian banks	Small–medium Armenian businesses Armenian banks
Proposed finance corporation	GOA USG	Izmirlian Foundation Eurasia Foundation	Small–medium Armenian businesses
Izmirlian–BSTDB joint venture	GOA	Izmirlian Foundation BSTDB Netherlands Management Cooperation Programme	Medium–large Armenian businesses
Lincy Foundation			
SME loan program	GOA USG	Lincy Foundation GOA Armenian banks	Medium–large Armenian businesses Armenian banks
Foreign investment, loan/equity program	GOA USG	Lincy Foundation GOA	Foreign investors Local partners of foreign investors

insufficient progress in developing laws to protect creditors in Armenia (Grigorian 2003). The pervasiveness of bad loans and difficulties in collecting collateral likely contributed to a high mortgage level attached to the loans under the Lincy SME loan programs and, consequently, to the relatively low levels of loans made under this program (Seiranyan 2001a).

The GOA appears to have played a more direct role—beyond legislation—in determining the conditions under which the Lincy Foundation's SME loan program would operate. With no direct experience in the area of SME support and despite alternative suggestions, the GOA chose to direct the grant to the emergent domestic banking industry (Seiranyan 2001b). This decision resulted in lackluster performance, since the emergent banking industry apparently lacked the expertise and the appropriate oversight to identify and subsequently nurture potential entrepreneurs on the scale envisaged. ABC also suffered from GOA interference, nearly collapsing after a powerful government official directed loans to questionable companies. This experience suggests two propositions: (1) effective DBS is handicapped when homelands lack developed and well-regulated financial institutions; and (2) DBS performance may be inhibited by interference of the homeland government with agent, client, or service selection.

Adopted-country governments. Both the United States–based Lincy Foundation and the Eurasia Foundation, the US partner of the Izmirlian Foundation, were required to abide by certain regulations established by the USG. According to one Izmirlian project respondent, these were "too numerous to mention," and the Lincy Foundation appears particularly preoccupied with conditions that the Internal Revenue Service placed on projects it funded. While these regulations posed no real conflict with the organizational missions of the social entrepreneurs, the oversight and paperwork involved with regulatory compliance demanded considerable management time. Despite Lincy's preference for hands-off management of its funded loan programs, checking for compliance with the IRS rules was one area that this relatively new philanthropic foundation actively oversaw. Thus, adopted-country interference is likely to affect the efficiency rather than the effectiveness of operations, suggesting an additional proposition: (3) DBS efficiency may be diminished by the need to adhere to regulations and/or reporting requirements set by the adopted country.

Input Sets

As apparent from Table 6.1, key entities that comprise the input sets of the different projects include social entrepreneurs—philanthropic institutions and diaspora investors—as well as their agents—Armenian and international banks, the GOA, and foreign and international development organizations.

Social entrepreneurs. The dominant role of the social entrepreneurs was to provide funds for the business-development projects. Many foundations in the twenty-first century do not want to provide ongoing funding, even to successful projects, in order to encourage grant recipients to become more self-sufficient (Dees 1998). The case of DBS in Armenia, however, is particularly marked by the apparent timidity of many social entrepreneurs who withdrew relatively rapidly from projects that exhibited start-up problems. Social entrepreneurs are typically presumed to posses a long-term vision. Lincy, potentially the largest player, quickly left the field, claiming that it never planned to stay. The result was little direct contribution to business development in Armenia and little organizational learning for the philanthropic foundation. Similarly, ABC was rocked by an exodus of investors. Although the organization adapted, it faced very limited funding. While the Izmirlian Foundation remained committed as of 2006, partners BSTDB and the Eurasia Foundation had given notification that they were leaving the field.

As altruists, social entrepreneurs in the area of DBS may react negatively to an unethical environment such as the one pervasive in Armenia at the time. As investors, they may be discouraged by the increasing dismal prospects for their investments. Since the social entrepreneurs in our case study came from successful business backgrounds, many may have been embarrassed to be participating in business ventures that were doing poorly, despite that fact that altruism may have partially spurred their involvement in the projects. Purely philanthropic projects are perhaps less problematic. After all, you look good if you donate money to a charitable cause; whereas you look ridiculous if you invest money in a business venture and lose it— however altruistic your motivation. Therefore, two related propositions may be added: (4) effective DBS requires that social entrepreneurs exhibit staying power when confronting initial challenges; and (5) diaspora members are more tolerant of losses and inefficiencies with philanthropic efforts than they are for business support projects.

Agents. The diaspora social entrepreneurs took a hands-off stance to their business support projects in Armenia, making the choice of agents to run the projects paramount to success. Both the Lincy and the Izmirlian foundations began operations by employing domestic banks as agents, but later established new operations that bypassed these banks. Arguably, utilizing domestic banks provided the foreign foundations with local partners that could provide assistance with identifying borrowers, evaluating potential loans and overseeing current loans as well as administering the disbursement and collection of funds.

Unfortunately, the domestic banking industry in Armenia was rife with problems. Even compared with other transitional economies, the financial sector in Armenia was underdeveloped, and supervision inadequate. Rolling

over nonperforming loans was a common way to overstate bank performance. Interest rates were prohibitively high, and some bank officers requested kickbacks in return for approving loans. Low-interest loans provided by
international donors and channeled through the domestic commercial banks
left even more room for kickbacks to be demanded (Grigorian 2003). Of the
twelve Armenian banks employed by the GOA to administer the Lincy
small-business loans, seven had gone bankrupt before the end of the program in 2003 (Baghdasaryan 2003). Foreign banks, on the other hand, were
seen as being able to provide more efficient and unbiased lending
(Grigorian 2003).

Besides banks, foreign and international development-organizations
appear in the input set of the projects associated with the Izmirlian
Foundation. Eurasia offered the Izmirlian Foundation a small-business loan
program already operational on which it could piggyback. Including the
Netherlands Management Cooperation Programme in the BSTDB joint venture more specifically targeted the potential management needs of SME
borrowers. An additional proposition emerges: (6) effective DBS requires
agents with experience in SME support, creation, and management.

In contrast to the Izmirlian decision to bypass domestic banks in favor
of a regional development bank, Lincy's decision to later bypass banks for
its second project put operating control directly in the hands of a new
agent—the GOA. This move resulted in no loans being made under the second program. The GOA appears to have had neither the expertise nor the
will to administer such a program. It has further been suggested that the
GOA, despite its ostensible courtship of diaspora investment, was closely
controlled by local business groups that discouraged the entry of new competition. In addition, the GOA appears to be very risk averse and concerned
about having the designated funds available to return to Lincy. The GOA
preferred to see the funds re-allocated instead to infrastructure programs
that would create immediate if not permanent employment and did not
require repayment. Governments are likely to be too distracted by conflicting agendas to prove the best agent for any particular business-support project. Similar to the poorer performance expected from greater government
intervention as a control entity, its employment as an agent appears undesir-
able as well, yielding another proposition: (7) host governments typically
lack the necessary experience and political will to be effective DBS agents.

Governance. As all the diaspora social entrepreneurs worked through
agents to manage their projects in Armenia, the issue of governance—monitoring and directing the behavior of agents—becomes salient. Honig (1998)
has proposed that lack of good governance can cause problems for philanthropic organizations involved in lending to small businesses in developing
countries. In our study, we observed relatively little oversight by social

entrepreneurs over their agents. Lincy limited its oversight to checking that proposed projects observed US regulations. Oversight at ABC was more an issue of crisis management, after which power was once again vested in a strong and relatively independent agent. The Izmirlian Foundation—the organization whose experience was relatively successful and the least disrupted—appears to have received the most information concerning agent operations, although this phenomenon may be largely attributable to the agent rather than to the social entrepreneur. The Black Sea Trade and Development Bank, chosen by the Izmirlian Foundation for one of its later projects, listed among its guiding principles consistency with sound banking principles, prudent banking practices, transparency, accountability, and effective corporate governance. Two related propositions are (8) effective DBS projects require adherence to strong general and industry-specific governance principles; and (9) effective DBS is enhanced by the use of agents from strong governance cultures.

Output Sets

As noted earlier, all the organizations selected for this analysis were ones that were funded by the diaspora and that declared they were supporting businesses in Armenia. All three philanthropic organizations targeted small- and medium-sized businesses at one time. As depicted in Table 6.1, however, the output sets of the various projects were sometimes more inclusive than simply SMEs. In the case of the Lincy Foundation loan programs, the GOA's desire to stabilize the financial sector resulted in a number of Armenian banks becoming part of Lincy's output set, to the likely detriment of potential SME clients. The more various the output entities, the more difficult it could prove to satisfy them within a single project. Alternatively, the success of the Izmirlian-Eurasia Small Business Loan Program with egg production in Armenia may have resulted partially from accrued experience and synergies gained from working with that particular sector. The experience suggests the following proposition: (10) DBS effectiveness is enhanced by targeting clients who are similar and by keeping the output set focused.

Even when clients were clearly designated, providing services to meet their needs could prove problematic. The Lincy SME loan program set loan amounts between US$100,000 and US$1million, a level far above the needs of small- and most medium-sized businesses in Armenia. The high collateral required by the participant banks to obtain the loan was a further hindrance to smaller businesses, as was the requirement to prepare a good business plan, the cost of which one estimate put at US$10,000–$15,000 (Seiranyan 2001b). This mismatch between the program's target market and the requirements for participation could be another reason that the fund remained underutilized.

Perhaps the greatest lost opportunity to provide service to SMEs in Armenia was the fact that none of the social entrepreneurs became actively involved with the clients beyond providing the funds that were eventually channeled to them. The lack of hands-on management by diaspora social entrepreneurs—or even serious interest in the operations of the businesses supported by their projects—robbed these businesses of key advantages that investor "angels" often contribute to new enterprises. Major investors usually provide advice and help enterprises find key personnel, suppliers, and customers. SMEs in countries like Armenia need more support than just money, but such support, if present at all, was very little. For all the business expertise of the diaspora social entrepreneurs, virtually none was transferred from them to the businesses they funded. These shortcomings are reflected in two additional propositions: (11) effective DBS addresses the specific needs of targeted clientele; and (12) effective DBS requires integration of a service portfolio that assists clients with financing and marketing as well as with the management of operations and human resources. Such a portfolio can be delivered directly by the social entrepreneur or by an agent or a broader network of providers.

In addition to having little direct impact on SMEs beyond limited financial support, the diaspora social entrepreneurs, with the exception of the vast infrastructure investments funded by the Lincy Foundation, failed to target improvements in the macroenvironment. None used their influence—individually or, better yet, combined—to lobby for governmental reform in key areas such as governmental corruption, weak legal infrastructure, or the oversight of financial markets, problems that affected not only their projects directly but also indirectly, by their costs to client firms. Despite sharing and voicing common problems, none of the organizations ever worked together to address these common problems. This lack of collective action stymied their ability to act as effective change agents in the transitional environment, and suggests two final propositions: (13) effective DBS may require proactive attention to influencing the macroenvironment, including policy frameworks; and (14) ensuring supportive macroenvironment may require coordinated efforts among DBS projects.

Conclusion

Table 6.2 identifies the performance gaps of the three social entrepreneurs. Some of the missed opportunities were clearly beyond their control, determined by the institutional context of host and homeland. Other missed opportunities provide lessons for further ventures in this field. The Armenian Business Corporation mobilized the contributions of multiple diaspora members to finance joint ventures with local companies. Of the

Table 6.2   Armenian Diaspora SME-Support Project Performance

	ABC	Lincy	Izmirlian
1. Level of homeland financial development	–	–	–
2. Lack of homeland interference	+	–	+
3. Lack of adopted-country interference	+	–	–
4. Resiliency of social entrepreneurs	–	–	+
5. Tolerance for losses	–	–	–
6. Experience of agents	+	–	+
7. Nongovernmental agents	+	–	+
8. Strong governance	–	–	–
9. Agents from strong governance cultures	–	–	+
10. Homogeneous client set	–	–	+
11. Services congruent with needs	+	–	+
12. Broad service portfolio	–	–	–
13. Attention to macrolevel change	–	+	–
14. Coordination to enable macrolevel change	–	–	–

three organizations, it best served the broader diaspora constituency seeking to be involved in homeland development, but its small size and constrained resources limited its economic impact and left it unprotected in a transitional legal environment. The Izmirlian Foundation focused on choosing experienced agents, and arguably, both the foundation and its agents had more clout with the GOA. As such, it avoided making the early mistakes that nearly crippled ABC. The Lincy Foundation, for all its size and influence, failed to establish and run a truly successful SME support project. Nonetheless, by diverting funds to infrastructure projects to improve the macroenvironments, the foundation may have accomplished more to help Armenian SMEs than did the loan and investment projects of the other organizations.

This Armenian case study suggests that there is a dilemma inherent in DBS to the homeland. Diasporas want to support businesses in ways that do not require direct involvement, but the more direct the involvement, the better the result. Diasporas can suffer from donor fatigue despite their altruistic attachment to the homeland. Consequently, they search for ways in which their contributions can be channeled from consumption to productive investments, and many diaspora members are intrigued by the idea of making small investments in homeland companies. If diasporas choose to simply donate money for this purpose, the choice of agent is key. Relying on an underdeveloped banking industry or stock market appears counterproductive. The best choice is likely to be a development organization that has obtained some expertise in this area. Yet even good agents can pose problems for social entrepreneurs, not least of which are conflicts of interest. The Izmirlian Foundation eventually faced the loss of its two agents in

Armenia. One, a development NGO largely financed by the USG, proved to have only an intermediate-term interest in business development in the country. The other, an international bank, clashed with the foundation over profitability goals and methods.

As the introduction to Part 2 makes clear, it is more than financial support that makes diasporas valuable to emerging businesses in the homeland. It is their integration into global markets and their socialization into good governance that make them attractive as potential leaders and mentors of the local private sector. To deliver on this potential requires active participation. Short of participating in foreign direct investment, diaspora social entrepreneurs should consider creating organizations or networks that target needs of homeland businesses beyond mere funding: business incubators, short-term business mentoring, and lobbying for a better institutional environment for business.

Notes

1. Vartan Hovhannisian, "Interview with Mr. Oskanian, H1 Television Orakarg (Agenda) Program, February 8, 2003; Anonymous, "Interview with James D. Aljian, Chairman to the Lincy Foundation," Hetq Online, November 1, 2003; Edik Baghdassaryan, "How Lincy Foundation Money Is Managed," Hetq Online, September 24, 2003; Manuk Hergnian, "Interview with Paul Korian," Radio VEM, www.vem.am (accessed September 9, 2003); Manuk Hergnian, "Interview with Vargen Setrakian," Radio VEM, www.vem.am (accessed September 26, 2003); and Anonymous, "Kirk Kerkorian, Armenian-American Philanthropist," *Armenian Business Review* (Winter 2001).

2. E-mail exchange with Armen Der Torossian, ABC board member, September 25, 2003.

3. Armenian Business Corporation (ABC), "Shareholder's Packet 2001," p. 2.

4. Comments made by Hovsep Seferian at a press conference, Hovsep Journalists' House, Yerevan, Armenia, October 26, 2000 (internal company document).

5. E-mail exchange with Armen De Torossian, ABC board member, September 25, 2003.

6. Sona Hamalian, "Izmirlian Foundation Awards $3 Million to Eurasia Foundation's Small Business Loan Program," Eurasia Foundation press release, May 4, 1999, www.eurasia.org (accessed December 1, 2003).

7. Ibid.

8. Personal interview with Bill Grant, director of the Small and Medium Enterprise Development Program, Eurasia Foundation, Armenia office, September 18, 2003.

9. Black Sea Economic Cooperation, *Black Sea News* 2 (December 2002): 1.

7

Homeland Export and Investment Promotion Agencies: The Case of Afghanistan

Liesl Riddle and Valentina Marano

The substantial decreases in trade and investment barriers associated with globalization have not only engendered greater economic opportunities worldwide; they also have fostered competition among nations to promote exports and attract investment capital. In many nations, public and private sector organizations are taking active roles in promoting their nation's exports or encouraging foreign investment into their country. These export promotion organizations and investment promotion agencies often play an important role in economic development. EPO and IPA activities can improve national trade balances; increase employment quantitatively and qualitatively; and improve firm-level competencies, efficiencies, and performance.

A substantial literature stream has emerged—mostly within the field of marketing—that examines the activities, impact, and effectiveness of EPOs and IPAs. This literature is silent, however, about the role, actual or potential, that EPOs and IPAs could play in promoting diaspora homeland-product/service purchases or attracting diaspora foreign investment. Yet diaspora homeland product/service consumption and homeland investment are well-documented phenomena, and research has demonstrated that diaspora purchase and investment motivations can differ from those of buyers and investors outside the diaspora community (e.g., King and Gamage 1994; Gillespie et al. 1999). Diaspora contributions to homeland economies are increasingly viewed by homeland governments as key to national economic development. Their role in jump-starting foreign investment may be particularly salient in countries emerging from conflict. The growing body of knowledge about diaspora involvement in homeland economies begs the question, How can the economic potential of the diaspora be effectively tar-

133

geted, cultivated, and coordinated by homeland organizations? Drawing on the experience of one country that has sought answers to this question, this chapter reviews current practices and proposes an agenda for what more could be done.

Over twenty years of war and isolation have devastated Afghanistan's economy and infrastructure. As of this writing, businesses within Afghanistan struggle to survive amidst limited access to energy, credit, skilled labor, and land. These harsh realities, coupled with perceptions of security risks, often discourage foreign-buyer and -investor interest. But several diaspora Afghans have been undaunted by these challenges. Diaspora members have boosted Afghan export sales and pioneered much of Afghanistan's postwar, private sector investment. Increasingly, Afghan organizations—within both the public and private sectors—are seeking ways to better communicate and work with the diaspora in order to further encourage sustainable homeland economic involvement. A central challenge faced by these organizations is the lack of information about best practices in diaspora marketing in EPOs and IPAs.

In this chapter we first discuss how export and investment promotion organizations can contribute to national economic development. Next we turn to the case of Afghanistan, chronicling the challenges that Afghan organizations have faced in encouraging diaspora homeland economic involvement. Then we outline a scope of work for future research to examine export and investment promotion programs targeted toward diaspora communities.

Export and Investment Promotion and Economic Development

Export Promotion Organizations

An increase in a country's export intensity and diversity strengthens its economic health by improving the national trade balance, increasing available foreign exchange, reducing dependence on traditional exports, and contributing to a more dynamic and competitive business community (Hill 2007). An increase in national exports can create particularly beneficial employment effects for small and/or poor countries with limited domestic markets.

EPOs seek "the creation of awareness of exporting as a growth and market expansion option, the reduction or removal of barriers to exporting, and the creation of promotion incentives and various forms of assistance to potential and actual exporters" (Seringhaus and Rosson 1990, 5). EPOs also encourage demand for a nation's exports by marketing national industries to foreign buyers and brokering relationships between foreign buyers and home-country exporters (Seringhaus and Rosson 1990). Seringhaus and Botschen (1991, 117) outline four specific export promotion organization objectives:

1. to develop a broad awareness of export opportunities and to stimulate interest for export in the business community,
2. to assist firms in the planning and preparation for export market involvement,
3. to assist firms in acquiring the needed expertise and know-how successfully to enter and develop export markets,
4. to support such foreign-market activity tangibly through organizational help and cost-sharing programs.

EPOs provide training, information, and operational support to encourage nonexporters to engage in exporting activity and increase the regularity and intensity of exports for exporting firms. Through conferences, classes, and Web sites, EPOs enhance firms' motivation to export (Seringhaus and Rosson 1990). They provide information about requisite export procedures, regulations, and paperwork; consumer demand, potential buyers, distribution networks, and foreign-market competition; credit and financing involved in international transactions; and product, promotion, and technology trends in the global marketplace (ITC 1986). They also offer operational support, such as export logistics training, marketing assistance, trade missions, financing support, foreign-buyer visits, providing contacts, and regulatory assistance (Diamantopoulos, Schlegelmilch, and Tse 1993).

Czinkota (1996) has developed a conceptual model to illustrate how export promotion programs contribute to firms' export performance. These programs affect performance through their effect on a firm's organizational and managerial abilities. Export promotion programs enhance a firm's market knowledge and connections and their human and technical resources. They also deepen managers' international knowledge, exposure, and commitment.

Several authors note the potential importance of export promotion organizations as catalysts of economic growth, particularly in developing countries (e.g., Seringhaus 1984, 1993; Moini 1995; Ahmed et al. 2002). Much of the economic base of developing economies consists of small- and medium-sized enterprises with little to no experience in the export process. Studies have empirically linked the use of EPO services to improvements in firms' export competencies, strategies, and performance, particularly for SMEs and larger nonexporting or sporadically exporting firms (e.g., Reid 1984; Seringhaus 1984, 1993; Riddle and Gillespie 2003; Francis and Collins-Dodd 2004).

Investment Promotion Agencies

A spirited debate exists in the international business and development litera-
tures regarding the extent to which, and under what circumstances, foreign
direct investment contributes to economic development. The potential benefits of foreign direct investment identified in this literature include
increased employment, technology spillovers from multinational firms to
local enterprises, increases in the depth and breadth of local human capital,
and an enlargement and invigoration of the local competitive business environment (Hill 2007). Moran, Graham, and Blomstrom's (2005) recent
analysis of this literature notes that the salubrious effects of foreign direct
investment on recipient countries are greatest when such investment occurs
in an open market, when investments made by multinationals are well integrated into their firms' respective global supply chains, and the country's
overall trade is increasing.

IPAs encourage foreign direct investment into a country through five
sets of activities. First, they seek to promote the country as an attractive
investment destination to potential investors. Thus, many IPAs produce
focused advertising campaigns, hold public relations events, and cultivate
relationships with journalists to encourage strong publicity about their country (Wee, Lim, and Tan 1992). Second, IPAs offer investor-facilitation and
investor services. IPAs often serve as "one-stop shops" for investors, assisting them with expediting approvals, obtaining sites, brokering relationships
with local firms, and so on (Brossard 1998). Investment generation is a third
function of IPAs. Investment leads are generated via direct mail or telephone
campaigns, investor forums or seminars, and individual presentations to targeted individuals (Wint 1993). IPAs also engage in policy advocacy within
their home countries, conducting business surveys, lobbying, and putting
forward policy and legal proposals (Wells and Wint 2000).

Few studies assess the impact of specific IPA services on the investment decisionmaking process. Brossard's study (1998) of investors in
Belgium, France, Ireland, and Switzerland found that a majority of
investors claimed that IPA services played a significant role in the decision
to invest. The survey particularly emphasized the importance of IPA-provid-
ed information and networking services to the investment decision. Wells
and Wint (2000) and Morisset (2003) provide empirical evidence of a positive association between investment promotion and national foreign direct
investment levels. Morisset and Andrews-Johnson (2004) quantify the positive association between a country's IPA activities and its foreign investment inflows. Controlling for a variety of factors, including the investment
climate and market size, they conclude that "for each 10 percent increase in
the [investment] promotion effort, the level of foreign direct investment
increases by 2.5 percent" (2004, 13). Wint (1993) argues that investment

promotion activities are critical for developing countries that compete with more attractive, developed markets for foreign investment.

EPOs, IPAs, and Diasporas

As the discussion above reveals, EPOs and IPAs engage in similar sets of activities. Their common objective is to build bridges between foreign entrepreneurs/firms and entrepreneurs/firms in their home countries. Both types of organization are engaged in *target marketing*. EPOs market the idea of exporting to local firms. They also target foreign buyers, seeking to enhance the country-of-origin image for the products produced by their country. IPAs market their country's potential as an investment destination to prospective foreign investors, typically large multinational corporations. Both EPOs and IPAs offer *knowledge-provision services* as well. EPOs provide local firms with knowledge about exporting and foreign buyers/distributors with information about exporting firms in their country and the products that these firms produce. IPAs provide knowledge about the business environment and investment process to foreign investors. Further, both EPOs and IPAs provide *networking services*. EPOs bring buyers and exporters together; IPAs introduce investors to numerous local contacts, brokering relationships with government officials, partners, suppliers, and other local entities. Both organizations also engage in *advocacy services*. EPOs articulate the interests of exporters, and IPAs represent the interests of prospective and current foreign investors to the national government. Because of the natural synergies between EPOs and IPAs, in some countries EPO and IPA functions are subsumed into a singular organization. In other countries they remain separate organizations with varying degrees of interaction and coordination.

Research regarding EPOs and IPAs primarily focuses on the origins of these organizations (e.g., Gillespie and Riddle 2004), interorganizational cooperation and competition (e.g., Riddle 2001), the basket of services that these organizations provide (e.g., ITC 1986; Wells and Wint 2000), firms' awareness of their services (e.g., Ahmed et al. 2002), and their performance (e.g., Francis and Collins-Dodd 2004; Morisset and Andrews-Johnson 2004). Research in this field has not yet explored the role of these organizations (potential or actual) in fostering economic ties between diasporas and their homeland economies.

As reviewed elsewhere in this volume, diasporas can offer various types of capital to homeland economies that contribute to greater homeland exports and foreign investment. Diasporas transfer financial capital and increase homeland exports through their purchases of homeland products (e.g., Mundra 2005) and homeland tourism, and the use of other homeland services (e.g., King and Gamage 1994). In many countries—particularly

those perceived to be especially risky or cumbersome business environments—diaspora homeland investment may constitute a significant proportion of a homeland's foreign direct investment total (Gillespie et al. 1999;
Gillespie, Sayre, and Riddle 2001). Many diaspora communities also contribute material remittances (in-kind donations), many of which are sent to
homeland organizations.

But diasporas also contribute other forms of capital that enhance homeland exports and foreign investment. Diaspora members may enhance
homeland-firm managers' social capital, extending their social network and
market reach through contacts in their countries of residence (Kyle 1999;
Uduku 2002; Cheung 2004). These contacts may smooth the way for homeland firms' exporting activities. They may also encourage investment by
reducing foreign investors' uncertainty about local partnership opportunities
in the homeland country.

Further, diasporas can strengthen the level of human capital in the
homeland economy. This, in turn, can increase exports and investment in
homeland countries by increasing homeland firms' managerial efficiencies
and effectiveness (Seguin, State, and Singer 2006; Carr, Inkson, and Thorn
2005). Diaspora members have participated as mentors to homeland-firm
managers, provided training programs to homeland firms, and served as
consultants to government officials striving to improve the business environment in homeland nations.

As illustrated in Figure 7.1, EPOs and IPAs can serve as a bridge
between diasporas and their homeland economies. The following case illustrates the opportunities that diasporas can offer homeland economies and
the challenges that EPOs and IPAs face in leveraging these opportunities.

Diaspora Economic Involvement in Afghanistan

Afghanistan's economy has improved since 2001, owing in large part to
more than $8 billion in international assistance, the recovery of the agricul-

Figure 7.1 EPOs and IPAs: Bridging the Diaspora-Homeland Divide

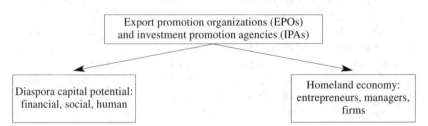

tural sector, growth in the service sector, and the reestablishment of market institutions. But the country still remains one of the poorest countries in the world and is in need of increased exports and investment. As of this writing, per capita GDP was a mere $350; over half of the country's population lived in poverty. Unemployment was estimated to be at least 40 percent. Licit trade was dominated by the agricultural sector; less than a quarter of GDP was generated by manufacturing, most of which was small-scale and substandard production of textiles, soap, furniture, shoes, and fertilizer (Central Intelligence Agency 2007). The country was the world's largest producer of opium, and illicit trade was estimated to compose one-third of total economic activity in Afghanistan (Blanchard 2006).

A survey conducted by the Afghan American Chamber of Commerce (Atash 2004) revealed that most businesses operating in Afghanistan were small, sole proprietorships (74 percent). Most businesses were new, in operation for less than five years (64 percent). Over one-quarter were engaged in some level of export activity (29 percent). The survey revealed several challenges faced by businesses in Afghanistan, including a lack of access to capital, energy, and land; poor infrastructure; corruption; security concerns; and barriers to export. In a study of Afghanistan's investment climate, the World Bank identified additional challenges, such as an evolving legal system, a cumbersome tax regime, lack of transparency in customs administration, and a complex property market (World Bank 2005a).

Although President Hamid Karzai declared Afghanistan "open for business" as early as in 2002, the country continues to struggle to encourage exports and lure investors into what Karzai himself refers to as Afghanistan's "fresh, needy, greedy market" (Morarjee 2006, 2). By the mid-2000s, the country began to focus much of its export- and investment-promotion attention toward the Afghan diaspora, hoping that their altruism might override concerns about the daunting business environment. The following section describes the origins and composition of the Afghan diaspora, organizational attempts to market Afghanistan to the diaspora, diaspora economic involvement in Afghanistan, and the challenges faced by Afghan organizations when targeting the diaspora community.

The Afghan Diaspora

Historically, Afghanistan has been a land of passage and migrations. The country's population comprises a complex mix of ethnicities and cultures. Migration has been described as a "way of life" for many Afghans; transnational migration patterns are now well organized to the extent that they have become a major element in the social, cultural, and economic life of many Afghans (Stigter and Monsutti 2005). At least five discernible types of migration involve the people of Afghanistan, namely "internal immigration, emigration, repatriation, transit, and cycling (repetitive repatriation-emigration)" (Hanifi 2006, 100). These types of migration stem from different motivations and have different consequences for the communities involved.

The destruction and conflicts of the past twenty-five years have given a dramatic rhythm to migration waves to and from Afghanistan. The World Bank (2005a) reports that during the past twenty-five years, more than 30 percent of the Afghan population has been externally or internally displaced. During the 1970s hundreds of thousands of Afghans moved to the Middle East, attracted by increased labor opportunities created by the oil boom (Stigter and Monsutti 2005). The first significant out-migration took place between 1980 and 1986, after the Soviet invasion of Afghanistan (Jazayery 2002). Although about 2 million refugees returned to Afghanistan when the Mujahideen took over in 1992, protracted fighting among Mujahideen factions and the 1994 arrival of the Taliban instigated a second large out-migration wave.

As of this writing, although 2.4 million Afghans have been repatriated, an estimated 3.4 million Afghans remain outside the country. The lack of reliable demographic data in Afghanistan and other countries where Afghan diaspora members reside makes quantifying the Afghan diaspora a difficult task. Estimates for the Afghan diaspora by country are summarized in Table 7.1.

There are two different subpopulations in the Afghan diaspora: those living in affluent countries, such as Europe, the United States, Australia, and the United Arab Emirates, and those living in proximal states, such as Pakistan and Iran (Jazayery 2002). This distinction is important (as suggested by Milton Esman in Chapter 5), since these two groups have very different compositions and conditions of life in exile, and differential potential in terms of their contribution to the reconstruction of Afghanistan.

Diaspora Afghans in Pakistan and Iran primarily originated from rural

Table 7.1   The Afghan Diaspora Around the World

Country of Residence	Estimated Number	Source
Pakistan	2.5 million	US Department of State 2005
Iran	1 million	US Department of State 2005
United States	100,000	Hanifi 2006
Europe	100,000	Jazayery 2002
Central Asia and Russia	150,000–300,000	Jazayery 2002
India	40,000–50,000	Jazayery 2002
Australia	20,000–30,000	Jazayery 2002
Japan	10,000–20,000	Jazayery 2002
Arab Gulf countries	100,000	Ezz Al Deen 2006

Afghanistan, where they had been "small farmers, village artisans, tenants, or were lower middle-class shopkeepers, civil servants and bazaar crafts-men" (Braakman 2005, 7). Most ended up in refugee camps dependent on international aid, although some members of the former Afghan urban mid-dle class tried to build a self-sufficient existence in the cities (Braakman 2005). Most diaspora Afghans residing in Iran found employment as manual workers on construction sites or farms. After the fall of the Taliban, the Iranian government increased its policy of intolerance toward Afghan refugees; most are now ineligible for free education, health services, or food rations. There is even talk of possible "forced repatriation" (Human Rights Watch 2002).

The minority of the few hundred thousands who were able to reach Europe, North America, Canada, New Zealand, and Australia mostly belonged to the "wealthy urban educated Pashtun or Tajik elite and middle classes, especially from the capital, Kabul" (Braakman 2005, 8). Much of the elite moved to Canada and the United States, while mostly the middle class moved to Europe.

A relatively new community, the Afghan diaspora is slowly developing a transnational identity. Social cleavages exist within the community, even within individual countries of resettlement. As Maryam Qudrat, women's affairs officer at the embassy of Afghanistan and author of the book *Torn Between Two Cultures: An Afghan-American Woman Speaks Out*, explains:

> There certainly are rifts in the community, and those are sometimes defined by the time-line, in terms of when they migrated. So the first immigrants and latest immigrants belong to different layers of society. Another rift comes from where people are located socioeconomically. And people tend to stay within those layers. Sometimes diaspora is defined geographically: you have the Afghan Americans on the West Coast and the Afghan Americans from the East Coast.[1]

Hanifi (2004) similarly observes that "there doesn't seem to be a sort of sys-tematic circulation of Afghans through the diaspora communities—Virginia Afghans visiting California Afghans, those from Germany visiting those from Australia, et cetera."

Some individuals within the Afghan diaspora community have sought to engender stronger intradiaspora identity, ties, and purpose through the creation of diaspora-oriented Web sites. These sites create "digital diaspo-ras," which reinforce and deepen diaspora group solidarity, foster intradias-pora and diaspora-homeland relationships, and mobilize the diaspora for homeland political, economic, and social participation (Brinkerhoff 2004). Examples of these Web sites include AfghanistanOnline, Rebuild-Afghanistan, and Afghans4Tomorrow.

Attracting Diaspora Economic Involvement in Afghanistan

The Afghan government places the diaspora at the forefront in its economic reconstruction plan, particularly in terms of foreign investment attraction into the country. As Khaleda Atta, acting commercial attaché of the embassy of Afghanistan describes:

> The government's vision about the reconstruction of the country involves a three-tiered system of private investment, and the first tier is supposed to come from the Afghan diaspora itself. The second investment tier are the regional neighbors, and the third and final investment level would be foreign direct investment from countries further out, including the United States and Europe. Because of their cultural ties, their linguistic ability, their religious sensitivity, their connections to the local communities, the government's logic goes, members of the Afghan diaspora have the best chance to make successful investments in Afghanistan.[2]

These sentiments about the diaspora's importance are echoed by Suleman Fatimie, vice president of the public sector IPA, the Afghanistan Investment Support Agency (AISA), which has functioned as the Afghanistan government's voice to the diaspora. In addition to the above-stated resources that the diaspora brings to the investment situation, diaspora members provide "know-how, trade expertise, experience—much-needed new blood for the Afghan economy."[3]

Created in September 2003 with financial support from the German government, AISA is a "one-stop shop for investors," whose mission is to "facilitate and promote investment and aid the development of competitive private enterprise and thereby robust and sustainable economic growth in Afghanistan" (AISA 2007). Box 7.1 provides a list of the services that AISA offers. The organization is divided into five departments: licensing and legal support, investment promotion, research and analysis, media and public relations, and industrial parks development authority. Diaspora Afghans constitute 90 percent of AISA's management staff.[4]

The reduction in the wait time for an investment license "from weeks or months to five to six days" was one of "AISA's greatest achievements" (Burnett 2004, 31). According to the World Bank, Afghanistan now is ranked sixteenth among 145 countries for ease of opening an enterprise (World Bank 2006b).

Most of AISA's diaspora-marketing efforts have centered on investment-promotion "road show" events. AISA's first road show took place in Amsterdam in June 2004; over 400 diaspora members attended. In October 2005, AISA organized an investment-promotion road show in cooperation with the Afghan Ministry of Commerce, the embassy of Afghanistan in Washington, D.C., and the US Department of Commerce. The event was replicated in Europe in February 2006, covering the cities of Copenhagen; the

---

Box 7.1   Afghan Investment Support Agency Services

- All necessary permits, licenses, and clearances
- General information on investment opportunities
- Judicial details on investment, tax, labor, insurance, and environmental laws/regulations and social/ecological standards
- Financial information regarding banking facilities, labor costs, and investment incentives
- Support in the acquisition/leasehold of land
- Assistance in custom clearance of material related to investment
- Online investment inquiry/information and license application
- Conferences and symposiums on important investment-related issues
- Announcement of investment opportunities via the foreign missions in Afghanistan and the Afghan embassies overseas
- Research, surveys, and reviews on issues that are considered to be of vital importance to investors
- Regular consultations, dialogues, seminars, and workshops with stakeholders

---

Hague; Hamburg and Munich, Germany; and Paris. The objectives of these road shows were to increase diaspora awareness about the opportunities for investment in Afghanistan and to link Afghan business owners through informal networking with potential US and European investors.

The Afghan International Chamber of Commerce (AICC) has also reached out to the diaspora community, particularly through its overseas chambers—the Afghan-American Chamber of Commerce (AACC) in Washington, D.C., and the Afghan Business Council in Dubai. AICC gathers funding from a wide variety of sources, including private parties and government agencies, nongovernmental organizations, and membership fees. The mission of the Chamber is to "advance and promote the economic environment for business, encourage investment and advocate responsive government, quality education, and transparent business dealings while preserving Afghanistan's unique culture and values" (AICC 2007).

AACC was initially formed as the Afghan-American Business Association in 1996. With US Agency for International Development funding and technical assistance from the Center for International Private Enterprise in 2002, AACC's mission narrowed to address "the critical need for peer-to-peer contact with the Afghan business community as a cornerstone of developing a free market economy in Afghanistan" (AACC 2005, 5). Its Web site states that AACC is "the leading organization facilitating US-Afghan business, investment, and trade ties" (www.a-acc.org).

AACC has hosted several events targeted to promote Afghanistan's exports and attract investment into Afghanistan. For example, in October 2005 it sponsored the United States–Afghan Business Matchmaking

Conference. The goals of this conference were to foster joint venture, partnership, financial, government, and other relationships for potential investors in Afghanistan. AACC's Afghan Business Dialogue seminar series generates awareness about opportunities in the Afghan economy for potential buyers and investors. Seminar topics include USAID and World Bank procurement procedures, opportunities in the energy sector, and an overview of the Afghan privatization program. The organization also maintains an English-language Web site with information regarding Afghanistan's economic climate; export/import regulations, procedures, and paperwork; legal and tax regimes, and so on.

The Afghan Business Council of Dubai was created in 2005, a result of the joint efforts of the Afghan community in the United Arab Emirates, the Afghan government, the US government, and AACC. It serves as a trade and investment link between the Gulf countries and Afghanistan. In early 2006 it hosted a conference called "Defining Trade and Investment Opportunities in Afghanistan," which was attended by hundreds of companies in the Gulf region.

Diaspora Economic Contributions and Challenges

As former Afghanistan finance minister Ashraf Ghani observed, the diaspora is a "key to reviving the collapsed manufacturing and commercial sectors" of Afghanistan (Burnett 2004, 31). Some of the largest private sector investments into Afghanistan have been created by diaspora members. Perhaps the largest and most well known diaspora investment is the $25 million Coca-Cola bottling plant established by Habib Gulzar, an Afghan living in Dubai (Burnett 2004). Kabul's first shopping mall was opened in 2005 by an Afghan American.[5] Among Afghanistan's thirteen commercial banks, two were founded by Afghans from Dubai.[6]

Maryam Qudrat describes the diaspora's economic interest in the homeland:

> It is such a fortunate time for Afghanistan, because even though the country has suffered such a devastation and trauma, it has this pool of hyphenated Afghans who not only are qualified to help, but they also have the will and the interest to help. That's quite an amazing miracle that all these people want to offer. And this does not happen for personal benefit, given that the country doesn't have a whole lot to offer. It's not a very desirable place to be. But there are all these people who are drawn toward it. Obviously this attention needs to be coordinated in some way.[7]

But cultivating diaspora altruism and coordinating diaspora investment has been challenging for the Afghan organizations working on the country's economic development. To date, in the early 2000s, much of the focus of these organizations has been placed on encouraging diaspora repatriation to their homeland and on the large-scale investments they might bring to the country. As Ashraf Haidari, first secretary at the embassy of Afghanistan observes: "The government has tried to facilitate the return of the diaspora cooperating with international organizations. But the number of people who actually went back with these programs is extremely low."[8]

Several of our contacts mentioned the repatriation issue as an obstacle when probed for the challenges involved with diaspora homeland investment. Khaleda Atta explains the challenges in diaspora investment associated with diaspora repatriation: "Many of them have families that they need to take care of [in the host country]. Then there are time/resource constraints. Some have also resettled, but it is much more common to find people who once they establish a project in Afghanistan, continue going back and forth when they can."[9] Diaspora repatriation might also not always be ideal for Afghanistan's development, since "Afghanistan's remittances are an important aspect of the diaspora's contributions. Afghanistan needs those remittances!"[10]

Our interviews with several Afghan government officials, development experts, and Afghan diaspora members revealed that Afghan organizations are searching for better ways to target and leverage the diaspora. They are seeking best-practice models of programs and services successfully offered by export and investment promotion from other countries. But scant research exists on this important topic. In the next section we explain how traditional EPO and IPA activities may need to be tailored to fully unlock the economic potential of the diaspora. We conclude by detailing a plan for future research to uncover best practices in EPO/IPA diaspora marketing.

Homeland Export and Investment Promotion Programs for the Diaspora

Afghanistan is certainly not alone in its attempts to motivate diaspora economic homeland involvement. A broad array of nations have sought to involve their respective diaspora communities in economic development, including other postconflict societies, such as Liberia and the West Bank/Gaza; smaller countries, such as Armenia and Vietnam; and large emerging markets, such as China, India, and Mexico.

The emotional identification and attachment that diaspora communities feel toward their homeland may make diaspora community members prime targets for homeland product/service purchases and investment. But, as the Afghan case illustrates, diaspora communities pose both challenges and opportunities for homeland organizations engaged in export and investment promotion. These challenges and opportunities may require these organizations to adapt their existing activities. In other cases, these organizations may need to develop new ways of thinking and behaving in order to capitalize on the tremendous advantages that diasporas offer their homelands. Specific differences between typical EPO/IPA activities and diaspora EPO/IPA activities include target marketing and the provision of knowledge, networking, and advocacy services. Table 7.2 summarizes these differences.

Target Marketing

EPOs and IPAs typically target most of their marketing efforts toward foreign buyers and multinational corporations. They promote their country

Table 7.2   Difference Between the Typical and Diaspora EPO/IPA Focus

	Typical EPO/IPA Activity	Diaspora EPO/IPA Activity
Target marketing	Foreign distributors/ buyers and multinational corporations whose motivation is pecuniary	Transnational individuals whose motivation is both pecuniary and altruistic
Knowledge-provision service	Foreign- and local-market research, information about export and investment procedures and processes	Information needs may be less general and only required in key areas where diasporan lacks knowledge; especially for first-generation diaspora members
		Identifying ways to harness and disseminate diaspora members' knowledge of markets and investment procedures and processes
Networking service	Brokering partnerships and offering contacts with service providers and government officials to individuals with few or no contacts in the market	Networking needs may be less important and only required in key areas where diasporan lacks knowledge; especially for first-generation diaspora members
		Identifying ways to leverage diaspora members' existing contacts
Advocacy service	Representing the interests of local entrepreneurs and firms to local government	Representing the interests of transnational entrepreneurs and firms to local and foreign governments and multilateral agencies

through traditional business-to-business channels, including trade-fair booths, presentations and direct mail to business associations abroad, and one-on-one presentations to prospective buyers/investors. Diaspora marketing requires a more consumer-marketing approach. To effectively target the diaspora, EPOs and IPAs must identify the channels that are most salient for diaspora communities, including the Web sites they frequent, publications they read, organizations they belong to, events they attend, and so on.

Successful diaspora marketing efforts require more than just promotion channel adaptation. The marketing message may also need to be amended. Nondiaspora buyers/distributors and investors are motivated by pecuniary interests; therefore, a key component of EPOs' and IPAs' value propositions is their ability to decrease the costs associated with a foreign purchase or investment. But diasporans may be motivated by pecuniary as well as altruistic interests. Successful marketing messages for diaspora communities may also emphasize the diaspora's opportunity to contribute a sustainable, peaceful, prosperous homeland future. In some cases, economic participation could be positioned as the diaspora's duty to help the homeland.

Most important, to fully leverage the possibilities that diaspor homeland economies, EPOs/IPAs should consider creative ways to and transmit diaspora capital—financial, social, and human—to ho economies that do not require diaspora repatriation or large amounts or financial resources from a singular diaspora member. This activi require EPOs/IPAs to create new services that scale-up smaller indiv diaspora capital contributions.

Knowledge-Provision Services

Traditional EPOs/IPAs provide information about export/investment procedures and processes to foreign firms with limited information about the EPO/IPA's home country. Diasporas, particularly first-generation immigrants, possess greater knowledge about the homeland business environment than the nondiaspora buyer or investor. To effectively meet diaspora information needs, EPOs/IPAs must discern what specifics the diaspora members lack about the homeland economy that impede their economic involvement. Then they must determine ways to transmit that knowledge to diasporans.

Diasporas can enable EPOs and IPAs to extend their knowledge-provision services in new directions. EPOs and IPAs can identify ways to harness and then disseminate diasporans' knowledge of foreign markets, buyers/distributors, entry mode rules, and regulations, as well as potential investors to firms in the home country.

Networking Services

EPOs and IPAs typically serve as relationship brokers between foreign firms with few or no contacts in the home market. EPO/IPA networking services may be particularly useful to diaspora members who lack strong homeland familial ties. But the networking needs of well-connected, first-generation diaspora buyers and investors may be less broad or intense. To effectively meet diaspora needs, EPOs/IPAs will need to identify what types of contacts these diasporans typically lack. EPOs/IPAs can seek ways to leverage diaspora members' existing contacts; they can serve as networking conduits, providing virtual and real links among diasporans interested in homeland economic involvement. EPOs/IPAs may also extend their networking function by playing a coordination role among organizations engaged in homeland material remittances, particularly regarding donated items for businesses. This service could heighten diaspora members' and homeland firms' awareness of EPOs/IPAs and their activities. Such activities may also strengthen EPO/IPA reputations as organizations serving all homeland organizations, not just the large and well-connected ones.

Advocacy Services

Both EPOs and IPAs provide advocacy services, representing the interest of local entrepreneurs and firms to the government. But the transnational context of diasporas extends the boundaries of EPO/IPA constituencies beyond national borders. This may broaden EPO/IPA advocacy responsibilities to include representing the interests of transnational entrepreneurs and firms to foreign governments and multilateral agencies.

Conclusion: Areas for Future Research

EPOs/IPAs—with some modifications in their traditional approaches—can form a bridge between diaspora capital potential and homeland entrepreneurs, managers, and firms. Homeland organizations, such as those in Afghanistan, that seek ways to integrate the diaspora into their economic development plans would benefit from greater knowledge about the ways in which EPOs and IPAs around the world have cultivated and transmitted diaspora capital to their homeland economies.

Future research should investigate the following questions:

- How is the diaspora perceived by EPO and IPA leadership? To what extent are diasporas viewed as important in their country's economic development? Why or why not?
- To what extent do EPOs and IPAs actively target the diaspora? Why? How?

- What types of diaspora-targeted campaigns and services created by EPOs and IPAs have succeeded or failed? Why?
- How involved—and in what ways—do diaspora members want to be in their homeland economies?

A multimethod approach will be required to fully probe these questions. In-depth interviews with leadership in different EPOs/IPAs could provide insights about their attitudes toward the diaspora and its economic potential. A cross-national survey of EPOs and IPAs could identify EPO/IPA diaspora-oriented activities. Survey data could be utilized to isolate strong case studies for in-depth investigation, including case studies of positive and negative diaspora marketing experiences. Case studies could not only chronicle the development and design of successful diaspora marketing activities from the point of view of EPO and IPA officials but could also measure the response and impact on diaspora community members and homeland entrepreneurs, managers, and firms. Surveys of various diaspora communities could help quantify the development opportunities that diaspora communities can provide. They could also be used to create a database of diaspora contacts that homeland firms and organizations could draw upon when seeking networking and investment opportunities.

It is hoped that the proposed research will uncover creative ways to effectively target, cultivate, and coordinate the substantial economic-capital opportunities within the diaspora. This information would benefit all countries seeking ways to better leverage the development opportunities that their homelands offer.

Notes

The authors would like to thank Mr. Torek Farhadi, senior strategy officer, Middle East and North Africa Department, International Finance Corporation. Mr. Farhadi is a former finance adviser to Afghan minister of finance Ashraf Ghani and to Afghan Central Bank governor Anwar Ahady. Mr. Farhadi provided invaluable comments on this manuscript.
1. Personal interview with Maryam Qudrat, April 28, 2005.
2. Personal interview with Khaleda Atta, April 11, 2006.
3. Personal interview with Suleman Fatimie, May 28, 2006.
4. Interview with Khaleda Atta.
5. Ibid.
6. Interview with Suleman Fatimie.
7. Interview with Maryam Qudrat.
8. Personal interview with Ashraf Haidari, April 14, 2006.
9. Interview with Khaleda Atta.
10. Interview with Ashraf Haidari.

Part 3

Beyond Remittances: Knowledge and Networks for National Development

THE CHAPTERS IN this volume have touched upon a wide range of contributions diasporas can make to their homeland's development. These include remittances (including social, in-kind, and collective), knowledge transfer, related philanthropic support and interventions, and more specific business/economic investment and support. As illustrated in Parts 1 and 2, these contributions are particularly salient and highly motivated in countries emerging from conflict. While they may at times represent segmented and narrowly targeted assistance, the cumulative effect of diaspora interventions may significantly influence national-level development and recovery, as described for Liberia (Lubkemann, Chapter 3).

In other instances, diasporas' national-level contributions may represent more systematic and coordinated efforts. Chapters 8 and 9 illustrate two such cases, which combine diasporas' material contributions of remittances and knowledge transfer with policy influence and the leveraging of networks inclusive of diaspora-homeland government relations and beyond. Specifically, the cases of rural Morocco (1985–2005) and Dominica demonstrate the importance of diasporas' transnationality in linking opportunities, resources, and expertise from the host land to homeland actors, including governments.

To place the lessons from these examples in context, the remainder of this introduction reviews literature on homeland government policy options vis-à-vis the diaspora, networks for diaspora homeland contributions, and diaspora organizations.

Homeland Government Policy Options

Home-government perspectives on diaspora activities differ, depending on the diasporas' agenda for influencing the homeland. In some cases, governments consider them an interference with state sovereignty. In other cases, governments see them as important contributors to social, political, and economic development. Accordingly, some states (e.g., India, Mexico, and the Dominican Republic) actively court the participation of their diasporas, while others (e.g., Cuba) ignore or view them as enemies.

The stance of national governments with regard to their diasporas varies according to a range of factors, including the national ethos of the country of origin, the makeup of the diaspora (e.g., refugees versus economically motivated emigrants), the importance of economic remittances to national development, and citizenship laws (Shain 1999). For example, countries that include migrants as "official members of their political communities" include Mexico, Colombia, Brazil, Ecuador, and Portugal (Levitt

2001a). Not surprisingly, the legal rights of immigrants and the implications of dual citizenship are contested subjects (see Neuman 1996; Benhabib 1999). States are increasingly challenged by the tension between preventing brain drain and controlling the activities of diaspora communities, on the one hand, and, on the other, not limiting their potential economic contributions (see Alexseev 2002).

Many governments seem to prioritize remittances and the direct transactions that come with them over brain drain.[1] More and more, home governments are soliciting remittances and offering policy incentives (e.g., dual citizenship, tax-free investment opportunities, and matching grants) and investment options (e.g., remittance-backed bonds and foreign-currency accounts) to encourage diaspora contributions (see, for example, Orozco with Lapointe 2004; Lowell and De la Garza 2000; Pires-Hester 1999). For example, through hometown associations, resources can be channeled to specific development projects, sometimes identified by the targeted communities themselves, and/or coordinated with government funds and expertise (see Orozco 2003; see also Smith 2001; Shain 1999). The Mexican government introduced a "3X1" matching incentive program to encourage developmental investments, where HTA investments are matched at local, state, and national levels (see Orozco with Lapointe 2004).

Policy frameworks can foster incentives for diaspora development contributions to the homeland. Lowell, Findlay, and Stewart (2004) identify three policy areas for optimizing skilled migration: migration management, the "diaspora option" (originally proposed by Meyer et al. 1997), and democracy and development. Migration management seeks to create disincentives for skilled migration. Related policies have evolved from an emphasis on value recovery through taxation and repatriation programs (i.e., the return option; see Meyer et al. 1997; Meyer 2001) to host-country immigration regulations and international agreements limiting the immigration of skilled individuals from targeted countries (see Lowell, Findlay, and Stewart 2004; Gamlen 2005; Iredale 2001), and to addressing the causes of migration, that is, tackling economic and political development challenges (Lowell, Findlay, and Stewart 2004). More conventional return policies persist, and their targeted design and application are encouraged, for example, for retirees and students (see Pellegrino 2001).

The diaspora option encompasses several potential approaches. This policy framework conceives the skilled diaspora as an asset to be captured (Meyer et al. 1997), and is the primary focus of this volume. Gamlen (2005) distinguishes three types of related diaspora engagement strategies: remittance capture, diaspora networking, and diaspora integration. Remittance capture can be achieved by offering various investment options and supporting incentives, including remittance-backed bonds, foreign-currency accounts, investment tax breaks, exemption from import tariffs on capital goods, duty-free shopping bonuses, and free passport insurance. Diaspora networking refers to cultivating links between the homeland and its diaspora.

The diaspora integration strategy recognizes the diaspora as a constituency that is marginalized from the homeland. Related policies include, for example, the extension of citizen rights such as voting, and the organization of diaspora summits and diplomatic visits to diaspora organizations in their host countries. Mexico, a leader in the diaspora option generally, has created positions for elected diaspora representatives in state parliaments. Diaspora integration policies confer social status, political influence, and legitimacy to the diaspora and its potential efforts to contribute to the homeland. Zambia's president, Levy Mwanawasa, provides an example that combines remittance capture with diaspora integration strategies. In an address to the Zambian community in the United States, he stated: "I know you expect me to say come home. I am not going to do that. I have no jobs to give you. Work here and send money home" (qtd. in Manda 2004, 74).

Finally, policies for democracy and development include strengthening institutions and human rights, education, and targeted development; promoting civil-society participation in the policy process; and intergovernmental agreements and harmonization, bilateral and multilateral agreements, and the General Agreement on Trade in Services (GATS) (see Lowell, Findlay, and Stewart 2004; see also Iredale 2001). This policy area encompasses a broad range of potential actors: home- and host-country governments, international and intergovernmental organizations, NGOs, and diaspora organizations themselves. Democracy and development in the homeland at once serves to address the causes of migration for some, and provides incentives for diaspora contributions by enabling these contributions and enhancing a sense of efficacy that they can have an impact.

Networks

While individual diasporans can contribute to households and philanthropy to support homeland development, their impact is greatly enhanced when they take place in the context of broader networks. For example, in some cases the volume of remittances may be enhanced and productive investments may be increased when remittances are pooled or coordinated—for example, by a diaspora organization.

Professional Networks

The importance of networks to mobilize and enhance the effectiveness of diaspora contributions has been most explored in the literature on brain gain, or knowledge transfer and exchange. In emphasizing networks, Meyer

(2001) stresses the implications of social capital. With specific application to knowledge networks, he applies Callon's (1991) concept of sociotechnical or technoeconomic networks to describe how such networks link heterogeneous entities—including equipment, norms, and organizations—such that the potential of each link within the network is only as valuable as what it can mobilize in the network as a whole.

The body of research on intellectual, scientific diaspora networks is increasing. In 1997 Meyer and associates published the first study of a diaspora knowledge network, focusing on Colombia. Only two years later, Meyer and Brown (1999) identified forty-one expatriate knowledge networks tied to thirty different countries. These are specific efforts to link diaspora professionals to the homeland for the purpose of transferring knowledge. The networks were categorized into four types: student/scholarly networks, local associations of skilled expatriates, expert pool assistance through the UNDP's Transfer of Knowledge Through Expatriate Nationals (TOKTEN) program, and intellectual/scientific diaspora networks. Of the forty-one identified, fifteen were classified as intellectual/scientific diaspora networks with an explicit purpose of promoting the economic and social development of the homeland.

Many associations of skilled expatriates are evolving into formal professional associations, which are becoming increasingly active in intellectual/scientific diaspora networks. The highly skilled may rely more on such professional networks, as well as on school-based networks and formal recruitment and relocation agencies, than on kin-based ones (Vertovec 2002). In fact, such reliance is more likely to yield a match of skill levels to jobs than is reliance on networks based on personal ties, which tend to foster ethnic profession and destination niches that can yield brain waste (see Poros 2001). These professional associations, or networks, need not be diaspora-specific in order to play a role in fostering knowledge transfer to or exchange with the homeland. While experience varies among professions, professions are increasingly international (see Iredale 2001).

The most notable examples of knowledge transfer and exchange highlight the role of diaspora identity-based professional associations (see Saxenian 2002a). These include, for example, the Silicon Valley Chinese Engineers Association, the Indus Entrepreneur, and the Korean IT Forum. These associations fulfill a range of social network roles, including facilitating the settlement—professional and otherwise—of recent migrants, professional and technical advancement, ethnic identity formation and maintenance, and entrepreneurial investments in the homeland. Saxenian (2002a) particularly highlights their role of bridging homeland producers to the global economy.

The experience of professional networking bridging diasporas to the homeland confirms the power of heterogeneous networks that facilitate the role of diasporans as interlocutors between host-land and homeland actors, and between tacit and technical knowledge from the host land, on the one hand, and culture, relationships, and adaptation in the homeland, on the other.

The Intermediary Role

Intermediaries are important to facilitate both entry into knowledge networks and the successful application of skills and knowledge in both host- and homeland. Intermediaries may include formal recruitment and relocation agencies as well as professional associations, among others. Meyer and Brown (1999) argue for a coordinating body to facilitate knowledge transfer: "The function of such a coordinating body would be to collect, organize and maintain the information needed for the systematic search of partnerships, but also to manage and promote the interests and actions of the multiple entities present in a network of this kind" (13).

Examples from diaspora-homeland knowledge exchange in China, the Philippines, and Afghanistan demonstrate a range of options for fulfilling intermediary functions. In China (see Biao 2006), the intermediary role is enacted by several types of actors. Government examples include the Ministry of Science and Technology, which facilitates the matching of local needs to diaspora skills through the dissemination of its *Science and Technology News* to overseas Chinese professional (OCP) associations; and the many websites at national and local government levels. Nongovernmental associations in China may also play an intermediary role, such as the Overseas Talents Serving the Homeland program of the Chinese Association for Science and Technology. OCP associations, like other diaspora organizations, play a critical role for knowledge exchange with China, for example, promoting matching by organizing delegations and inviting Chinese scholars for knowledge exchange in the host land. In fact, the government of China increasingly relies on OCP associations for broader communication with the diaspora.

Filipino diaspora organizations play similar roles (see Opiniano and Castro 2006). Both the Science and Technology Advisory Council of Japan (a Philippines government–initiated, volunteer-based overseas professional association) and the Brain Gain Network seek to connect overseas Filipino professionals with homeland counterparts. While some Filipino NGOs have directly solicited assistance from Filipino diaspora associations, more commonly, diaspora associations act as intermediaries by conducting their own needs assessments, networking with Filipinos at professional conferences, and promoting their philanthropic programs to potential beneficiaries. The Society of Afghan Engineers and Afghans4Tomorrow play intermediary roles and, like some of their Filipino counterparts, also initiate the design of philanthropic projects that draw upon diaspora skills and knowledge.

Diaspora Organizations

Diaspora organizations are increasingly playing this coordinating and inter-mediary role both within the highly skilled diaspora and with those diaspo-rans who may be of lower education and incomes but who share a strong inclination to support the homeland. Diaspora organizations can engender a sense of solidarity and community identity and may represent both bonding and bridging social capital. Bonding social capital can generate trust (Coleman 1988, 1990) and the shared identity required for collective action (see also, Ostrom 1990). As evidenced by diaspora organizations (e.g., eth-nic professional associations, and philanthropic organizations), bonding social capital enhances the likelihood of diaspora contributions, whether for productive investment, knowledge transfer/exchange, or philanthropy. For example, Biao (2006) suggests a correlation between those OCPs who join overseas ethnic professional associations and those who maintain contact with the homeland.

Bringing diaspora members' material resources, skills, and capacities together requires an organizational or networking base (see Klandermans and Oegema 1987), which enables diaspora members to contribute their perspectives, skills, and resources to the collective effort. Strong ties that bridge individuals between the home- and host land may be crucial to increasing the volume and effectiveness of knowledge exchange. Again, Biao (2006) highlights the importance of bonding social capital between OCPs and individuals from knowledge institutes, who benefit from their knowledge exchange/transfer (83 percent of surveyed OCPs cited personal contacts as the most valued factor in their participation in knowledge exchange). This and other cases illustrate that bonding social capital is important for both informal exchange and for facilitating access to formal opportunities offered by government and knowledge institutes. In short, bonding social capital is instrumental in cultivating and enhancing the impact of bridging social capital.

While diaspora organizations (DOs) are highly varied, most tend to be volunteer based and relatively unsophisticated, and achieve results, if any, on small scales, through very personalized networks. In a speech at the "Diasporas as Wealth Creators Conference," Carlo Dade of the Canadian Foundation for the Americas (FOCAL) described diaspora organizations as "typically all-volunteer groups with minimal administrative skills and mini-mal organizational structure" (Dade 2006, 3). Portes, Escobar, and Radford's (2005) study of DOs from Colombia, the Dominican Republic, and Mexico found that less than half of these were registered as formal non-profits and four-fifths of them had no paid staff. Still, 45 percent did have legal status, and some of the diasporas were more organizationally sophisti-cated (Colombia, followed by the Dominican Republic) than others

(Mexico). Whether aimed at quality of life in the home- or host land, many of them are likely to suffer from various forms of voluntary failure. Salamon (1987) outlines four voluntary failures: (1) philanthropic insufficiency, rooted in NGOs' limited scale and resources; (2) philanthropic particularism, reflecting NGOs' choice of clientele and projects; (3) philanthropic paternalism, where those who control the most resources are able to control community priorities; and (4) philanthropic amateurism.

Just as these failures apply less and less to the NGO sector as a whole (Brinkerhoff 2002; Brinkerhoff and Brinkerhoff 2002; see also Hulme and Edwards 1997), however, so, too, are we likely to see an increasing sophistication and capacity within the diaspora organization sector. This already occurs somewhat naturally as individual diaspora communities evolve. In one of the few—if only—studies of diaspora organizations as of this writing, Portes, Escobar, and Radford (2005) find that more established immigrants prefer more formal and institutionalized initiatives. Sometimes these are reflections or extensions of traditional US nonprofits, such as Lions and Kiwanis clubs. Moya (2005) compares the evolution of immigrant associational life with the voluntary sector more generally, noting that, historically, the growing variety of associations that developed in diaspora led to increased specialization of these organizations (see Ross 1976; Smith and Freedman 1972; from Moya 2005).

The sophistication of individuals' participation is also likely to increase with progressing integration. The literature on voluntary associations finds that membership increases with education, income, and professional employment (Moya 2005). It should be anticipated, then, that as diaspora members progress educationally and economically in the adopted homeland they, too, may join more associations. More-educated diaspora members are also more likely to organize for homeland interventions that are national in scope (Portes, Escobar, and Radford 2005).

Lessons from Morocco and Dominica

The following chapters illustrate how government policy and action, networking and mediation within diasporas and between diasporas and the homeland, and diaspora organizations facilitating this networking and mediation can contribute to homeland development on a national scale. The chapters take the issues of diasporas and development from a focus on individual types of contributions, actors, and contexts to a broader, integrative level. In doing so, they offer new perspectives and interpretations of these contributions and phenomena (Iskander, Chapter 8), and illustrate how diasporas can assist in helping the homeland escape from one of its most intractable vicious cycles concerning migration and development: the interaction of remittance dependence and brain drain (Fontaine with Brinkerhoff, Chapter 9).

In Chapter 8 Natasha Iskander reifies remittances as constituted by social processes within complex networks of diverse and multisectoral actors, inclusive of diaspora organization mediation. She suggests the target of intervention for enhancing the development impact of remittances is not the remittances, the individual remitter, the transfer mechanism, or even the funneling of its application to development purposes. Instead, it is the social process that not only links the remitter to a recipient household and community but also the process that determines its application as negotiated among migrants, recipient households and communities, and a host of other public, private, and potentially philanthropic actors. By regarding remittances in this way, the example of rural Morocco in 1985–2005 demonstrates their potential to contribute to development on a much grander scale, even at the national level.

In other words, as long as policymakers, including government and development industry actors, remain fixated on the object of remittances and the individual application choices recipients make, they will miss the true potential of remittance contributions to development and likely miss important opportunities to further national development agendas in partnership with diasporas. Indeed, when the focus is on specific development objectives and means to those ends, instead of engaging in a cocreated process that generates meanings and outcomes previously unimagined, the true potential of diaspora-inclusive development efforts is limited and may be wasted. Iskander's chapter is an important albeit ignored illustration of the migration and development nexus that is so talked about yet poorly understood.

The case of rural Morocco and its diaspora's contribution to homeland development unfolds over the course of twenty years (and counting) and is the result of substantial investments on the part of the government of Morocco to build relationships with its diaspora, and to negotiate and implement partnerships for development. In contrast, Thomson Fontaine with Jennifer Brinkerhoff (Chapter 9) provide a snapshot of the very early stages of such processes for a small island state caught in an all too common vicious cycle of remittance dependence, limited homeland employment and advancement opportunities, and continued out-migration and brain drain. The case of Dominica suggests an alternative approach to diaspora contributions to homeland development that is not grounded in selected communities but takes as its starting point national development and national initiatives. Both chapters take a historical view. Whereas Iskander traces the evolution of one diaspora group's experience in one country (France) and of its support to and impact on homeland development, Fontaine with Brinkerhoff trace the general history of migration and its impact on

Dominica and provide an overview of diaspora organizing within and across several receiving countries.

Both chapters document the evolution of the respective diaspora-homeland government partnerships. In the Moroccan case, the diaspora first developed and demonstrated its development model (in partnership with other actors) and only later sought to influence the government's policy and approach. In Dominica the diaspora has sought a more formal partnership with the government from the outset of its national development organizing efforts and has established somewhat of a quid pro quo relationship, with the diaspora demanding certain policy changes and related benefits while it continues to initiate its own development projects and respond to specific requests from the government. The partnership with government has culminated in the production of a diaspora policy paper, wherein the diaspora has articulated its vision for Dominica's development and the diaspora's role in it—at the request of the government.

The Dominica diaspora's efforts are also more systematic, with a structured approach targeting particular sectors (e.g., committees on economic development, agriculture, health, and education) and priority issues (e.g., crime prevention), while partnering with government and forging relations and cooperation with local residents. Further, the diaspora is innovating ways to connect diaspora youth to youth in Dominica and supporting other cultural efforts to instill a shared pride in the Dominican culture and identity and sustain it among generations of migrants. This diaspora's organizing efforts, structured mechanisms for facilitating development contributions and partnerships, and specific initiatives provide a wealth of examples for other diasporas to consider.

Beyond the multiactor partnerships these chapters illustrate, another approach for thinking about how to maximize diasporas' contributions to homeland development is to better link their efforts to the international development industry. Manuel Orozco (Chapter 10) concludes this volume by reiterating the various mechanisms by which diasporas contribute to homeland economic development (intentionally or not), and outlining the impediments to linkages to more-formal development efforts.

—Jennifer M. Brinkerhoff

Note

1. For example, see Kaukab (2005) for the Pakistan case; and Manda (2004) on Zambia.

8

Diaspora Networks for Creating National Infrastructure: Rural Morocco, 1985–2005

Natasha Iskander

A s migrant remittances worldwide have risen to stratospheric levels, the aggregate role of countless small transfers of money in national economic growth has become impossible to ignore. Development scholars have produced a spate of increasingly sophisticated models of how remittances affect economic performance, as well as a growing body of qualitative analyses of the ways that transfers of money, but also of knowledge, social networks, political influence, and even cultural values, affect economies of migrant-sending countries. Likewise, policymakers have rushed to apply the prescriptions those efforts have yielded to design policy that directs migrant resources to uses whereby they can have the greatest positive effect on economic growth. Both the policy interventions and the models on which they are based, however, share a fundamental assumption about migrant resources, monetary and nonmonetary, that seriously undermines their usefulness: policymakers view migrant resources as fungible as capital that is unchanged by its transfer across local and national contexts. Moreover, they cast remittances as the vector of change, placing them at the center of an impact model in which remittances—like proverbial meteors, large and small—cause change as they collide into receptive locales.

In this chapter I present an alternative view of migrant resources as constituted through the actions of migrants. I argue that remittances are not merely transferred; they are *made*. Their import for local and national development cannot be read off the remittances themselves, with forecasts dependent on the assumption that outcomes are predictable given certain preexisting conditions. Rather, I maintain that the significance of remittances for development is shaped by the ways in which migrants and their communities engage with them; it is the social processes through which actors infuse remittances with meaning and choose how they will use them that are the drivers of economic change. Furthermore, I argue that because remittances are constituted, policy interventions are most effective in forging a link between emigration and development when they actively connect with the social processes through which local actors determine the value of migration-generated resources. Instead of merely directing remittances to a limited predetermined set of uses that the state or donor institutions deem economically beneficial, this approach allows policymakers to participate in the envisioning of new previously unimagined uses for remittances and, in doing so, to magnify the value of remittances themselves by using state resources to extend the reach of the social processes through which they are constituted.

The experience of Moroccan emigrants from the mountainous Souss region in the rural south of the country illustrates that remittances are a constituted resource and demonstrates the potential that this attribute represents for policy. In the 1980s and 1990s, Soussi emigrants acted as catalysts for the transformation of rural infrastructure provision in their homeland. In partnership with their communities of origin, they engaged migrant resources in order to generate innovative solutions for infrastructure provision. Drawing on the social networks, wages, and labor-organizing experience Soussi emigrants had acquired in French industrial cities, they came up with new technical and social approaches to supply their isolated and long-neglected hamlets with electricity, water, and roads.

The Soussis' modest initiatives would ultimately spark the redesign of major national programs for the provision of basic infrastructure in rural Morocco, and would lead to the restructuring of the government agencies charged with implementing those programs. Soussi migrants deliberately pulled state actors into their conversations about how to transform both monetary and nonmonetary remittances into new infrastructure schemes. The Moroccan central government's involvement in the social processes through which migrants and their communities determined what their remittances would mean for local development caused it to revise its own narrow and conventional views about how it could deploy its resources to provide infrastructure to about 65 percent of the nation's 35 million residents, dispersed in the mountainous terrain of Morocco's arid countryside.

The results of the engagement between Soussis and the Moroccan government have been nothing short of dramatic: within one short decade the Moroccan government quadrupled its electricity coverage from about 20 percent of rural residents in the late 1980s to almost 80 percent by 2004; it adopted a compendium of ecologically sustainable approaches to irrigation and water distribution, doubling by 2005 rural access to water for drinking and agriculture; and it revamped its national rural roads program, redrawing road placement in its construction plans in keeping with its new priorities, and replacing kilometers paved with social impact as its primary measure of success (ONE 1999, 2004; Daoud 2005; World Bank 2004a; Levy 2004; van de Walle 2004).

This chapter addresses Moroccan emigrants' role in the reform and expansion in one area of infrastructure provision—rural electricity—to flesh out the notion of remittances, both monetary and nonmonetary, as constituted. In the first section, I provide a conceptual treatment of remittances and of the processes through which their value is socially created, borrowing from management and organizational behavior analyses of the movement of resources within extended firms. The second section focuses on how the engagement between emigrants and villagers constituted three kinds of resources generated by migration—knowledge, funds, and labor organizing experience—to build an innovative rural electricity solution. In the third section I describe how the state's participation in migrant-initiated processes in constituting remittances changed the government's strategy for electricity provision; the state appropriated the insights that it drew from its engagement with migrants around rural electricity delivery to modify its knowledge base about the design of rural electricity networks, to retool the funding schemes to bankroll rural electricity provision, and to amend its view of the social organization needed to support the new power distribution systems. The case presented here is based on six months of fieldwork in Souss, Rabat, and Paris stretched over several years, between 2001 and 2005, and on substantial documentary research in archives of both the government and nongovernmental institutions.[1] In the final section I discuss the implications that a view of remittances as constituted has for designing policy to link emigration to local economic development.

Constituting Remittances

The scholarship on migration and development is organized around a defining assumption: migrant resources—monetary (see Orozco 2001), social (see Levitt 1998), political (see Goldring 2002; Popkin 2003), knowledge based (see Saxenian 1999, 2005; Schiff 2005), or network based (see Portes 1999)—are remitted back to communities of origin, and those remittances then have an impact on local economies that can be predicted given existing local conditions. The literature documents well how migration channels resources to migrant-sending countries and communities. It further demonstrates how local institutional structures and practices direct the impact of those resources, much like water canals direct the flow of water for irrigation (see Durand, Parrado, and Massey 1996; Chaudhry 1989). It has also shown how those resources can and do change local social and economic relationships and processes (see Edwards and Ureta 2003).

The most recent literature on this topic is more nuanced in its analyses, and observes that migrant resources set in motion local transformations that are subtle, sometimes indirect, but profound, affecting communities over time—like a stream of water that gradually erodes and ultimately redefines the local landscape. These studies, qualitative and ethnographic for the most part, show how migrant resources have revamped the architecture of institutions as basic as family and property rights (Kanaiaupuni and Donato 1999; Nuijten 1998), reshaped modes of production (Guarnizo 2003; de la Garza and Lowell 2002), and shaken up deeply held worldviews (Glick-Schiller and Fouron 2001). Furthermore, they call into question the notion that migrant resources flow only in one direction, back to communities of origin. Studies on transnationalism show that migration-generated resources—money, ideas, networks—move back and forth between different nodes or expressions of a community, such that migration makes these communities transnational (see Levitt 2001b). Moreover, the practices of moving resources from one area implicated in the local migration processes to another, in themselves, create transnational social fields that "exist within but [are] constituted apart from the larger states and societies in which they are constituted" (Smith 1995, quoted in Pries 2001, 34).

Both the canonic studies and the latter revisionist batch share two defining assumptions: first, migrant resources are always generated *elsewhere*, and are merely *transferred* back (Hart 2002). In this view, migrant resources are not altered by their trajectory; they arrive intact to affect a passive locale, whether the locale in question is a community or a nation. Building on this understanding of migrant resources as traveling unadulterated across space and into a locale, the second assumption is that the remittances themselves are the cause of local change. While local institutional structures and practices may set the stage for the kind of impact remittances have, migration resources are the catalyst for economic development, or in some cases, for economic dependency and distortion (Hart 2002; Guarnizo 2003). So even while these perspectives acknowledge that remittances may often have subtle and complex effects, they always identify remittances as the force that carves out new curves in a social or economic landscape that is otherwise static and receptive. Consequently, the overwhelming concern in the field has been to hone analytic models so that they might better assess, explain, and predict the effect that migrant resources have on communities or countries of origin (see Taylor 1992; Acosta 2006; Page and Adams 2004).

These twin assumptions of remittances as unchanged by their transfer and as the instigator of economic change have defined migration and development policy. They have given rise to the analogy of migrant resources—especially monetary remittances—as flows, and, like any flow, the perception is that the resources can be rerouted without altering their makeup in any way or distorting the effect that the redirected remittances are predicted to have for economic growth. Thus, the overwhelming concern of governments and multilateral institutions in designing policy in this area has been to develop tools to channel migrant resources to uses where they are forecast to have the most positive impact. On the whole, policy interventions are designed to achieve two goals: first, to increase the volume of remittance flows by lowering transaction costs and removing any friction that obstructs their movement; and, second, to divert some portion of remittance flows away from household consumption, often viewed as "unproductive," to investment or savings in the country of origin, uses viewed as generators of economic growth. In none of these policy initiatives is the action of the state viewed as changing the good transferred: money is money is money, supremely fungible and its material essence impervious to change. The same is true of knowledge, social networks, and even political influence: policy efforts to capitalize on them are not deemed to have any effect on the basic makeup of those resources.

Other analyses of what happens to resources when they are moved from one context to another take a very different view and contend that their transfer alters their intrinsic character. This notion is well developed in organizational behavior analyses of the transfer of resources through the various branches of large multilocational firms, and the findings in those studies provide helpful guideposts for an examination of the way migrants and their communities ascribe value to remittances, and how the social process involved can lead to economic development. These organizational analyses demonstrate that the value of a resource grows out of the way in which it is employed.

Research on knowledge transfer has been particularly compelling in its illustration of the ways that knowledge is situated in the everyday practices of the organizational settings in which it is used; it is embedded in local languages, practices, routines, and social relationships (Kogut and Zander 1992). Observations of groups of workers that perform specialized tasks, sometimes called occupational communities, stress, for example, that the knowledge required to complete their work is inlaid in the groups' shared jargon, in conventions for the appropriate way of completing certain jobs, and in the norms governing social exchanges of members as they work together on a task (Dougherty 1992). Many scholars have taken that observation further and have argued that knowledge is more than just embedded group languages, procedures, relationships, and routines; it is part and parcel of them. They posit that knowledge is enacted through practice and has no meaning or value separate from the actions or contexts in which it is used. Knowledge, they note, is in fact indistinguishable from social exchanges (Lave and Wenger 1991; Orlikowski 2002). Even knowledge as seemingly codifiable and abstract as mathematical formulas, for example, is only intelligible and useful when related to social contexts; the numerical concepts that are the building blocks of algorithms depend on socially constructed understandings for measuring quantity, as well as culturally specific, although widespread, conventions for counting, like the use of the concept of zero. As Lave and Wenger observe in their monograph on learning and knowledge transfer, "Any 'power of abstraction' is thoroughly situated, in the lives of the persons and in the culture that makes it possible" (1991, 34).

As a result, epistemologists increasingly maintain that it is impossible to separate out knowledge as a good that can be picked up and moved from one organizational location to another (von Hippel 1994; Cook and Brown 1999; Orlikowski 2002). They suggest knowledge is more than just "sticky," more than just difficult to extract from specific settings because of the way it was interwoven in local practices. They argue that knowledge actually undergoes a transformation when it is transferred from one situated context to another, one that is so fundamental that it ultimately changes basic aspects of the knowledge being transmitted (Bechky 2003; Lave and Wenger 1991). Observers of this process are referring to more than the slippage of translation, where certain concepts are truncated or lost because the palette of another (literal or practice) language cannot capture them; they are referring to more than the clumsiness of making tacit knowledge explicit, a process that hopelessly blunts subtle understandings in order to encode them (Polanyi 1967). What they are pointing out is that the way that people engage with knowledge in order to communicate it in a situated context different from their own alters what that knowledge actually is (Bechky 2003; Carlile 2004; Kellogg, Orlikowski, and Yates 2006).

Many of the resources that migration makes available to migration communities may seem more materially tangible, more fixed—and less elusive—than knowledge. However, as sociologists of economic change have observed, even though the money, social networks, and political leverage generated through migration appear more concrete, they share the same situated and contingent qualities of knowledge (Zelizer 1997; Hart 2002). Just like knowledge, what those resources are, intrinsically, depends on the ways they are enacted and woven into practice (Giddens 1984).

Zelizer (1997) forcefully illustrates this contingent and situated quality of seemingly concrete resources in her study on the relationship between the social and economic values of money. She argues that even though money's usefulness in society and in production is wholly derived from the appearance of having a constant, objective worth, it nevertheless acquires value only through the social interactions in which it is used or invoked symbolically. So profoundly inscribed is money by the social and cultural ways in which it is used, she posits, that one cannot accurately refer to money as being a single currency. Rather, she concludes, to capture money's social and economic functions, it makes more sense to talk about money as a social medium with multiple currencies, some of which are "as unexchangeable as the most personal and unique object" (1997, 17). In other words, the way money is used, both materially and symbolically, shapes what money is, and variations in the practices of using money transform an apparently undifferentiated resource into distinct, nonfungible objects that are not just valued differently but that invoke different registers of value altogether. Thus, shifting money from one use to another often requires a dramatic change in practice and the meanings with which it is infused (Somers and Block 2005).

What is true of resources like money and knowledge in their particular social, economic, and geographic contexts is even more so in migration communities where the repeated exchange of resources is what weaves communities together across space. Just as the organizational behavior studies suggest, the resources themselves are defined through practice—the way migrants and their communities use them define what they are. Financial remittances sent home to support a child, for instance, express and maintain familial relationships and identities in ways that are different from monies sent to support a quranic school in the village mosque where the same child is learning to read. The remittances in this example, earmarked for different functions, will have different and symbolic value, and people in the community will engage with those resources in ways that reflect that difference in worth.

Moreover, just like the movement of knowledge or funds within a firm, the transfer of resources across context depends on the practices that translate those resources from one place to another: currencies must be exchanged; the local knowledge that is tacit and implicit in one setting—a French urban neighborhood, for example—must be made explicit in another, in a Moroccan village, for example; and the relationships that make up transnational social networks must be sustained using practices that are culturally intelligible and acceptable in specific contexts. The practices that both migrants and their communities use to move resources, especially practices to reconcile different ways of understanding and using money, knowledge, and relationships, fundamentally transform those resources, redefining what they are, their perceived value, and the potential uses ascribed to them.

As the case of infrastructure innovation in the Moroccan countryside will show, practices through which migrants and their communities move and use remittances can enhance those resources significantly; they can infuse them with meanings that turn them into catalysts for economic development and social change. The resources themselves are not what cause local change; remittances in and of themselves do not flow into a given locale to either spark or hinder economic growth. Rather, the social processes that move those resources and give them meaning are what create change; they—not remittances they move and constitute—are the link between migration and development. Indeed, it was precisely the processes through which Soussi migrants and their communities transferred and transformed remittances that turned their abandoned drought-depressed region into a hotbed of infrastructure innovation.

Electrifying Remittances

In the mid-1980s, no more than a fraction of Morocco's rural inhabitants had electric power. While data for the 1980s are sketchy at best, they indicate that rates of electricity access were abysmally low, with coverage estimated at anywhere between 4 to 18 percent. The data from the 1990s are more reliable, having been drawn from a series of government and aid agency studies. Although they still display some variation,[2] they clearly indicate that the rates of electrification for the Moroccan countryside lagged far behind those for similar income countries in the region (ONE 1999; World Bank 1990, 1998). By 1990, Algeria had achieved 70 percent rural electricity coverage and Tunisia was close behind with 60 percent (World Bank 1990).

The Moroccan government explained away its poor performance by contending that hooking up dispersed villages to the national electricity grid across the country's craggy rural topography was prohibitively expensive, and that the alternative of setting up self-standing diesel-generator or solar-powered systems diverted too large a proportion of local revenues from other government functions (World Bank 1990). In the early 1980s, prodded by the World Bank, the Moroccan central government embarked on a rural electrification program, but by all accounts, it was a half-hearted effort with little impact: between 1982 and 1996 the state connected only seventy villages per year to electricity services, with most villages selected located on the outskirts of urban centers and often on the verge of being swallowed up by the burgeoning towns anyway (ONE 1999, 2004). At that rate, it would have taken Morocco over 300 years to provide electricity to its 34,000 villages. As a former director of the National Office of Electricity, Driss Benhima, tersely conceded, "Between 1960 and 1990, it [rural electrification] was not a priority" (qtd. in Daoud 1997, 40; Daoud 2005).

Faced with government inaction in the provision of electricity, a group of emigrants from the Souss region decided in the mid-1980s to fund and erect self-standing networks in their villages of origin. The emigrants had been working at the Péchiney company, a group of aluminum-processing plants in the Argentière valley in southern France since the late 1960s and early 1970s. A little less than two decades after they first joined the factory, Péchiney, a casualty of the mortal blow that the oil shocks of the 1970s dealt French heavy industry, was first nationalized and then was forced to restructure and close most of its plants. As part of its severance package to hundreds of laid-off workers, the now politically accountable parastatal granted start-up funds for small firms to its former employees. The Soussi emigrants decided to take the funds and set up firms in their villages of origin rather than trying to rebuild their lives in Argentière.

Because the funds, though paid out to individual workers, were disbursed to spawn a microenterprise-based economy to replace the closed factories, Péchiney refused to give them to the Moroccan workers. With the help of the CFDT (Confédation Française Démocratique du Travail), a major French labor union, the emigrants took Péchiney to court. After a protracted and acrimonious legal battle, the Soussi plaintiffs were awarded their capital and began planning for the microenterprises they would establish on their return to their villages. They envisioned grocery stores and gas stations, small agro-processing outfits, and marginal agricultural improvements to their family plots.

Very quickly, however, it became clear to the emigrants that even their relatively modest projects would fail without electricity. Already organized because of their legal struggle against their former employer, they shifted their focus from the creation of small firms to the provision of electricity. In 1984 they pooled a portion of their severance award and set up a small association, Retour et Développement (Return and Development), to build electricity networks in their villages in the heart of the Souss (Daoud 1997). The migrants later renamed the organization they established Migration and Development (M/D) because they began to feel that the word *return* in the previous name sounded too much like an exhortation. And as the first project led to many others, the new name happily captured the ongoing nature of their development efforts (Daoud 1997).

The Soussi emigrants' idea of building informal electricity networks was not new. Villages throughout the Moroccan countryside had cobbled together electricity networks powered by local generators. In fact, external consultants contracted by the National Office of Electricity estimated that in 1993, about 2,000 villages had set up informal electrification schemes, most often bankrolled through emigrant remittances (Berdai and Butin 1993). The networks tended to suffer, however, from two serious and mutually reinforcing shortcomings. First, the independent systems used equipment of a quality that was so poor that electricity provision was sporadic and dangerous; low-hanging cables, frayed and too weak to carry the voltage that passed through them, along with faulty connections and unreliable circuit breakers, produced blackouts as well as accidents that were frequently fatal. Second, informal electricity networks tended to serve only those families that had contributed funds for their construction—by most estimates, somewhat more than 20 percent but rarely above 50 percent of residents (M/D 1992).

Poorer families, excluded from service, relied on "found" energy sources; they scavenged for wood from already denuded slopes, aggravating rapid deforestation. This compounded increasingly regular droughts that were imperiling local agriculture. The stripped soil was unable to absorb and hold the seasonal rainwater that fed Moroccan agricultural production. The growing scarcity of water meant that families with access to the informal electricity networks relied ever more heavily on motor-powered water pumps, which drew water up from deep and rapidly falling underground water tables, to irrigate their fields. As they did so, they overtaxed their already maxed-out village electricity network, often causing damage that necessitated costly repairs. The expenses for the repairs thinned out the participants in the network, excluding those families that could not contribute additional funds to fix the system and relegating them to the ranks of those who relied on "found" energy. In a vicious cycle, as the number of families who foraged for wood increased, their collective impact on the environment and on the availability of water was augmented, which in turn compelled families that depended on electric water pumps to use them more intensely, causing short circuits and other malfunctions in the electricity network, which eventually required expensive repairs. In a pattern that was all too common, the network became too costly for an ever-smaller group of families to maintain and was abandoned (Missaoui 1996; M/D 1996).

The emigrants of M/D wanted to do things differently. Having observed electricity schemes in villages neighboring their own fall into disrepair and disuse, they resolved to build a network that fulfilled two criteria: first, an affordable, reliable, and safe network; and second, access for all villagers regardless of their ability to pay.

To accomplish this goal, the emigrants drew on three kinds of remittances: the technical knowledge about electricity networks they procured through the social networks they had forged in France, the funds they had earned and collected abroad, and the experience many of them had acquired as worker organizers in the French labor movement's conflict with Péchiney (Daoud 1997). In and of themselves, those resources were significant. It was the way the migrants and their communities engaged with them, however, that made the resources valuable for the construction of their electricity network, so valuable in fact that it turned their plan to build a modest electricity network into a laboratory for infrastructure innovation.

Transforming Knowledge

In 1985 the Soussi emigrants decided to build their first electricity network in the village of Imgoun, a small hamlet of about a thousand residents that was home to the founder of M/D. The village was perched on a rugged mountainside approximately two hours away by all-terrain jeep from the nearest town that had electricity and a well-stocked regional market where supplies to maintain a network could be acquired. To get help with the technological hurdles represented by setting up a safe and sustainable electricity network in that setting, M/D contacted the French Agency for Energy Management (Agence Française pour la Maitrise de l'Energie [AFME])—a French governmental agency, later renamed the Agence de l'Environment et de la Maitrise d'Energie—through the social networks that the M/D emigrants forged during their legal battle with Péchiney.

The leadership of the AFME had long-standing ties to the CFDT, the union that supported the emigrants in their struggle against the aluminum magnate, and by the time the M/D emigrants began exploring energy options for Imgoun, the union boss of the CFDT, Michel Roland, was named president of the AFME. The energy agency mediated a relationship between M/D and Electricité de France (EDF), then a French government producer and distributor of energy in France and, on a much smaller scale, in selected sites of North and West African countries. EDF, interested in exploring new decentralized energy solutions that the company could market widely, promptly sent thirty-seven volunteers to Imgoun to assist the emigrants and villagers in building their informal electricity network (Daoud 1997). A couple of AFME engineers, retained as consultants to the Moroccan government on the issue of rural electrification, joined the EDF volunteers of their own accord because they were interested in the design challenges the Imgoun project represented.

According to the plan, the EDF engineers would bring their technical expertise to come up with an energy network to fit Imgoun's specific topographical and economic constraints. Knowledge was not simply transferred to the village, however. Instead, the way that the M/D emigrants and Imgoun's residents engaged with the French technicians and with their knowledge reformulated both the standard technical guidelines for electricity networks and the procedures used to design the networks for varied settings. The migrants and the villagers hosted the EDF electricians in their houses, shared their meals with them, and involved them in Imgoun's daily rhythms of agriculture, water collection, and cooking and housekeeping (Daoud 1997). They engaged the technicians in extended and wide-ranging conversations about how residents used power and its relationship to the deforestation of nearby slopes. Those conversations revealed that the heaviest usage of power would be for everyday household functions ranging from cooking to lighting. Based on those findings, the technicians, the emigrants, and the villagers abandoned the idea of a solar-powered system, which would have drawn on a plentiful but undependable energy source, and opted instead for an electricity system that drew on a more reliable diesel-powered generator. Together, they began to draw up a blueprint for the new system.

While they built the network, they revised the plan many times over; they improvised with materials, modified the design to deal with the topographical challenges of connecting houses on steep slopes, and adjusted machine components to make the generator and the distribution system easy to maintain and repair. The process through which villagers employed the electricians' technical knowledge, and through which the technicians drew on Imgounis' local knowledge, was highly iterative and in the end, so profoundly transformed their technical and social conceptualizations of electricity that neither party could have imagined the electricity network they ultimately constructed prior to their engagement. Moreover, as their knowledge base was revised, work practices were also amended. Instead of drafting a complete design for a network based on industry standards and abstract engineering principles and then only afterward constructing it on the ground, they learned to adopt a more improvisational approach in which obstacles that emerged in building led to a change in design, which in turn led to a change in construction strategy.

The final product diverged significantly from the construction standards mandated by the Moroccan government as well as those used by the EDF itself—both of which were formulated with an urban setting in mind—but nevertheless complied with the logic that underpinned those standards: the network was safe, and it was reliable. The dimensions of the network and of the physical structures to support it were based on the real and projected electricity consumption in the village, and were therefore smaller than the norm. Thinner than usual cables were strung on poles that were only 6 meters tall instead of the required 10. The poles, stripped eucalyptus trucks, were bought locally, and substituted for the compulsory concrete columns that were impossible to transport up the dirt road that led to the village and were difficult to pour on site. Electricity was transmitted along this network at a frequency one-third the intensity specified by the industry standard, and the circuit breaker was secondhand and refurbished.

After the project, Jamal Lahoussain, one of the emigrant founders of M/D, reflected on how the perception of what technical options were viable shifted with the Imgoun project: "The standards of the National Office of Electricity were too draconian. They imposed them on the villages. In the end, even EDF found that they were excessive and that they did not take technological evolution into account" (qtd. in Daoud 1997, 37). The rough poles and slack wires that now wove through the village, rudimentary though they appeared, represented a significant technological advance. They embodied a new way of thinking about rural electricity provision, one that grew out of the particularities of the locale to which energy would be supplied rather than on the design of the network that would distribute the power (M/D 1996).

From Remitting Funds to Funding a Project

The funds required for the construction of the electricity network were relatively modest, but the labor that the M/D emigrants expended in collecting them was substantial. The way the emigrants assembled the project money informed its significance and its material value for the electricity network, as well as for the economic development of Imgoun more broadly. Wary of shouldering the entire financial cost of the network and of replicating the social divide that had emerged in other villages between those who paid for electricity service and those who did not (and who were thus excluded), the emigrants insisted that 40 percent of the monies required to erect the network be collected in Imgoun. The source of the money contributed could of course be remittances, but what mattered more to M/D was that the money be donated through families still living in Imgoun so that the genesis of the project would be rooted in the village rather than in the cities of France. Moreover, they insisted that every family contribute some amount to the project, either in cash or in kind, but scaled the donation requested according to household income. These conditions transformed the electricity project from an emigrant initiative to a community project and ensured that the electricity produced would always be considered a public good, whose creation all in the village had supported and on which all in the village could thus draw, for as long as the network still stood.

The emigrants raised the remaining 60 percent of the funds required among themselves, each of them contributing a percentage of the severance capital they had received from Péchiney. They also fund-raised among French donors, appealing to the French organizations involved in the Imgoun electricity project—AFME and EDF—for monies. Additionally, they registered as an immigrant nongovernmental association with the French government and successfully applied for a grant through the government's Fund for Social Action, an endowment established in 1981 to support immigrant integration in France (Daoud 1997).

By drawing on sources of funds other than their remittances, sources both in Imgoun and in France, the emigrants transformed the conception of the project from a remittance-funded migrant initiative to a village project in which emigrants participated as members of the village community. Their multifaceted fund-raising approach recast emigrant remittances, converting them from a financial lifeline on which the village depended to one resource among many that the village could tap into for the electricity project, as well as for any future projects carried out in Imgoun. Moreover, the relationships that emigrants established with foreign funders, and that the villagers cemented when they hosted EDF technicians in their homes, augmented the value of the funds donated, changing them from a delimited sum of money earmarked for a specific purpose to a potential source of financial

support for additional development initiatives that the village would launch
in coming years.

Organizing Electricity

With the funds collected and the electricity network constructed, the
remaining challenge for the village of Imgoun was to develop a system to
maintain the network. The generator that powered the network needed to be
refilled and recalibrated almost daily; the costs of the benzine had to be collected in a manner that adhered to the principle of equal access to electric
power regardless of income; and the equipment itself had to be monitored
for usage damage, and repairs had to be completed quickly, with the outlay
recovered. Taken together, these tasks represented a significant logistical
and organizational hurdle.

The M/D emigrants brought their labor organizing experience to the
problem; several of the emigrant activists recounted that their participation
in numerous strikes against Péchiney during its plant closures in the 1980s
and then in their subsequent mobilization against the company to obtain
their severance grants made clear to them that the way people organized to
address obstacles mattered just as much as the outcome they achieved. The
extensive deliberations they held among themselves and with the union that
was supporting them persuaded them that it was essential, even if laborious,
that all the villagers, as users of electricity, should have some say in how the
network was run and how fees were collected. They recalled that their
lengthy and sometimes meandering discussions during their French labor
struggle made their mobilization durable enough to last even when confronted with Péchiney's intransigence, but also flexible enough to incorporate new insights about the companies' vulnerabilities and to experiment
with creative strategies. In a call that ran counter to patriarchal village
norms, they insisted in particular that women and youth in Imgoun contribute to decisions about the network's management. Additionally, emigrants remarked that their French organizing experience underscored the
value of collaboration between people with different skill sets and knowledge bases in the design of effective strategies, and were adamant that people with the ability to read, write, and interpret engineering drawings be
given as much voice as village elders whose pronouncement carried the
weight of law in Imgoun.

While the insights the emigrants gleaned from their activist experience
in France alone were valuable, both the emigrants and the villagers engaged
with them in Imgoun transformed those observations into an organizational
form robust enough to maintain the electricity network over the long term.
Together, they used the lessons the emigrants articulated to reinvent the
jema'a, a traditional council of elders that had for centuries pronounced

binding verdicts in disputes and governed the management of communal resources (like water and pasture access) in villages throughout the Souss region. Often celebrated as a form of protodemocracy, the jema'a elected its leader each year, and most decisions were made by consensus (Mernissi 1998). Membership, however, was limited to male village elites, the senior heads of families with landholdings expansive enough to qualify (de Haas 2003). By 1985, however, when ground was broken for the electricity network, the jema'at in the Souss had been seriously weakened owing to a series of political blows and administrative measures the monarchy's control had inflicted on the rural south over the previous two decades (de Haas 2003; Lugan 1992).

The emigrants and the villagers resuscitated the injured institution by reinventing it. They applied the lessons the emigrants brought with them about organizing and transformed the arthritic jema'a into a vibrant village association. In the new association, all villagers—regardless of income, landholdings, age, or gender—were automatically vested as members, with equal rights to speak and participate in the consensus-based decisionmaking processes. Moreover, villagers with certain skill sets, notably literacy, were assigned the task of supervising the implementation of the associations' decisions. By reviving the jema'a, they implicitly classified electricity as a communal resource, akin to water and pastureland, over which all residents had usufruct rights. But by amending the council makeup, they redistributed the authority over how those rights would be defined from a handful of notables to include some of the most marginalized members of the community (M/D 1996; Daoud 1997). As an M/D document would later summarize: "[T]he association enables everyone to get involved in the development of the village, and reduces the hierarchical inequalities between rich and poor, between young and old" (M/D 1992).

After protracted rounds of discussion, the village association decided that tariffs for electricity usage would be modulated according to household income, with wealthier residents charged more per kilowatt hour to subsidize usage by poorer families, who would pay somewhat less than the net cost. Tacked on to the fees would be a proportional tax, both to cover a modest salary for two or three schooled young men who would monitor and keep records on the day-to-day function of the network, and to feed into a contingency fund for any necessary repairs.

The sociotechnical model that the emigrants and villagers together developed for energy provision quickly expanded to villages surrounding Imgoun. M/D was rapidly overwhelmed with requests from nearby villages for help with electricity networks. It managed to assist an average of ten villages a year in establishing electricity provision between 1985 and 1996, at a time when the Moroccan central government succeeded in providing less than seventy with electric power per annum. Inundated with petitions for assistance, the emigrant association began to look to the state to fulfill its long-neglected responsibilities to the Souss. As one M/D emigrant activist explained:

> We want to take the state by the hand and bring it here. We don't have the resources the state does; we can never accomplish what the state can. What we want is for the state to do the work of the state *here*. Once the state takes responsibility for something—like providing electricity—there is no need for us to continue [doing that]. (Interview, January 2004)[3]

Bringing the State by the Hand

To "bring the state by the hand" to their communities, the M/D emigrants began by involving the Moroccan central government indirectly in their processes of constituting migration resources. Two engineers from the AFME who assisted M/D with its Imgoun electricity network served as the first bridge between the migrant development organization and the government. The Moroccan government contracted the AFME for technical assistance to improve its badly limping rural electricity program, and the French AFME technicians brought the new technological and organizational understandings about electricity provision developed in Imgoun to bear on their consulting work. The exchange was, as one AFME consultant recalled, "informal, indirect." It was a casual, even lackadaisical, consideration of ideas brought to the table by politically neutral French technical assistants and was far from being bureaucratically sanctioned (Interview, August 2004).

Soon, however, the Moroccan government's dismal performance in rural electricity provision compelled it to search more intentionally for successful and affordable approaches to rural electrification, and the exchange of ideas with M/D grew more institutionalized. The government's National Program for Rural Electricity, launched in 1982 at the behest of international donors, was a miserable failure; the state was able to supply only 287 new villages with electricity between 1982 and 1987, about 60 per year, and even that modest effort proved too expensive for the government to envision on a grand scale (World Bank 1998). In 1987 the Moroccan Ministry of the Interior tasked the AFME with helping design a pilot program for rural electrification in the hopes of developing new models for electricity distribution. The government was particularly keen on experimenting with rural energy strategies that did not require villages to be linked to the state network (Ministry of the Interior, Kingdom of Morocco, and AFME 1987; World Bank 1988, 1990; Grosclaude 1990; AFME 1988).

Although none of the 200 pilot sites selected for the program were located in the Souss, M/D was able to influence the government's scheme by using its own collaboration with AFME technicians to invite government officials into the villages where the migrant organization had erected inno-vative electricity networks. M/D actively engaged the government on the development of new electrification strategies for the duration of the pilot program's existence, from 1987 to 1995. Government engineers regularly visited M/D sites to draw insights from the electricity experiments, and M/D regularly, albeit informally, drew them into the process of constructing new electricity networks. Additionally, government electricians used the mature, well-functioning M/D electricity networks to test the viability of various electricity-related strategies (like the use of fluorescent bulbs) (Berdai and Butin 1993, 1994; Butin and M/D 1993).

Over time, M/D's imprint on the government pilot program became increasingly clear. Because M/D's sway stemmed from its back-and-forth exchange with government engineers, its influence occurred not through a direct application of M/D innovations but, rather, through the government's appropriation and reinterpretation of the insights the migrant organization generated about rural electrification. In a process strikingly similar to the one that occurred when migrants and their communities of origin engaged with the monetary and nonmonetary remittances, the new knowledge about rural electricity provision that government technicians gleaned from M/D villages was not merely transferred to government pilot sites; it was trans-formed as it was applied.

The effect of the engagement between the government and M/D emerged in three main areas of the government scheme. First, the pilot pro-gram began to reflect the understanding that electricity-generation and -dis-tribution technologies had to be adapted to local contexts, and that the mod-ifications needed would more likely than not emerge during the process of construction. Moroccan government bureaucrats, however, proved much more deliberate in trying to balance topographical, economic, and social specificities of individual villages against the goal of adhering to state elec-tricity network standards. Second, as the Moroccan government employees experimented with different funding and cost recovery arrangements in their pilot sites, they drew on the principle advanced in Imgoun and at other M/D villages that all community members should have access to electricity, irrespective of their ability to pay. Rather than press wealthier villagers to subsidize their poorer neighbors, however, the directors of the pilot program preferred to advance various pay-by-installment and loan schemes.

Third, the French engineers and their Moroccan colleagues gleaned from the example of Imgoun the importance of a viable social organization to the maintenance of an electricity network over the long term. Thus, asso-ciations in pilot sites were established at the encouragement of bureaucrats working to implement the pilot project. The degree of protection from gov-ernment influence of these pilot associations is a matter of debate, but the significance of government recognition that an autonomous social organization could be valuable at a time when the monarchy was carrying out some of its most ruthless suppression of nongovernmental organizations since independence cannot be minimized. So heavily did the fist of the government fall, in fact, that the late 1970s and 1980s have been dubbed the "leaden years."

In the mid-1990s, as the pilot program was drawing to a close, an unprecedented opportunity for rural villagers to "take the government by the hand" and bring it to areas it had long abandoned suddenly emerged. The Moroccan national energy sector entered a crisis so severe it led to a fundamental reorganization of power production and distribution in the kingdom. Energy production and distribution had been a state concern since the mid-1970s. Years of underinvestment led to the sector's progressive breakdown, and by 1994 the state was forced to begin rapidly privatizing energy production along with most of its energy distribution franchises.

With privatization, the National Office of Electricity (ONE), the administrative body that had been charged with producing and distributing the kingdom's electricity, lost its reason for being. But dismantling the public sector and turning out its several thousand employees, or even a sizable fraction of them, was not a political option, especially at a time when the monarchy's preparations for an upcoming succession made it fragile. To stay afloat and maintain its employment levels, the ONE adopted rural electricity as its new mission, and in 1996 the agency launched a massive rural electricity program, called the Programme d'Electricifation Rurale Globale (PERG). The goal of the program was to provide electricity to 90 percent of households in rural Morocco by 2010. To meet its ambitious target, the ONE invested heavily in the program and restructured its bureaucracy around its new organizational vocation (World Bank 1998; Bentaleb 2002; Interviews, March–August 2004; Triki 1994, 1993a, 1993b; Mossadeq 1996a, 1996b).

What distinguished the PERG from its predecessors were the lessons incorporated into its program design; it drew on the insights generated through the decadelong engagement between government engineers and M/D activists around the construction of rural electricity networks. But just as occurred with the pilot program, the lessons were not simply adopted wholesale; they were transformed when the ONE translated them into a scheme that could be deployed on a national scale. The government reinterpreted the three main insights that the pilot program had generated about the technologies used, funding sources, and the social organization necessary to maintain the network, and incorporated them into the PERG in reinvented form.

The PERG built on the pilot program's observation that electricity networks were most cost effective when they corresponded to local needs. The PERG was based on new national electricity standards that were written as guidelines, with defined ranges, to allow for some local variation in topography and electricity usage patterns. Furthermore, the ONE embraced the idea of community cost-sharing and expanded it to a national level. While levying a tax on electricity usage by urban households to cover 55 percent of the cost of hooking up new villages, the ONE required the local township to contribute 20 percent of the expense, and the consumer to bear the remaining 25 percent (ONE 1999, 2004). Finally, the PERG's design reflected a government acknowledgement, though limited, that community management of electricity networks was important to keeping them functional and cost effective over the long term; and the program formally mandated some degree of community management, chiefly in the form of fee collection (ONE 1999, 2002).

With the PERG, the government reversed its three-decades-long losing streak in the field of rural electricity provision. Impressively, the ONE surpassed its own expectations of performance, connecting 80 percent of rural households to electricity by 2004 instead of the forecast 70 percent (ONE 1999, 2004), all the while managing to stay well within the budgetary bounds the agency set for the program. The PERG's success stemmed from its program design and the grounded insights around which it was conceived. Without the lessons generated from the emigrants' electricity initiatives in Imgoun, and later in surrounding villages, the state would likely not have had access to the conceptual bases that allowed it to create an effective national rural electricity provision scheme.

Lessons for Reconstituting Remittances

A group of emigrant workers, laid-off from their manual production jobs in France, built a rudimentary electricity network in an isolated hamlet tucked away in the Atlas Mountains and changed the way a nation provided electricity to hundreds of thousands of its citizens. Similar processes and successes occurred with respect to water capture and distribution and road planning. By the 1990s the way that emigrants and their communities engaged with migration-generated resources contributed to the conceptual understandings on which three new major state initiatives to alleviate rural poverty were built: the national program to provide rural electricity (PERG), the national program to provide water to rural areas (Programme d'Approvisionnement Groupé en Eau Rurale, PAGER), and the national program to construct rural roads (Programme Nationale de Construction de Routes Rurales, PNCRR) (van de Walle 2004; Levy 2004; World Bank 2001). Combined, the programs had yearly operating budgets that totaled several hundred million dollars.

In constituting remittances, emigrants cast themselves as protagonists of their history, of their own local processes of development, and of their homeland's effort to eradicate rural poverty, and in ways that were far more profound than simply bankrolling community projects or subsidizing their family members' expenditures. As the M/D director explained in a moving reflection on the meaning of participating in development, emigrants reclaimed a sense of themselves as agents that did more than channel resources back to their communities of origin:

> The act of doing local development work, that's something very important. Important not only for the village, in terms of what they [the migrants] do and what comes into being in the village, but also for their concept of themselves, their personality. . . . Doing development work, it's revealed to them that they . . . can be actors. *This is over and above the money that they bring, over and above what they can do, the skills that they have and that they can bring back.* (Lahoussain Jamal, qtd. in M/D 2002, 273; emphasis added)

The experience of M/D in the Souss demonstrates that remittances have no value independent of that with which migrants and their communities infuse them as they transfer them, use them, and reinvent them. Contrary to the prevailing models used to understand the relationship between migration and development, remittances are not the vector of economic transformation and cannot have, in and of themselves, any impact, positive or negative, on economic development. Rather, it is the process through which migrants and their communities relate to remittances and imbue them with meaning and worth that is the catalyst for economic development. The way that Soussi migrants and their communities engaged with the emigrants' knowledge, funds, and organizing experience transformed those resources into something more, and that process of transformation galvanized social and economic change in the Souss region of Morocco.

The infrastructure innovations authored in a handful of Soussi villages had national-level impacts because the emigrants were able to draw the state into their process of transforming remittances. The Moroccan government appropriated the resources migrants had reinvented, and reinvented them in turn, transforming very local insights about infrastructure provision into foundational concepts that could be built into a national program. The fact that the state engagement with Soussi emigrants and their community revamped rural infrastructure provision through Morocco suggests important lessons for the design of migration and development policy.

First, migration and development policies that are built on the notion that remittances—monetary and nonmonetary—are fungible resources and that focus on channeling remittances to uses viewed as supportive of economic growth are forgoing the main potential that migration offers for economic transformation. The promise that migration offers for development lies in the ingenuity and innovation that can emerge as emigrants and their communities engage with remittances, and the best way for governments to reap the benefits of that creativity is to support and join the process of constituting remittances.

Second, policies that foster state engagement with migrants and their communities, and with their process of constituting remittances, must be open in their design and evolving in their character. For the innovations that surface in migration communities to affect development on a large scale and in an enduring manner, they have to be incorporated into government policy. In Morocco this openness happened by historical accident. Morocco's repeated failures in rural infrastructure provision and the rapid collapse of its national electricity service forced an otherwise authoritarian regime to remain receptive to new approaches to rural electrification. Had it not been, however, for ongoing amendment of the pilot program's rural electrification strategy and the embrace of a completely new electrification approach with the 1996 national rural electrification program, the insights would never have been formally integrated into government infrastructure provision. The ideas that emerged in the Souss would have died in the Souss.

Third, and finally, government can amplify the resource that is the process of transforming remittances and spread it to the nation as a whole, including to areas that experience no significant out-migration. And in so doing, it can make the relationship between migration and development into the relationship that connects every village and every neighborhood in the nation to the process of re-imagining and reinventing what development can be.

Notes

1. The information on the case drawn from ethnographic observation and interviews are not noted in the text but should be assumed. When supporting information is drawn from documentary evidence (articles, reports, and so on), the citations are noted in the text. When these citations are provided, it does not indicate that they are the sole source of the data provided; they were always corroborated through interview information.

2. The Moroccan National Office of Electricity estimated that only 18 percent of rural Morocco was connected to electricity in 1994 and the World Bank measured that access as somewhat higher, at 25 percent.

3. The exchanges between Moroccan emigrants and the Moroccan state documented in this chapter vacillated between collaborative and conflictual. Many of those who participated in conversations with the state did so at some political and personal peril. As a result, the confidentiality of the people I interviewed is maintained throughout this chapter. Where necessary, the organization, place, and month in which the interviews occurred are noted.

9

National Development Planning: The Case of Dominica

Thomson Fontaine
with Jennifer M. Brinkerhoff

This chapter explores what happens when a country's economy is almost entirely dependent on remittances, thus encouraging a national culture of out-migration. The presumed outcome is often consistent with the traditional orientation of the migration and development literature: few prospects, if any, of retaining skills and knowledge and developing a locally driven economy. Indeed, some countries for whom these characteristics are strong, though not necessarily universal, have evolved a human-capital export model. This is the case, for example, for the Philippines, which maintains several nursing programs with the primary purpose of exporting labor and thus creating a continuous stream of remittance inflows. Such a scenario risks creating a vicious cycle, where diasporas' contributions are limited to remittances, as out-migration, including brain drain, is encouraged. What is a nation to do to escape such a vicious cycle, and how might its diaspora help?

Dominica is a good case for exploring this question. Dominica is ranked among the top five countries in the world with the highest rates of net migration, having lost most of its population in the last decades of the twentieth century. It is considered to be the only country in the world in the recent past to experience negative population growth owing to voluntary migration. So widespread is the phenomenon it is estimated that every household on the island has at least one family member who has migrated. Dominicans often view migration as a rite of passage, with a vast number leaving to seek further studies, while others do so in search of employment opportunities or to join family members. Building on a sound primary and secondary education system in the country, a large number of those migrating have gone on to distinguish themselves in their adopted homelands, in areas as diverse as business, medicine, information technology, and law.

Over the years these diaspora Dominicans have played a consistent role, both on an individual and group basis, in contributing to the local economy. Traditionally, this support has involved the provision of financial and material resources to family and friends, the setting up of businesses, and promoting and preserving Dominica's rich cultural heritage. Undoubtedly, the large volume of remittances has helped to mitigate adverse external shocks, maintain macroeconomic stability, and reduce poverty. But these efforts, as in other countries, do little to prevent continued migration and to reduce remittance dependence.

Within the Dominica diaspora a recent focus has evolved to forge new partnerships across the various destination countries, and to commit to the task of nation building. Diaspora Dominicans are beginning to appreciate their common destiny regardless of geographical location, realize their potential, and understand and appreciate the expanded role they can play in helping make a difference in their homeland. Several new initiatives undertaken by the Dominica diaspora provide a glimpse of the opportunities that exist and hint at the diaspora's aspirations. Among these initiatives are efforts aimed at harnessing the tremendous human potential that exists in the diaspora. Dominica diasporans are acting on a belief that small independent efforts toward a common goal can succeed in turning a country around. These efforts are promising, since new ways are being found to utilize the diaspora's considerable resources in helping to develop the homeland.

While diaspora efforts to move beyond remittances are still in their early stages, the Dominica diaspora's initiatives suggest a way out of the out-migration trap and toward national planning and development. As noted at the outset of this volume, empirical research on migration has largely focused on the impact of remittances and the effect of brain drain on source countries. This chapter, in addition to examining these effects, will look at the diaspora's broader impact on Dominica's development prospects. The most recent wave of migration has created tremendous opportunities, which if properly managed, can do a great deal to reverse the damaging effects of the brain drain and contribute significantly to the development of Dominica. The Dominica experience illustrates the diaspora option for migration policy and is consistent with the diaspora approach recommended by Mishra (2006), where countries seek to increase the benefits of emigration, drawing on the diaspora to build networks for trade, tourism, and investment promotion; harness its knowledge, skills, and assets; and attract higher and more efficient forms of remittances.

Following a review of the remittance and brain drain literature, the case of Dominica will be presented, including a history of its migration, remittance dependence, and diaspora initiatives. Dominica's experience suggests a much greater potential for diasporas to contribute to the national development of their homelands than remittances alone imply. It further illustrates how migration brain drains can be converted to brain gains. These contributions are facilitated when the diaspora is able successfully to partner with its homeland government.

Perspectives on Remittances and Brain Drain

Historically, most analyses of migration and development impacts have examined brain drain and remittances in isolation. This section reviews some of the more recent literature on these topics, which suggests a convergence that will enable more sophisticated analyses of diasporas' potential contributions to homeland development.

Remittances

It is a well-established fact that migrating populations with families in the home countries traditionally send support in the form of remittances in cash and in kind. Quite a lot of research has sought to estimate the levels of such assistance as well as its impact on recipient economies, given its relative importance to other foreign-aid flows. Giuliano and Ruiz-Arranz (2005) found that migrant remittances can substitute for a lack of financial development in developing economies and hence promote economic growth via investment. The World Bank estimates that in 2004 over US$150 billion was remitted to developing countries by the diaspora, with the Caribbean accounting for around $40 billion (Ratha 2005).

The literature also has explored the conditions under which the financial sector infrastructure—and, in particular, transaction costs—influence the propensity to remit. Several authors stress the link between a fully functioning financial market and promotion of economic growth (see, for example, King and Levine 1993; Beck, Levine, and Loayza 2000). On the other hand, agents may compensate for the lack of development of local financial markets using remittances to ease liquidity constraints, channel resources toward productive investments, and hence promote economic growth (Giuliano and Ruiz-Arranz 2005). The savings of returning migrants may be an important source of start-up capital for microenterprises (see, for example, Dustmann and Kirchkamp 2001).

Brain Drain

Early literature on brain drain effects supports the view that skilled-labor migration is detrimental to those who remain in the country (Grubel and Scott 1966; Bhagwati and Hamada 1974; Kwok and Leland 1982). The argument is as follows: the economy suffers if the migrants' contribution to that economy is greater than their marginal product, an effect that is compounded if the education of the skilled emigrants was partly funded by taxes on residents. Extending this analysis, several authors reformulated the negative effects of brain drain in an endogenous growth framework (Miyagiwa 1991; Ul Haque and Kim 1995). While it is well known that brain drain leads to a loss of productivity and taxes, and sometimes negatively affects the provision of key public services (such as education and health), historically, it has been difficult to empirically assess the full extent of its effect on countries. Attention has focused on estimating emigration rates of the highly skilled. Carrington and Detragiache (1998, 1999) developed such estimates for sixty-one developing countries based on US Census data, OECD data on immigration per country of origin, and data describing the skill structure in sending countries (Barro and Lee 2000).

Other studies focus on the possibility that migration may foster human-capital formation and growth in the sending country (Stark, Helmenstein, and Prskawetz 1997; Beine, Docquier, and Rapoport 2001). According to this beneficial brain-drain argument, more people at home may enroll in domestic education, since the prospects of migration through education opportunities increases the expected return of human capital. In the end, the increased acquisition of education contributes positively to growth and economic performance in that country.

A more recent effort to determine the effect of brain drain in developing countries calculated the "augmented emigration loss" for several Caribbean countries. These countries have lost 10–40 percent of their labor force to migration to OECD countries. Even more alarming, in many countries this migration includes over 70 percent of the labor force with more than twelve years of schooling. On the other hand, in 2002, the region received about 13 percent of its GDP through remittances (Mishra 2006). Despite these significant resources, using simple welfare calculations, Mishra (2006) confirmed a brain drain from the region that is not compensated by remittances.[1]

A broader World Bank study (Özden and Schiff 2005) sought to determine the effects of migration and to identify migration policies, regulations, and institutional reforms that will lead to improved development outcomes. The International Migration and Development Research Program was divided into a number of focus areas, including (1) the impact of migration and remittances on development indicators, including poverty and inequality, investment, and so on; (2) brain drain; (3) temporary migration, including under the General Agreement on Trade in Services; and (4) the links among migration, trade, and foreign direct investment (FDI). In other words, this research took remittances and brain drain as its starting point, but sought to integrate these into a more comprehensive analysis of the net impacts on migrant-sending countries.

Thus, more sophisticated attempts to gauge brain drain as general losses to the homeland are evolving and include incorporation of other potential contributions and losses, among them, remittances. While difficult to measure, increasing attention is given to one such potential contribution: temporary knowledge-exchange, sometimes referred to as brain circulation, where migrants return intermittently or temporarily to contribute their knowledge and expertise (see, for example, Gamlen 2005; Saxenian 2002a; Pellegrino 2001). Recent studies combining these potential gains and losses include case analysis of China, the Philippines, and Afghanistan (Wescott and Brinkerhoff 2006); and an investigation of health-sector brain drain in South Africa (Clemens 2007).

Dominica, Its Diaspora, and National Development

The experience of Dominica and its diaspora hints at a net gain for the homeland, particularly when accounting for the diaspora's more recent efforts to contribute to national development. Following is a review of Dominica's migration history, diaspora remittances, and brain drain. The case section concludes with a description of the diaspora's organizing efforts for national development.

The History of Dominica's Migration Movement

Dominica is ranked among the top five countries in the world having the highest rates of net migration, with a record high in 1989 of –32.7 per 1,000 of the population (Figure 9.1). Over the last 100 years, Dominicans have migrated in ever increasing numbers in search of employment opportunities, as was the case in the early nineteenth and twentieth centuries, and, in the early twenty-first century, in pursuit of higher education. In the 1800s many went to work in mines in Venezuela and French Guinea, and in the early 1900s, some left to build the Panama Canal while others migrated to Aruba and Curaçao. From 1959 to 1962 the country recorded an unprecedented wave of migration to the United Kingdom, with an estimated 14 percent of the population migrating to that country. At the time, the majority of emigrants were drawn from the rural areas and left with hopes of starting new lives for themselves. The exodus came to an end only after the British authorities imposed immigration restrictions on the Caribbean in 1964.

The second major migration wave took place between 1983 and 1992, when an estimated 25 percent of Dominica's mean population migrated. About 80 percent went to the United States, where, approximately 8 percent of the population was granted US immigrant visas and another 35 percent were issued with nonimmigrant visas. Other migrants went to Canada (2%),

**Figure 9.1 Dominicans' Net Migration Rate, 1985–2005
(migrants/1,000 population)**

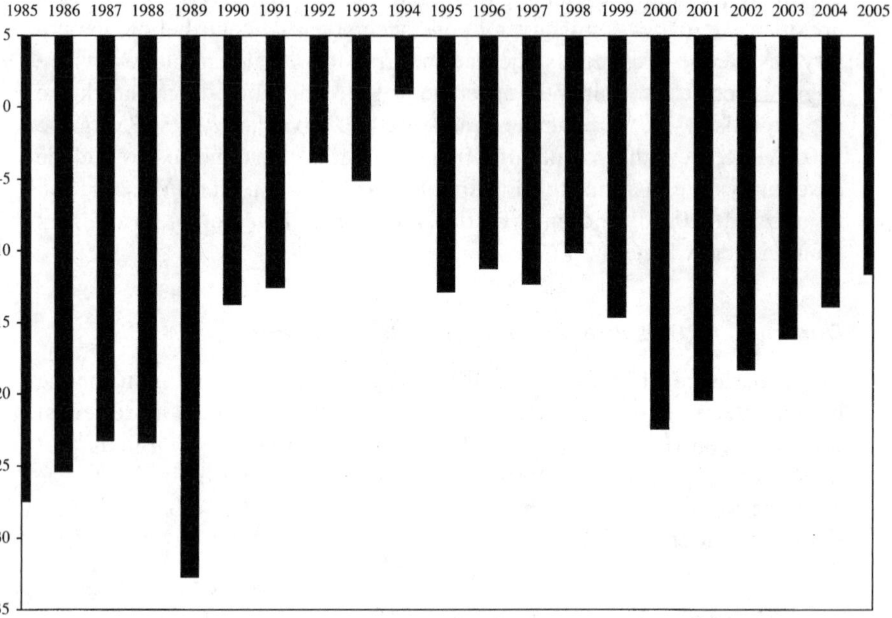

Sources: Central Statistics Office (2006a); CIA, World Factbook, at http://geography.
about.com/library/cia/blcdominica.htm.

the US Virgin Islands (5%), and the French Caribbean Islands of
Guadeloupe and Martinique (10%).[2] An interesting feature of migration
during this period was the large number of persons holding degrees as well
as a flow of students going to universities in the United States. Many of the
migrants chose the United States because it was relatively easy to secure a
visa and to access universities in that country.

Because the relatively more developed economies of the French
Caribbean were just minutes away from Dominica, they proved to be attractive countries of choice for migrants. Jobs were fairly easy to come by, and
the Dominicans also had few problems in assimilating because of the shared
Creole language. Accordingly, many of the migrants settled there, particularly in Guadeloupe, and the flow of official migration slowed only when
the French authorities moved to impose visa restrictions in the late 1980s.
Even then, illegal migration continued.

The third major migration wave started in 1996 and continues to this
writing. From 1996 to 2006, an estimated 35 percent of the mean population
migrated, resulting in a net reduction of the overall population (the migration

rate exceeded the rate of natural increase of the population). The main factors contributing to the exodus are a slowing economy and a correspondingly high rate of youth unemployment, estimated at 40 percent, combined with relatively easy entry into the United States and Canada. Approximately 85 percent emigrated to the United States.[3] Dominica's 2005 population was estimated to be at least 10 percent lower than its 1990 level. Overwhelmingly, recent migrants are either skilled or recent graduates from secondary schools who went on to US universities. Although no detailed studies have been done, anecdotal evidence based on the number of graduates applying for jobs in Dominica suggests that less than 1 percent of university graduates receiving their training in the United States return to Dominica upon graduation. Recent efforts to organize this tremendous skill-set to focus on Dominica's development have drawn extensively from the most recent migration period.

Remittances and the Dominica Economy

Since 2001 the level of remittances to Dominica has more than doubled, keeping pace with the expanding migrant population. Interestingly, a significant amount of the remittances from the French Caribbean and the US Virgin Islands are in-kind (consumer products, groceries, and so on) (Figure 9.2). Dominica ranks among the world's top twenty recipients of remittances relative to GDP, and it currently constitutes the major source of external financing (IMF 2005; and Central Statistics Office 2006b). Indeed, the level of remittances has consistently exceeded FDI and official government transfers and has more recently equaled export receipts (Central Statistics Office 2006b). The flow of formal remittances from the diaspora continues to exhibit an increasing growth rate.

Between 1991 and 2004, remittances increased from 7 to 14 percent of GDP, while FDI declined from 10 to 4.5 percent of GDP; official government transfers increased marginally from 7.7 to 8.5 percent of GDP; and export earnings fell from a high of 37 to 15 percent of GDP. During 2003 the level of remittances exceeded export earnings for the first time. The declining export levels are linked to the demise of the banana industry, and anecdotal evidence points to an increased level of remittances as the economic situation worsened on the island (Figure 9.3 and Table 9.1).

By helping to improve Dominica's development prospects, mitigate against adverse external shocks, and maintain macroeconomic stability, diaspora remittances have had a direct impact on income and poverty levels. While no formal surveys have been conducted, one can easily observe families that would not otherwise be able to achieve a given level of consumption, successfully maintaining certain lifestyles based solely on the income received from remittances. The inflow of remittances similarly serves to mitigate the adverse effects of the country's high rates of unemployment. In

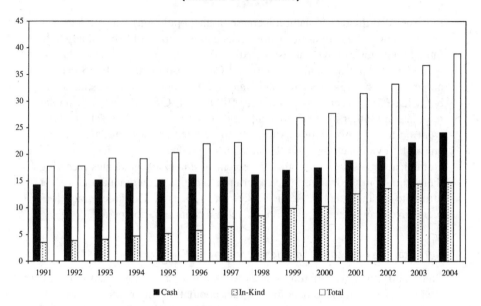

Figure 9.2 Dominicans' Cash and In-Kind Remittances, 1991–2004 (millions of US dollars)

■ Cash   ⊡ In-Kind   ☐ Total

Sources: Central Statistics Office (2006b), and Fontaine's calculations.

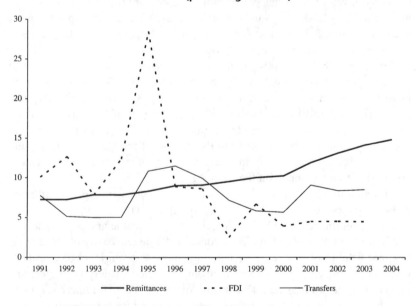

Figure 9.3 Dominicans' Remittances, FDI, and Official Transfers, 1991–2004 (percentage of GDP)

—— Remittances   ▪ ▪ ▪ FDI   —— Transfers

Sources: IMF (2005); Central Statistics Office (2006b).

Table 9.1   Dominicans' Remittance Transfers, FDI, Exports, and GDP,
1991–2004 (millions of US dollars)

	Private Remittances	FDI	Government Transfers	Export Revenue	GDP
1991	17.8	15.2	11.7	55.6	150.7
1992	17.8	20.4	8.2	54.6	161.1
1993	19.3	13.2	8.4	48.8	168.8
1994	19.2	22.6	9.2	47.1	182.8
1995	20.3	54.1	20.6	49.3	190.1
1996	22.0	17.8	23.0	51.3	200.3
1997	22.3	21.1	24.3	52.3	244.8
1998	24.7	6.5	18.6	62.0	259.2
1999	26.8	18.0	15.6	55.7	267.4
2000	27.7	10.6	15.3	53.5	270.9
2001	31.5	11.9	24.0	43.4	264.1
2002	33.3	11.4	21.2	41.8	253.5
2003	36.7	11.6	22.1	39.0	260.3
2004	40.2	10.8	24.1	43.5	265.6

Sources: IMF (2005); Central Statistics Office (2006b).

addition, there has been increased investment in physical and human capital, since remittances have enabled increased spending on education, health,
and nutrition. Recent construction booms in Dominica have been fueled in
large part by emigrants returning from the emigration wave of the 1960s.
More than forty years after migrating to the United Kingdom, a substantial
number of the immigrants have reached retirement age and are returning to
build homes and spend retirement in their country of birth.

As for easing liquidity constraints and supporting productive investments, a substantial amount of the cash returned by migrants is kept in local
bank accounts and has thus benefited the local banking system. Further, evidence shows that contrary to the common perception that remittances are
largely for consumption purposes, a sizable amount to Dominica goes to
financing private investment. Remittances to Dominica have proved an
important source of start-up capital for microenterprises. Registration documents filed with the Business Registrar's Office and the Ministry of Legal
Affairs suggest that more than 60 percent of the small-business start-ups
draw on remittances from the diaspora or result from the savings of emigrants returning to Dominica. Remittances have therefore served to alleviate credit constraints on the poor and have improved the allocation of capital. The level of remittances is expected to continue in the foreseeable
future as waves of upwardly mobile, highly educated migrants, the majority
schooled in developed countries, along with those less skilled continue to
establish residence in developed countries.

Dominica's Brain Drain

Over the years Dominica has joined a number of other Caribbean countries that have lost scores of their best and brightest to emigration. Starting in the mid-1970s, large numbers of students just out of secondary schools began to leave for studies abroad. Most of these studies were financed by local banks providing student loans and private family support. In addition, successive governments provided hundreds of scholarships and other incentives to facilitate study abroad.[4] Unfortunately, the overwhelming majority of those receiving such scholarships have not returned to the country. Although the government usually requires the students to be bonded, most have opted to repay the bond in lieu of return or have simply ignored its repayment. While no definitive studies have been undertaken to determine the cost over time to the country, it is clear that the continued subsidization of overseas education has been at a huge cost to the country.[5]

Students returning with university degrees to Dominica often complain that there is limited opportunity to harness their newly acquired skills. For the most part, the government is the largest employer in the country, and for many years it has restricted new employment. At the same time, the private sector has not been sufficiently developed to accommodate large numbers of individuals holding degrees. Thus, taking advantage of a relatively hassle-free process for immigration to the United States, Great Britain, and Canada, the overwhelming majority of persons holding degrees have simply migrated to these countries. In fact, Docquier and Marfouk (2004) found that Dominica had the fifth-highest rate of migration from the Caribbean of persons having a tertiary education. They also ranked Dominica among the top twenty countries in the world having the highest rate of skilled-person emigration (Docquier and Marfouk 2005). The data confirm the trend noted earlier and point to the potentially damaging effect to the country of losing so many skilled persons.[6]

On the other hand, there is evidence supporting a beneficial brain drain (see, for example, Stark, Helmenstein, and Prskawetz 1997; Vidal 1998). Students seeing the success of those who have migrated and hold degrees, use that as an incentive to invest more heavily in their own secondary education. In their view, education offers a unique opportunity for migration and the chance at a better life.

Combining remittances with out-migration, the benefit from remittances far exceeded the emigration loss. As noted above, Mishra (2006) calculated the "augmented emigration loss" for several Caribbean countries and found that the loss from the emigration of highly skilled workers confers a positive externality, thus increasing the overall loss due to migration. This emigration loss was then compared with the measurable benefit of remittances to the home country. With respect to Dominica, the benefit from remittances far exceeded the emigration loss. When, however, the estimated cost of education expenditure was added to emigration loss, the losses exceeded the benefit of remittances to the home country.

The potentially damaging impact of such a large migration of skilled persons from Dominica has been mitigated to some extent by the readiness of the migrants to contribute, not only through remittances but also through a concerted effort to give time, skills, and training to the development effort of their homeland. This desire is often manifested by the great interest in participating in different diaspora groups and the willingness to be considered "Dominican" even after having been away for several years. More recently, that patriotic flavor has taken on an added dimension with the ease of communication, particularly via the Internet, which has facilitated the coming together of disparate Dominica diaspora groups across the globe.

Organizing the Diaspora for National Development

Migration patterns for Dominicans show that the majority have moved to the larger population centers in their adopted countries. For instance, most migrants to the United States have moved to New York, Miami, and Boston. In the case of Canada, migration has been largely to Toronto, and in the United Kingdom to London. Having large numbers of Dominicans in an essentially localized area has provided opportunities for organizing. In all of these large population centers, there are several Dominica diaspora organizations focused on coordinating support to their home country. These Dominica associations (as they are often referred to) usually engage in fund-raising and rely on donations to send cash and in-kind assistance to Dominica.

Early organizations, such as in London, focused almost exclusively on providing support to public institutions like hospitals and schools. They also responded generously to natural disasters. It is widely believed, and there is evidence to support, that the diaspora's role following the onslaught of hurricanes serves to mitigate the loss from those disasters. Typically, during these emergencies, support in the form of cash and transfers to families and institutions increases to compensate for local loss. These findings have been confirmed, for example, in Haiti (Fagen 2006).

With advancements in communications, diaspora organizations moved quickly to coordinate and harness the skill set that existed throughout the various Dominica migrant populations. Christian (2002) catalogs the rise of the national development consciousness among Dominican overseas communities. According to the author, the education reforms in Dominica during 1961–1979, the upsurge of black nationalist and liberation politics in the 1970s, the growth of the Internet, the increased access to college education in the United States by Dominicans in the 1980s, and the advent of

Dominica-specific websites—all contributed to a new dynamism in Dominica diaspora involvement in development initiatives on the island.

The Dominica diaspora in the early twenty-first century was increasingly fixated on seven aims: (1) good governance on the island; (2) economic activity favoring local control of the means of production; (3) the right to vote for Dominica diasporans; (4) integrity legislation to outlaw corruption in public office; (5) increased investment by the diaspora and government incentives to spur the same; (6) protection of Dominica's natural environment; and (7) the building of a technologically advanced economy on the island. These are all illustrated through specific projects documented on Dominica diaspora Internet sites.

There has been a deliberate attempt by diaspora organizations to go beyond simply sending remittances to Dominica to tap into the wealth of human resources that exists within the diaspora. These highly educated and upwardly mobile migrants possess the requisite skills that can be used to further the development process in their country. Foremost among those efforts was the setting up in 2000 of a database of skilled persons within the diaspora under the umbrella of the Dominica Academy of Arts and Sciences (DAAS), and a year later an online diaspora news magazine, *TheDominican.net*.[7] The primary mission of the DAAS is to gather the resources of overseas Dominicans in its skills directory and promote specific research and development projects, which benefit the island. In addition, the Dominica Sustainable Energy Corporation (DSEC) was formed to promote the use of environmentally friendly energy-generating processes; and the National Development Fund was offered as a means of streamlining financial assistance.

On December 8, 2001, several hundred Dominica diaspora students, scientists, entrepreneurs, lawyers, political leaders, and others met in New York City for the first ever "Dominica Diaspora in the Development Process" conference.[8] The objective of the conference was to rally diaspora resources for nation building. This would be accomplished by harnessing intellectual capital and linking it to provide enterprise in banking, aviation, tourism, information technology, and agriculture, among others, in a quest for economic independence and self-reliance in the homeland.

At the end of the conference, attendees issued a declaration that called on the Dominica government to

- Provide better incentives to lure more diaspora investors and retirees to Dominica, including the provision of incentive packages for migrants to spend their retirement years in the country;
- Make use of the human resources compiled within the DAAS database in the crafting of public policy and to help overcome the dearth of technical capacity on the island;
- Extend its support to various diaspora initiatives, including to the

DSEC, the diaspora bank, and the Dominica Cadet Corps, and to health tourism development;[9] and
- Partner with the private sector and the diaspora movement for the common goal of national development.

Hailed as a success, this was the first time the Dominica diaspora was brought together in order to focus its efforts on Dominica's development. Among other things, it set the stage for establishing DSEC, tasked with promoting alternative natural sources of energy that would help reduce Dominica's dependence on imported fossil fuel. Since its inception, DSEC has undertaken a series of wind studies, which identified various locations on the island suitable for setting up wind farms. In late 2005 the company initiated discussions with the government that would permit the building of the first wind farm on the island. DSEC has also been instrumental in pushing for the end to the electricity generation monopoly, and is actively involved in guiding discussions on relevant legislation. In addition to its focus on wind energy, DSEC is exploring opportunities to capitalize on Dominica's vast geothermal potential.

Another important decision coming out of the conference was the need to set up a diaspora bank to channel diaspora resources to economic development purposes on the island. The bank would be targeted to serve small-business enterprises with a view to empowering indigenous business owners, thus spurring employment within the local community. Within a year of the conference, the required resources for starting the bank were identified and an application was made to the relevant authorities in Dominica. As of this writing, the license for starting the bank had not been granted.

Two years after the New York conference, another diaspora conference was held in Dominica. The emphasis was on strengthening ties between the diaspora and residents in the home country as well as on issues of education and crime prevention. Participants outlined a way forward for the diaspora movement and sought to formalize relationships with local businesspeople and other resource persons. A key feature of the conference was presentations by diaspora experts in education and crime prevention, including how these diasporans could contribute further to improvements in these sectors. The success of both conferences confirmed the role of the diaspora as a movement for economic advancement and social change in Dominica.

From the very beginning of its existence, the DAAS sought to serve as an umbrella organization for the disparate Dominica diaspora groups by promoting the notion of shared efforts toward a common goal of nation building. The DAAS formed various committees charged with performing specific functions. For instance, there are economic development, agriculture, health, and education committees. These committees are encouraged to include resident Dominicans among their membership and to develop specific programs within their particular area of expertise.

The diaspora's involvement in Dominica sometimes extends far beyond issues of economic development. In one instance, the diaspora demonstrated its capacity to act as a skilled emergency corps. Following an earthquake in Dominica in November 2004, the DAAS was able to draw from its database several structural engineers who offered their services at no cost to the government to check the structural integrity of buildings in the area hit by the quake. Beyond emergencies, when the government of Dominica began to explore the possibility of setting up a tertiary institution on the island, the Dominica State College (DSC), it turned to the diaspora movement to provide needed expertise. Several Dominican migrants who had served in management positions at universities in the United States were recruited to develop the concept, structure the curriculum, and launch the college. In the end, the DSC was established at considerably reduced cost to the government because the experts provided their services free of charge.

Another example concerns the revival of the Dominica Cadet Corps and the staging of a soccer tournament and youth camp in the summer of 2005 in Dominica. The Dominica Cadet Corps provides semimilitary training to young people and enforces discipline. After being defunct for over twenty-five years, it was revived through the initiative of Washington, D.C., attorney Gabriel Christian, who was also a founding member of the DAAS. Under the auspices of the DAAS and traditional diaspora organizations in Canada, the United Kingdom, and the United States, scores of young men, mainly children of migrants, were brought to Dominica to compete in soccer with local youth. It also provided an opportunity for the children of migrants to visit their parents' homeland and begin to build their own ties.

In January 2004 the government of Dominica asked the DAAS to prepare a "Diaspora Policy Paper."[10] After extensive consultations within the diaspora, the document was prepared within a few months. The paper provides a detailed analysis of the role of the diaspora in Dominica's development and outlines the future direction for its involvement. It urges the government to enact legislation to formalize the relationship between the diaspora and the country and work toward implementing its various recommendations, including these:

- Establishing an interministerial secretariat in Dominica to be responsible for managing and promoting issues related to diaspora affairs;
- Forming a committee of persons drawn from the diaspora, the local community, and a representative from Overseas Missions to present actionable measures by the government;
- Promoting a national discussion at home and abroad on the role of the diaspora (including returning migrants) in the national development agenda;
- Preparing a series of papers on issues of concern to Dominicans at

home and in the diaspora, including but not limited to trade, tourism, investment promotion, health services, youth unemployment and crime, and volunteerism and public service;

- Promoting direct diaspora investments in various sectors of the economy;
- Undertaking a concerted program to define Dominica by its unique features, history, folk and national heroes, myths and legends, culture, and other attributes that together foment and strengthen the links between the ancestral home and its sons and daughters abroad;
- Assisting public and private exchange efforts between resident Dominicans and those abroad in student exchanges, educational tours, and culture and sports programs (including a program of accrediting children of the diaspora to represent Dominica at international sporting and cultural meets); and
- Developing a program to coordinate and liaise between Dominica and other regional governments pursuing similar efforts to empower their diaspora to advocate overseas in matters of common interest.

The government intends to use the findings and recommendations of the Diaspora Policy Paper as the basis for formulating policy on key issues concerning the diaspora and as a way to further integrate its efforts in the development of Dominica.

Dominica: Remittances, Brain Drain, and Beyond

The review of Dominica's experience confirms both that the country is highly dependent on its diaspora's remittances and that brain drain is occurring. It also suggests how to recapture the brain drain, and tap the underlying motivations of remittances for deeper commitment to homeland development.

There is no question that remittances are crucial to livelihoods and the economy in Dominica. As noted, Dominica is among the top twenty recipient countries in the world for remittances relative to GDP, with remittances exceeding FDI and on a par with export receipts. Given the high unemployment rates, remittances may have a direct impact on poverty, and they may sustain families in times of natural disasters. They support the local economy by stocking the local banking system and benefiting as much as 60 percent of new business start-ups. But are these contributions sufficient to compensate for brain drain? And what prospects do they hold, alone, for national development?

Out-migration and brain drain are significant for Dominica. As described above, it is ranked among the top five countries in the world for net migration, among the top five countries in the Caribbean for the migration of those with tertiary degrees, and among the top twenty countries in the world for the highest rates of skilled migration. Dominica has a long history of out-migration, including incentives and encouragement to study abroad. While migrants have sought higher degrees, they also have taken their foundational education with them. It is not surprising that less than 1 percent return following their US degree, given the prospects for employment in Dominica in their fields of expertise.

These factors raise a serious question regarding notions of brain drain and concerns about the migration of the highly skilled: if these migrants were to be unemployed upon their return, is it really brain drain? Or is the contribution greater if the migrant remains outside of the country, employed in her or his field of expertise, and also applies that knowledge and those skills to Dominica's development on the side? The examples of the diaspora's mobilization for national development suggest the latter. Sending countries may experience a net gain when their skilled migrants remain abroad, owing not just to their remittances but also from their potential knowledge contributions. There are many uncertainties in this equation. It presumes that the diaspora is organized and willing and that the country is willing and able to receive these contributions. The latter may require a partnership with the homeland government, as is the case in Dominica.

The diaspora's experience suggest several factors that may be needed to establish such a development partnership. First, from an organizing perspective, the Dominica diaspora benefited from its large concentration in urban areas of settlement and from its use of information technologies for networking and mobilizing its members. Second, its initiatives have been driven by the specific skills, knowledge, and interests of its highly motivated members. These are discovered not only through the initiatives these individual diasporans take but also through the skills and knowledge databases the diaspora has established. These enable actors both in the diaspora and in the homeland to match skills with needs and to respond to specific requests. Third, the diaspora has benefited from existing patriotism and interest in giving back to the homeland. These are also cultivated and sustained through diaspora organizing, Web pages, and specific activities, such as youth exchanges as well as culture and sports programs.

The story of Dominica's diaspora so far is one of evolution. So, the fourth factor or lesson may be that diaspora development initiatives may start small and appear to be insignificant but may nevertheless grow into a powerful force for homeland development. Beginning with remittances and some support to microenterprises, the Dominica diaspora's development interests now represent a broad array, from good governance to green technology and ecotourism. Beyond sector-specific programs and activities, the diaspora now focuses on planning for national development. This process began with a call to action not only from the diaspora but from the government as well, both to solicit participation from the diaspora (with incentives) and to actively work with the diaspora on diaspora-initiated projects. The planning includes sector committees to address specific needs as well as integrated national development. And the diaspora's outreach to country actors now extends beyond government to private-sector and other-country experts. The partnership with government was perhaps fully operationalized with the government's request to the diaspora for a development-planning policy paper in 2004. The policy paper resulted in more specific requests for government action than the diaspora's initial planning conference yielded, including a more formalized relationship with the diaspora through an inter-ministerial Secretariat on Diaspora Affairs.

Beyond its policy/planning request, the government also introduces ideas and projects and looks to the diaspora to provide the needed expertise. This was the case, for example, in the creation of the Dominica State College. It remains to be seen if providing more opportunities for college education at home will reduce the demand for migration for study abroad. Projects such as this suggest increasing efforts to prevent the initiation in new generations of the vicious cycle of migration, brain drain, and remittance dependence. In other words, a fifth lesson is that diaspora contributions to development may also include explicit efforts to break these cycles and prevent migration in the first place.

A final lesson of the Dominica experience concerns the role of the homeland government. The Dominica diaspora's evolving partnership with its homeland government suggests that while diasporas can initiate development planning and related activities, the homeland government needs at least to be receptive. In the case of Dominica, the diaspora's initiative is leading to a partnership, where the government initiates its own efforts to tap the diaspora, for example, by explicitly requesting their expertise not only for specific sectors and projects but for national planning as well.

Conclusion

The Dominica diaspora movement continues to focus on issues of economic growth promotion, good governance, capacity building within the country, and conflict prevention and mitigation. By developing partnerships with government and the private sector in the home country, its efforts can continue to expand to benefit the country. This partnership, as demonstrated by the policy paper, can also lead to the designing of policies to maximize potential welfare gains from the diaspora. Successful design of such policies requires a careful analysis of migration patterns and detailed information, which can come only through much research and analysis. Research and analysis can help diaspora organizations to reverse the negative effects of brain drain; assist them to build a more systematic approach to harnessing diaspora potential, including using the diaspora to build networks for trade, culture, investment promotion, and tourism; and influence migration policies in developed countries, which continue to be largely protectionist.

Dominica's diaspora has initiated a movement for economic advancement and social change in the homeland. The diaspora is expected to continue to provide human resources, which are so critical to the development process. These are persons familiar with the country and its cultural and social nuances, and whose skills are needed for pivotal roles in its development. For their part, diaspora organizations are increasing their ability to organize and actively recruit from among their ranks. The government's task as a partner in this process is to take the lead in providing some focus and to support the enabling environment for these diaspora organizations to contribute to the homeland.

Dominica is not alone in its seeming entrapment in a vicious cycle of out-migration, disincentives for the return of the highly skilled, remittance dependence, and further out-migration. Other countries face similar challenges to greater or lesser degrees. The interdependence of incentive factors, contextual opportunities, and potential gains and potential losses to homeland families and national development is a subject in need of much further research. The experience of Dominica suggests a more nuanced interpretation of potential net gains to migration of the skilled and avenues for national development and possible escape from these vicious cycles.

Notes

1. Emigration loss measures the welfare loss due to movement of labor. It arises when the cost of employing the workers who migrate is less than the value of their marginal product. The surplus on these workers is therefore lost due to emigration, which imposes a cost on those who have stayed behind.

2. Based on Dominican census data and author's calculations. These and all of the following author's data calculations were made by Fontaine.

3. Based on Dominican census data and Fontaine's calculations.

4. The majority of students have pursued studies in the United States, the United Kingdom, and Canada, but hundreds have also been trained at Cuban universities. Still others have studied in India, other Commonwealth countries, Europe, and Japan.

5. For instance, each year the top student in the country receives a government scholarship referred to as the Island Scholarship. There are no restrictions on where the student can study. Most opt for the costlier private universities in the United States or Great Britain, which run into the hundreds of thousands of dollars, and they are neither bonded nor required to return to the country upon completion of their studies.

6. In that respect, Dominica is not unlike many other Caribbean countries. These countries accounted for thirteen of the top twenty countries in the world for emigration rates of skilled persons (seven of the top ten). A majority of the Caribbean countries have lost more than half of their labor force with a tertiary education, and more than 30 percent with secondary education.

7. *TheDominican.net* was founded in January 2001 by the primary author of this paper (Fontaine). It is focused on Dominican economic and social issues as well as the role of the diaspora in development.

8. A detailed analysis of the conference can be found in Christian (2002).

9. *Health tourism* refers to offering medical services at lower costs than might be obtained in industrialized countries (e.g., plastic surgery in Brazil, heart surgery in India), thus attracting "tourists" from abroad who purchase these services.

10. The Diaspora Policy Paper is available at http://da-academy.org.

Part 4

Conclusion

10

Diasporas and Development: Issues and Impediments

Manuel Orozco

A s the reality of globalization reaches more people than ever before, the role and impact of diasporas in development are becoming increasingly critical considerations in policy and politics. The movement of people is, as of this writing, more transnational than at any other time in history, and effective economic integration thus depends on the human links and connections that exist across borders. The same is true for development; it demands less territorialized strategies. This is the critical challenge for practitioners and volunteers alike. Following are some thoughts on the challenges and considerations to keep in mind when looking for opportunities to establish projects and partnerships with diasporas.

The UNDP defines development as a condition that creates "an enabling environment for people to enjoy long, healthy and creative lives" (UNDP 2006). A development player aims to find solutions to human needs and to offer alternative ways to promote self-sustainability. In more practical terms, economic development is a condition by which individuals and society at large enjoy a good quality of life, are free, have opportunities for upward mobility, and are able to improve their material circumstances. Three areas that enable these conditions are health, education, and material asset accumulation. In the context of transnational migration, deterritorialized development strategies should look at the intersecting issues and linkages to diasporas.

This concluding chapter presents thoughts on the potential for linking diaspora activities to development, reviews promising donor practices to date, and identifies continuing impediments to fully maximizing the potential of diasporas to contribute to formal development efforts. First, we turn to the lived experience of diasporas and their economic activities vis-à-vis the homeland.

The Reality of Diasporas in the Twenty-First Century

We live in a world characterized by the interplay between micro- and macrodynamics, creating the reality of "distant proximities" (Rosenau 2003). Distant proximities are real-life experiences that both integrate and fragment relationships outside and inside borders. Immigrant laborers are key protagonists of distant proximities; they integrate their home and host countries into the global economy as they seek to keep their families together. Their lives are also fragmented, however, by the experience of distance and separation from their families and nations. The end result is a transnational lifestyle, characterized by both opportunities and hardships that feature this paradox of distance and closeness.

Diasporas define themselves through relationships with the homeland, international entities, and host-country governments and societies, thereby influencing various dynamics, including development. One key consideration of the relationship between diasporas, migration, and development is that diasporas form, in part, as a response to changes in the composition of the international system (i.e., the global economy or the international political landscape), as well as development or underdevelopment. People leave their countries because of development conditions there, yet, as illustrated in this volume, they continue to engage with their homelands at various levels. Such engagement stretches the idea of development beyond territorial boundaries. Diasporas' substantive involvement in economic and social activities in their home countries is due, in part, to the dynamics of globalization and to new opportunities resulting from political and economic openings in their home societies. One of the resulting outcomes is the formation of transnational families and communities, defined as groups or families that maintain relations and connections that include home and host societies.[1]

In practical terms, a typical immigrant's economic linkage with the home country extends to at least four practices that involve spending or investment: (1) family remittance transfers; (2) demand of services such as telecommunication, consumer goods, or travel; (3) capital investment; and (4) charitable donations to philanthropic organizations raising funds for the migrant's home community (see Figure 10.1). Remittances are the first and most important economic activity. Although the determinants of sending do not vary between nationalities, the frequency and quantity of money sent fluctuate across groups. For example, Latinos and Filipinos in the United States send an average of $300 a month, whereas Southeast Asians in Japan send $671, and Ghanaians in Europe send $400 every six weeks (all dollar amounts in this chapter are US dollars) (Orozco and Fedewa 2005).

Migrants also manifest their links by staying in touch—calling and visiting their homeland. They purchase and consume foodstuffs from their home country, such as tortillas, beef jerky, cheese, rum, and coffee; and spend money on phone cards to call their families. Eighty percent of

**Figure 10.1 Immigrant Economic Practices
(annual expenses in US dollars)**

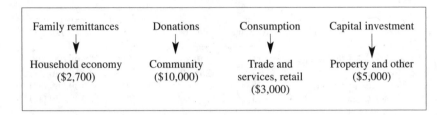

Latinos buy phone cards and speak to their relatives by phone an average of two hours a month. Two other practices involve donations and investment. In the case of donations, migrants raise funds to help their hometown as organized civil-society groups or hometown associations. These donations may amount to $100 to $200 a year per individual, and in some countries, like Mexico, donations on aggregate may translate to more than $50 million. Finally, migrants often are interested in investing in property or a small business, devoting between $5,000 and $10,000 to that activity. Figure 10.1 summarizes these economic practices.

Although these are predominantly concrete, material activities, they reflect individual and group exercises of migrants' transnational identity through symbolic and material commitments to the homeland. The implications of these experiences have raised interest and questions about their effect on development and the ways in which these interactions can be further leveraged to promote it. These practices generate significant revenue and benefits for many.

Take, for example, the cases of Salvadorans and Ghanaians. These migrant communities have been established for more than thirty years in the United States and have extended their links to the homeland at different levels. Tables 10.1 and 10.2 show estimates of the number of transnational activities that keep migrants connected with their home country. The highest volume of money spent is on remittances (which earns transfer companies a 10 percent revenue), but, as the tables show, other activities are also significant, given their impact on the two economies—even simple things like phone calls.

Considerations Linking Diasporas and Development

As the above discussion and examples confirm, the presence of millions of immigrants who are regularly connected to their homelands as well

Table 10.1 Percentage of Salvadorans Who . . .

	Percentage	Number	Annual Cost/ Expense per Person (US dollars)	Total Expenditures (US dollars)
Call on average 120 minutes	41	340,300	288	98,006,400
Send over $300	32	265,600	4,200	1,115,520,000
Buy home-country goods	66	547,800	200	109,560,000
Travel once a year . . .	24	199,200	700	139,440,000
and spend over				
$1,000	61	506,300	1,000	506,300,000
Have a mortgage loan	13	107,900	7,000	755,300,000
Own a small business	3	24,900	7,500	186,750,000
Help family with mortgage	13	107,900	2,000	215,800,000
Belong to an HTA	5	41,500	200	1,500,000

Source: Orozco (2005b).
Note: Number of Salvadorans remitting from the United States is 830,000.

Table 10.2   Percentage of Ghanaians Who . . .

	Percentage	Number	Annual Cost/ Expense per Person (US dollars)	Total Expenditures (US dollars)
Call on average 80 minutes	50	100,000	432	43,200,000
Send over $300	60	120,000	4,800	576,000,000
Buy home-country goods	80	160,000	200	32,000,000
Travel once a year . . .	50	100,000	1,200	120,000,000
and spend over				
$1,000	80	160,000	1,000	160,000,000
Have a mortgage loan	20	40,000	7,500	300,000,000
Belong to an HTA	20	40,000	200	8,000,000

Source: Orozco et al. (2005).
Note: Number of Ghanaians remitting from the United States is 200,000.

as the impact those connections have on local economies and communities are not negligible. The size of these migrant populations is likely to continue increasing, resulting in more and more funds flowing back to their home countries. Hence, taking diasporas into account when designing a development strategy is not only highly justified but necessary. The following section highlights five key issues related to linking diasporas and development. Box 10.1 summarizes corresponding recommendations.

**Box 10.1   Five Recommendations
for Linking Diasporas and Development**

1. Distinguish among the three dimensions of diasporas' links to development:
    development *in* the diaspora, development *through* the diaspora, and develop-
    ment *by* the diaspora.
2. Understand and specifically target the corresponding economic activities for
    each dimension.
3. Recognize the structural limits to diasporas' economic contributions to devel-
    opment and support necessary enabling environments.
4. Acknowledge the varied participation within diasporas; do not expect all
    migrants to participate in development activites.
5. Develop institutionalized communication mechanisms with diasporas.

---

1. The Dimensions of Diasporas' Links to Development

Little theoretical analysis exists regarding the link between diasporas and
development.[2] I argue that this link lies at a point where the economic
activities of migrants intersect in a way that transforms the material base
of migrants, their relatives, and their societies. This transformation takes
place along various dimensional spaces. Robinson (2002) speaks of the
relationship between diasporas and development as being three pronged:
(a) development *in* the diaspora, (b) development *through* the diaspora,
and (c) development *by* the diaspora. The first refers to the use of networks in the host country, which includes the formation of ethnic businesses, cultural ties, and social mobilization. Development *through* the
diaspora refers instead to "how diasporic communities utilize their diffuse
global connections beyond the locality to facilitate economic and social
well being" (Robinson 2002, 113). The third applies to the ramifications
of "the flows of ideas, money, and political support to the migrant's home
country" (123).

2. Linking Development to Migrant Economic Practices

A second consideration is the establishment of operational links with the
economic practices in which migrants engage. Within the context of changing dynamics and realities, there are important development alternatives to
consider. Donors can identify their role by understanding the activities of
diasporas, their dimensional space, and their nexus to development. In
doing so, they will be able to better operationalize policies and strategies.
Thus, the various relationships that immigrant communities have with their
home countries demand strategies that have a direct impact on issues relat-

ing to reducing remittance transaction costs; leveraging the capital potential of remittances through banking and financing; promoting tourism, nostalgic trade, and investment; and establishing a state policy that attends to a country's diaspora.

Table 10.3 offers a matrix depicting migrant economic activities and their three dimensions. These diaspora and development activities produce different dynamics. For example, in the context of remittances, development *in* the diaspora means to leverage the funds as a mechanism to provide financial access to migrants; whereas with respect to *through* the diaspora, remittances play an instrumental role in providing financial access to remittance recipients. Finally, the relationship between remittances and development *by* the diaspora concerns, for example, the role of ethnic minorities in providing remittance-related resources and services, such as establishing money transfer operations (MTOs).

3. The Limits of Diaspora Economic Activities in Promoting Development

While remittances and other economic exchanges primarily go to the poor, these interchanges alone are not a solution to the structural constraints of poverty. In many and perhaps most cases, remittances provide a temporary relief to families' poverty but seldom provide a permanent avenue to financial security. The literature on poverty and remittances has shown that the latter reduces poverty only to a certain extent.[3] Sustainable development through diaspora involvement depends on structural reforms addressing

Table 10.3   Three Dimensions of Diasporas' Links to Development

Development Activities	In the Diaspora	Through the Diaspora	By the Diaspora
Family remittances	Banking the unbanked	Financial intermediation; microfinance institutions	MTOs, e.g., Thamel.com
Consumption of goods and services	Supporting demand for products	Supply of home-country commodities	Small-business development
Investment of capital	Setting up minority-owned business	Technical training in remittance-receiving areas	Manufactured goods; nostalgic trade; tourism
Cash and in-kind donations	Capacity building	Project identification; networking	Social philanthropy

inequality in the home countries, as well as specific policies on financial democracy and asset accumulation.

Thus, when thinking about the intersection between development and migrant foreign savings, it is important to understand that the social and productive base of an economy significantly defines the ways in which remittances will effectively function in that economy. In other words, the robustness of the local economy will determine the leveraging impact of remittances. Remittances need to be understood exactly as what they are: foreign savings. As with any other source of foreign savings, like aid, trade, or investment, remittances interact with the structure of the local economy.

The extent to which local economies absorb foreign savings is the first question for development practitioners. Issues for analysis include the productive forces in an economy, the efficiency levels, how modern it is, what level of diversification/concentration of production exists within the various sectors, how entrepreneurship operates and is enabled, what technology tools exist or are missing, and the extent to which governments provide an enabling environment to motivate an interaction between investment and production (see Figure 10.2). Such analysis will highlight the urgency to create development strategies that link the local economies with the leveraging potential of diaspora or migrant foreign savings.

For example, comparative study of four semirural communities in Latin America showed that the productive base of their economies was unable to fully absorb these funds and the need to implement such strategies and policies was urgent (Orozco 2006b). These local economies are relatively fragile, with high costs of living, making it difficult for remittance recipients to save and mobilize those savings. In each community the entrepreneurial class caters little to the demands of remittance recipients, and its form of operation is relatively undeveloped. Moreover, governments and civil society do not provide recipient families with adequate support networks to help them cope with the realities of migration. As a result, nearly one-third of

Figure 10.2 Economic Interactions in the Local Economy

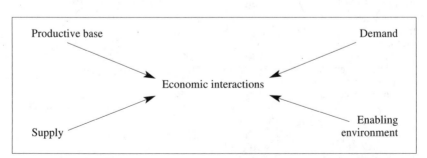

recipients reported that they were considering migrating and leaving their communities in the near future. Table 10.4 summarizes the economic profiles of the communities studied.

This analysis examined the extent to which the local economy exhibits substantive opportunities or failures that are enablers of migration and remittances. If an economy is unable to produce in a competitive context, its labor force will be depressed and eventually a portion will migrate in order to be able to provide for their families. Even once they are away and send money, however, the beneficiaries may be able to do only so much with that money insofar as the local economy provides an effective supply for the demand of services and products, and hence affects local (un)employment.

Table 10.4　Economic Profile of Four Latin American Cities

	Jerez, Zacatecas, Mexico	Salcaja, Quetzaltenango, Guatemala	Suchitoto, El Salvador	Catamayo, Loja, Ecuador
Basic Profile				
Population	37,558	14,829	17,869	27,000
Labor force (%)	41	37	34	31
Population ages 5–19 (%)	34.7[a]	36.81	34[b]	30
Main economic activities (%)				
Commerce and services	35	42	15.5	39
Agriculture	19	4[c]	52.2	20
Manufacturing	13	6	7.6	(est.) 8
Construction	11			
Proximity to major urban center	45 km to Zacatecas	9 km to Quetzaltenango	45 km to San Salvador	45 km to Loja
Cost of Living in US Dollars for . . .				
Food	219	228	209	201
Services (utilities)	60	44	40	43
Education	13	32	29	56
Health	40	41	34	68
Entertainment	27	3	40	35
Income				
Wages	323	303	125	162
Total earnings, including remittances	930	501	622	353
Monthly remittances, amount received	637	331	515	181

Source: Orozco (2006b).
Notes: a. Ages 0–14.
b. Ages 7–18.
c. Excludes subsidies.

Thus, remittances alone will not assure local development, suggesting a more urgent need for significant policy change than may be recognized as of this writing.

4. Participation Within the Diaspora

Understanding the level of engagement that diasporas can have in development is crucial. Assuming that everyone is involved or can be involved is unrealistic. When looking at the extent to which groups form organizations to promote development, at most, one-quarter of individuals who send remittances belong to some type of diaspora organization. Migrant levels of engagement, on the other hand, are far greater in other activities relating to family or personal investments. In addition, not all national groups have the same level of participation. Table 10.5 shows the variance in economic activities and practices across several Latin American countries (Colombia, Ecuador, El Salvador, Guatemala, Guyana, Honduras, Mexico, Nicaragua, the Dominican Republic, Bolivia, and Jamaica). Given these differences in engagement, considering partnerships with diasporas requires an assessment of how much can realistically be achieved with different groups.

5. The Need for Institutionalized Communication

Establishing a line of communication with migrant organizations is critical for creating an effective development partnership with diasporas. Both diaspora organizations and donors need to find a space for interaction and communication to bridge a divide that currently separates them, namely that diaspora groups are predominantly volunteer organizations. In order to develop successful partnerships, governments need to develop confidence-building tools and initiatives that demonstrate to migrants that governments are serious and committed to working with them. Confidence-building incentives should stress at least four components: (1) dialogue with leaders, (2) institutional resource investment for policy outreach, (3) institutional communication mechanisms that ensure systematic and legitimate contact with diasporas, and (4) the joint creation of an agenda of policy initiatives affecting both governments and migrants.

Policy Arenas for Engaging the Diaspora

The various relationships that immigrant communities have with their home countries demand strategies that reduce transaction costs; leverage the capital potential of remittances through banking and financing; promote tourism, nostalgic trade, and investment; and establish homeland govern-

Table 10.5 Levels of Transnational Engagement by Country of Origin (percentage of migrant remitters)

	Colombia	Ecuador	El Salvador	Guatemala	Guyana	Honduras	Mexico	Nicaragua	Dominican Republic	Bolivia	Jamaica
Calls once a week	80	98	41	56	42	57	66	70	77	33	75
Sends over US$300	27	33	32	43	33	8	46	13	17	21	42
Buys home-country goods	88	95	66	50	84	74	86	83	65	70	64
Has savings account	39	55	16	19	48	16	21	5	29	10	58
Travels once a year . . .	34	51	24	9	45	12	23	19	69	13	69
And spends over US$1,000	61	90	61	48	54	43	70	26	64	91	58
Has mortgage loan	12	14	13	4	18	12	3	6	6	36	15
Owns small business	5	1	3	2	8	4	2	3	3	4	2
Helps family with mortgage	21	24	13	1	21	8	5	7	13	31	16
Belongs to HTA	6	10	5	3	29	7	2	4	3	1	16

Source: Orozco (2005b).

ment policy that attends to a country's diaspora. These needs correspond to an array of policy arenas in which formal development actors can engage with diasporas.

1. Diaspora Outreach Policy

Diaspora outreach policy is key to any migrant-sending country's economic strategy. This should be the first step in addressing the linkages with the immigrant community living abroad. Such policy should, first, validate and legitimate the reality of the diaspora's migration status; and, second, explore policy opportunities to develop their condition and position in the home and host countries.

2. Business Competition

The transmission costs of remittance sending—fees incurred through the use of intermediaries—continue to be a significant concern to immigrants, development agencies, and others. Sending money to home countries entails costs, and pricing depends on the level of industry competition. As competition and volume increase, costs fall (Orozco 2006a). Therefore, it is important to analyze the structure of competition in corridors, identify obstacles that hinder competition, and promote options to reduce costs. Money transmissions are becoming less expensive, for example, through the formation of strategic alliances between money transfer companies and banks and between banks in Latin America and North America and the use of debit card technologies.

3. Banking the Unbanked

Many people in remittance-recipient societies lack access to the formal banking system. The effects of being unbanked include a higher susceptibility to greater transaction costs, and a lack of opportunity to establish credit records and obtain other benefits from financial institutions. Leveraging financial services among remittance recipients and senders can increase access to banking, and also expand credit through the mobilization of remittance savings. Microfinance institutions and credit unions in remittance-recipient countries demonstrate the potential to respond to this growing demand for financial transactions.

4. Investment and Microenterprise Incentives

Studies show that, on average, 10 percent of remittances received are saved and invested (IADB-MIF 2005, 2004, 2003a, b, c), putting some in a position to use their money for an enterprising activity. Both private sector and development players can insert themselves as credit partners for these potential investors. The effect is the provision of credit, supported by remittances, in local communities that lack the presence of active markets and production networks. Tying remittances to microlending enables local markets.

5. Hometown Associations as Agents of Development

The philanthropic activities of HTAs also have development potential. Some of the infrastructure and economic development work performed by these associations represents an opportunity for development agents to partner in local development. Governments can work with international organizations and HTAs to jointly support income generation schemes for local communities.

6. Tourism

Although a significant percentage of immigrants visit their home countries as tourists, typically there is still no tourism policy aimed at diasporas. The lack of such policy reflects government neglect and is a lost opportunity. Governments and the private sector can participate in joint ventures to offer their diasporas tour packages to visit traditional and nontraditional sites to rediscover and discover their home countries. They can also work out investment alliances with diasporas interested in partnering to establish joint ventures relating to tourism.

7. Nostalgic Trade

There is a significant demand for nostalgic goods, and many of the small businesses created by diasporas rely on the importation of such goods. Governments, development agencies, and the private sector, particularly local artisan businesses, find a natural opportunity to enhance their productive and marketing skills by locating their products with small ethnic businesses in North America, where a demand exists.

8. Macroeconomic Policy

Remittances respond to macroeconomic trends, such as changes in prices or the structure of a recipient country's financial system. Moreover, the ability of an economy to fully absorb migrant foreign savings will depend on the ways in which an adequate balance exists between macroeconomic policies and leveraging efforts on these flows. Governments, donors, and diasporas need to explore various policy opportunities that stimulate a country's economy as fertile ground to nourish the flows entering from abroad.

Current Practices Linking Diasporas to Development

Some positive experiences have resulted from experimentations in the policy arenas discussed above, through spontaneous developments or systematic initiatives coming from institutions in various parts of the world. This section reviews best practices and lessons learned, highlighting specific experiences from a range of actors worldwide.[4] The catalog of best practices provided here includes initiatives by four major players: governments, the private sector, NGOs, and international donor agencies (including foundations) (see Table 10.6). The initiatives include efforts related to remittance cost reductions, credit instruments, HTA donation facilitation, and incentives for migrant capital investment.

Broadly, these development actors are in the early stages of working in this field. Four institutions combined have invested nearly $50 million in grants to leverage remittances' development role. The Inter-American Development Bank (IADB) is the only institution that has gradually systematized its work. It is important to identify possible lessons learned from projects funded to date. Selected experiences are reviewed below.

Table 10.6 List of Best Practices in Remittance Transfers, Donations, and Other Activities

Player	Remittances	Donations	Other (Investments)
Government	BANSEFI (Mexico); Morocco Bank (Morocco); NRI (India); FDIC (USA)	Sedesol (Mexico); FISDL (El Salvador)	Por mi Jalisco (Mexico)
Private sector	Banco Salvadoreño (El Salvador); Banco Solidario (Ecuador); Banco Industrial (Guatemala); WF, BoA, Citi (USA)		
Nongovernmental organizations	FEDECACES (El Salvador); Oaxaca Bank (Mexico)		
Donors/ foundations	IADB; USAID; Ford Foundation; DFID, GTZ	IAF, IFAD, IADB, Rockefeller	

The Multilateral Investment Fund of
the Inter-American Development Bank

One of the pioneering institutions in addressing the link between remittances and development is the Multilateral Investment Fund (MIF) of the Inter-American Development Bank. The MIF has addressed the issue from a research, advocacy, and operational perspective. Since 1999 the MIF engaged in a series of discussions and studies about the impact of remittances in Latin America and the policy problem posed by high transaction costs. As its research and public discussion ensued, the Fund moved one step forward by taking the initiative to fund projects aimed at modernizing a financial infrastructure that could attract money transfers at lower cost, while addressing the financial needs of unbanked remittance-receiving households.

The MIF has funded over $70 million in projects in several countries in Latin America (e.g., Brazil, Colombia, Dominican Republic, Ecuador, El Salvador, Mexico, Nicaragua). Many of these projects are implemented by microfinance institutions or alternative savings and credit institutions. Table 10.7 identifies funding from the last two years.

The Fund has engaged in partnerships with other donors and institutions. For example, as of this writing, it has an alliance with the International Fund for Agricultural Development (IFAD) of the United Nations. In April 2004 the two institutions announced the creation of a $7.6 million fund aimed at supporting remittance-related projects that addressed microfinance and investment. Under this agreement, to which the MIF provided $4 million, local counterpart organizations, such as microfinance institutions and credit unions, are expected to commit $1.6 million to the projects they propose (IADB-MIF 2006b).

One of the successful cases resulting from IADB efforts is L@Red de la Gente project. In Mexico, for example, BANSEFI, the National Savings and Financial Services Bank, a quasi-government institution mandated to increase financial products and services to all Mexicans, entered into the remittance market and received funding to strengthen its technology and network of banks. In 2003 BANSEFI established a network of over 1,200 distribution centers, called L@Red de la Gente, together with popular banks, microfinance institutions, and credit unions to act as a remittance player. BANSEFI forged agreements with several MTOs, including GiroMex, Dolex, Vigo, and MoneyGram. It also linked its network to the US Federal Reserve System's Automated Clearinghouse (FedACH) International SM Mexico Service.

Under this scheme the members of L@Red de la Gente are offering remittance transfer services in mostly low-income urban and rural areas that experience significant emigration to the United States, and where the formal financial system has no coverage. In January 2005 BANSEFI was making 25,000 transactions a month and had opened accounts for 10 percent of the

Table 10.7   Projects Funded by the Multilateral Investment Fund, 2005–2006

Project	Country	Amount (US dollars)
Promoting Financial Democracy by Supporting FEDECREDITO	El Salvador	3,339,000
Create a Housing Finance Market for Transnational Families	El Salvador	5,250,000
Development of Services to Improve Remittance Access and Management	Bolivia	291,610
Remittances and Training for Brazilian Migrants and Their Beneficiaries	Brazil	470,000
Analysis of the Portugal/Brazil Remittances Market	Brazil	47,350
Remittances and Rural Development in Dominican Republic	Dominican Republic	321,500
Remittances and Rural Development in El Salvador	El Salvador	366,000
"More than Remittances"	Guatemala	198,000
Sociocultural Financial Services Adaptation	Guatemala	103,662
Enhance Development Impact of Workers' Remittances	Guatemala	5,200,000
Enhancement of Remittance Services to and Within Rural Haiti	Haiti	260,000
Support for Economic Development of La Piedad–Michoacan	Mexico	32,000
Pilot Project 3x1 for Migrants	Mexico	7,000,000
Direct Savings by Mexicans Living in the United States Toward Purchase of Housing in Mexico	Mexico	5,250,000
International Migration, Remittances, and Impact on Rural Communities in Zacatecas	Mexico	55,000
Facilitation of Access to Housing Finance for Recipients of Remittances	Mexico	1,700,000
Bringing Unbanked Remittance Recipients into Formal Financial System	Paraguay	222,000
Remittance Valuation of Peruvian Immigrants in Italy	Peru	49,000
Voluntary Return Migration Model Based on Entrepreneurship Development	Regional	3,975,000
Application of General Principles for Remittance Markets	Regional	1,759,300
Immigrant Remittance Corridors	Regional	167,500
Support for MIF Office	Regional	13,400
Improving Central Bank Remittance Reporting and Procedures	Regional	1,306,884
Total		37,377,206

Source: IADB-MIF 2006a.

individuals who had come in for remittance services, an improvement from the 6 percent who opened accounts in 2003. By May 2007 L@Red de la Gente had grown four times, to 120,000 transactions a month, and continued banking remittance recipients (see Figure 10.3).

**Figure 10.3 Mexicans' Remittance Transfers Through L@Red de la Gente,
January 2004 to March 2007**

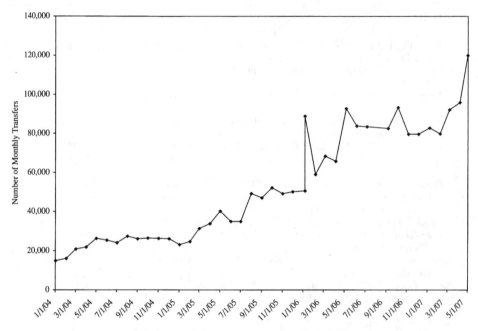

Source: National Savings and Financial Services Bank (BANSEFI), personal interview,
June 2007, Mexico.

Other IADB-MIF grantee institutions like FEDECACES, the federation
of credit unions in El Salvador, have targeted remittance recipients directly
as potential members of the credit union. Approximately 25 percent of
remittance recipients who choose FEDECACES to receive their remittances
are also FEDECACES clients.

International Fund for Agricultural Development

In addition to its work, reviewed above, in the area of remittances, IFAD
along with the MIF recently created a program to support binational rural
development projects in remittance-receiving communities. The program
supports funding in three areas: knowledge development for community-
based organizations and rural development, development of rural financial
services, and development of rural productive investment. Eligible institutions include NGOs, immigrant philanthropic groups working to support
their home communities, as well as savings and credit institutions.[5] IFAD

has expanded its remittance work worldwide not only in policy advocacy but also in operations.

Another example is the IFAD-EU-MIF facility. IFAD partnered with the European Commission, the Inter-American Development Bank, the Consultative Group to Assist the Poor, the government of Luxembourg, and the United Nations Capital Development Fund to launch a $10 million Financing Facility for Remittances to reduce rural poverty and promote development. The Facility aims to increase economic opportunities for the rural poor through the support and development of innovative, cost-effective, and easily accessible international or domestic remittance services within African, Asian, European, Middle Eastern, and Latin American countries. Its objectives are to improve access to remittance transmission in rural areas, link remittances to additional financial services and products, and develop innovative and productive rural investment channels for migrants and community-based organizations.

Through a competitive process, the Facility is awarding eligible institutions a maximum contribution per project of €200,000 (or approximately $260,000 for projects within the EU-LAC [European Union–Latin America and Caribbean] corridor). Research and practice has demonstrated that operationalizing projects to leverage remittances to maximize financial access through financial institutions does not represent costs above a quarter of a million dollars to banks or MFIs with an average of twenty branches. Through other experiences, we have learned that banking institutions can transform, on average, 5,000 remittance clients as bank clients within two years. Moreover, such efforts have demonstration effects on other financial institutions and encourage competition to increase financial services to this sector.

The United States Agency for International Development

USAID has followed the issue of remittances since 2000, considering it an area of attention within its programmatic plans. Some missions have decided to participate in projects related to diasporas and microfinance, banking, and hometown associations. The following section highlights some of USAID's work in Mexico and Jamaica, as well as the work of USAID's Global Development Alliance (GDA).

USAID in Mexico and Jamaica. In 2002 the Latin American regional office of USAID, began a pilot program on remittances focusing mostly on Mexico. USAID initiated four specific programs related to the financial aspects of remittances. These efforts seek to expand the financial services available to recipients of personal remittances. In September 2002, USAID gave a $500,000 grant to the World Council of Credit Unions, Inc. (WOCCU) to amend an ongoing project with Caja Popular Mexicana to help the latter connect to WOCCU's remittance services and market-related services to recipients. With a network of 330 branches in twenty-eight states, the credit union has distributed over $165 million in remittances to recipients in rural Mexico. Membership in the credit union has grown from 600,000 to over 1 million since 2003. At the same time, USAID granted $166,000 to Acción Internacional for their research examining the links between microfinance and remittances in order to gauge the interest of microfinance institutions in becoming involved in the service.

USAID has planned future projects that will include partnerships with microfinance organizations, cooperatives, and banks in order to extend banking services to low-income sectors in the countries and communities where the agency is engaged. USAID provided $900,000 annually from 2004 to 2008 aimed at improving financial services to low-income remittance senders and receivers. While USAID's projects related to remittances are, as of this writing, still in the early phases and the traditional results from development projects are not yet available, preliminary indications appear promising.

USAID is also working on a number of economic growth issues in Jamaica, with a particular focus on improving the business environment. One aspect of this effort focuses on access to financing through microenterprise and remittance programs. In November 2003 USAID entered into an agreement with the Jamaica National Building Society (JNBS), one of the country's remittance companies. Through this collaboration, JNBS introduced smart-card technology to reduce the cost of money transfers and create greater accessibility to funds. After eighteen months of work, 21 percent of remittance recipients were withdrawing their money with debit cards. As of June 2007 that number had doubled to 45 percent. Moreover, JNBS leveraged the savings created from the implementation of the smart card into development work. The building society participated with USAID in acquiring computers from US companies and donating them to different schools in Jamaica. JNBS helped pay for the costs in Jamaica of setting up computer connections and some technology training. Another USAID initiative has included the provision of technical assistance to USAID missions and governments in ways to better leverage remittances.

USAID's Global Development Alliance. GDA is the section of USAID dedicated to forging public-private alliances among governments, businesses, and civil society. As of this writing, GDA had not allocated a significant amount of resources to remittance and development programs, leaving that to the various USAID missions. In 2006, however, GDA partnered with FINCA (Foundation for International Community Assistance) and Hewlett

Packard separately to develop new technology, such as debit cards, to lower transaction costs of remittances. In late January of 2004, GDA announced a $600,000 grant to expand a public-private alliance with VISA and FINCA toward electronic microfinance. The program will take place over five phases, beginning in Central America, and will provide a business model that VISA and USAID will customize for other nations.

GDA's diaspora-related focuses are (1) increasing market-driven alternatives to large wire-transfer companies such as Western Union and Money Gram; (2) strengthening the capacity of HTAs and broker groups; and (3) developing alternate technology to reduce transaction costs of remittances. In 2006 GDA provided an estimated $1 million in funds for such activities. According to personnel interviewed for this study, the fact that until recently there was no single person dealing with the remittances and development issue within GDA constituted a significant barrier for the agency.[6]

The Ford Foundation

The Ford Foundation has a number of different programs, many of which focus on microfinance and access to financial services for poor people. The Foundation began making grants to broader projects dealing with remittances in 2002. Family and individual remittances, rather than collective (HTA) remittances constitute the Foundation's focus. It is interested in programs that allow individuals to build financial assets and enable financial institutions to become intermediaries in rural communities.

The Ford Foundation has ten migration and development programs with remittance components totaling an estimated $700,000 in grants. It typically spends a few hundred thousand dollars or more annually on such projects. Recipients of the Ford Foundation's funding include the Mexican Association of Social Sector Credit Unions, the California Credit Union League, and the University of California at Los Angeles's North American Integration and Development Center's effort to incorporate immigrants in Santa Maria, California, into credit unions to access financial services and find a means to send back money to the town of Santa Cruz Mixtepec, Mexico, through a microbank. Another aspect of the program works with HTAs to connect people to financial services in California.

The Foundation has worked with microfinance networks at the regional, Mexican, and Central American level. For example, it made a $235,000 grant to the Interdisciplinary Group on Women, Work and Poverty to support thirty-five student fellowships at Mexican universities to research how poor women use remittance income to improve their livelihoods and the welfare of their families. The Foundation also granted $60,000 to the organization Alianza para el Desarrollo de Microempresas, which has done significant work on remittance transfers.

The Ford Foundation's future plans will focus on the relationship between remittances and microfinance institutions. It is interested in promoting efforts that will shed light on how microfinance institutions can effectively deal with remittance flows. One particular area of concern for the Foundation is to determine how remittance activity will relate both technically and legally with unregulated microfinance institutions.

Development Initiatives in the Diaspora

Many initiatives focus on financial intermediation among remittance recipients, but remittance senders represent another, yet equally important, side of the equation. The Federal Deposit Insurance Corporation (FDIC) and the Consulate General of Mexico launched the New Alliance Task Force (NATF) in May 2003. The initiative comprises a coalition of over thirty banks, twenty-five community-based organizations, and government agencies, all striving to provide immigrants with necessary financial and education support services to access the US banking system. The NATF is made up of four working groups: Financial Education, Mortgage Products, Bank Products and Services, and Social Projects.

Prior to the launch, the Mexican Consulate had been promoting how the Matricula Consular could be used to promote banking services. This coincided with the FDIC's conclusion that immigrants' primary challenge to entering the banking system is obtaining the proper form of identification. The FDIC began presenting the *matricula* as an alternative and engaged in a two-year educational process with banks. Currently 118 banks nationwide accept both the *matricula* and the Individual Taxpayer Identification Number (ITIN) as alternative forms of identification to open bank accounts. Eighty-six such banks are located in the Midwest. Over twenty banks in the Midwest offer bank products with remittance features.

The NATF holds quarterly meetings in Chicago to take an inventory of who is doing what, share best practices, and report on new laws. Each of the working groups meets regularly. The Financial Education Working Group employs the FDIC's Money Smart financial curriculum to help adults outside the financial mainstream improve their money skills and create positive banking relationships. The program is offered in Spanish and three other languages. Future classes will be held on topics such as homebuyer information, predatory lending, taxpayer education, and use of alternative forms of identification, among others. Eighteen organizations including banks, nonprofits, and others will be involved. Banks, such as Bank of America, have donated ATMs for in-class simulation purposes.

The Mortgage Products Working Group helps banks develop loan programs for immigrants that can be held in the bank's portfolio as well as be sold on the secondary market. The NATF has created a New Alliance Model

Loan Product (NAMLP). It is intended for use by potential homeowners who pay taxes using an ITIN. The NAMLP is based on developed, unconventional mortgage programs to help immigrants qualify for existing home loan programs created by the Second Federal Savings and Loan Association in Chicago and Mitchell Bank in Milwaukee.

One of the highlights of the Bank Products and Services Working Group was the December 10, 2003, conference held at the Mexican Consulate in Chicago. Thirty national, regional, and community banks gathered for a showcasing of current and future remittance products. Bank of America, North Shore Bank, Mitchell Bank, and Fifth Third Bank featured their four different remittance products with four different features. These programs demonstrated that such products are both needed by the community and are a means to involve the "unbanked." The business case for banking the unbanked has been demonstrated, and there is real interest in the economics of the issue. The NATF has also been successful in receiving input from community organizations. While profits do not necessarily come from accounts for remittance senders, banks are looking to the long term. They want clients to enter the system and then cross over into other products like credit cards, auto loans, small-business loans, and so on, where the profits lie. There is a tremendous loyalty in the immigrant market; once individuals enter the system, they are unlikely to leave, and they usually bring in another ten to fifteen people.

In its December 10, 2003, press release, the Mexican Consulate highlighted the promising preliminary results of NATF. So far, more than $100 million in deposits have been invested in financial institutions that accept the Mexican *matricula*. Official reports from over thirty banks indicate that over 50,000 new bank accounts were opened in the Midwest by December 2003 by formerly unbanked customers, with an average balance of $2,000. The NATF estimates that new accounts represent over $100 million in deposits. By December 2003, over 35,000 immigrants in the Midwest had participated in education classes or workshops using the FDIC's "Smart Money" curriculum and similar financial education programs. In the 2002 tax filing season, almost 7,500 immigrant working families were served in the Chicago-area free tax-preparation sites, with earned income tax credit refunds of $9.3 million, saving immigrants $750,000 in preparation fees.

According to FDIC personnel interviewed, mortgage loans will be of major interest to banks. Banking the unbanked has been a three-stage process, beginning with (1) learning about the Matricula Consular and regulators' views, (2) offering remittance features to bring in clients, and (3) offering mortgage loans. Some banks are providing mortgage loans using ITIN numbers—six in the Milwaukee and Chicago area. To date, fifteen of the thirty-five NATF-member banks offer mortgage products that utilize ITIN numbers, totaling 659 loans—approximately $93 million in originations. The Wisconsin Housing & Economic Development Authority (an NATF member) purchases these loans in the secondary market from local banks in Milwaukee.

The FDIC has now expanded the program throughout the Midwest, California (Los Angeles), Texas (Austin), Iowa, Georgia (Atlanta), New York City, and Boston and has formed working groups in these areas. Moreover, the leadership of the FDIC created an advisory board, Economic Inclusion, that includes a component on remittances and financial access for migrants.

Impediments to Linking
Diasporas to Formal Development Efforts

These examples, coupled with diasporas' significant economic activities independent of the formal development industry, are cause for optimism in the quest to improve development outcomes by working with diasporas. Alongside this experimentation, however, one also finds reluctance among formal development actors to engage with diasporas. The policy and practice of engaging with the diaspora for the purpose of development remain in their infancy. While donors are engaging in experimental projects, an institutional strategy to link their work with diasporas is yet to emerge. Several factors may explain why this is the case. These impediments currently prevent the maximization of the potential of these linkages between diasporas and development. They originate from donors, within the diaspora, and in academe.

First, some development experts do not believe that migrants can participate in development schemes. Second, because of the limited knowledge that exists about organized diaspora groups, some donors have uninformed expectations about the results that these groups can achieve. For example, there are problems of symmetry between donors and diaspora organizations that need addressing. Third, diasporans' lack of development expertise, limited focus on how to become involved in development, and uncertainty about what to expect out of their involvement affects their ability to convincingly demonstrate to donors that they are suitable partners.

Fourth, academics who have studied diasporas have contributed little to developing a systematic approach that links diasporas and development. There is a lack of knowledge, theory, and method on how to bridge the assumed link. At times, academics themselves have made errors. For example, the term *collective remittances* is an example of an expression invented by academics that in actuality does not exist outside the minds of non-HTA practitioners. The appropriate term is *donations*. A similar problem surrounds the extrapolation of terms like *social remittances*. Fifth, the subject matter itself cuts across issues of migration and thus makes many uneasy about the political implications of doing migration-related work. Sixth, and finally, even when there are good intentions among donors, there is no communication among them, much less outreach. Box 10.2 summarizes these impediments.

**Box 10.2   Impediments to Linking Diasporas
to Formal Development Efforts**

1. Development experts' disbelief about migrants' role in development.
2. Limited knowledge about diasporas and their presence, work, and quality.
3. Lack of expertise and focus by diasporas.
4. Academic reluctance to develop theoretical frameworks and build related knowledge and methods.
5. Relationship to migration makes the subject matter political.
6. No or very limited communication or outreach to the diaspora.

Conclusion

The organizer of this volume, and the conference that led to it, intended to promote better understandings of diasporas, their potential to contribute to development, and how we might begin to consider how to better maximize this potential. This final chapter outlines an agenda for the arenas in which we might begin to more formally engage with diasporas and reviews experimentation in these to date. To meaningfully move this agenda forward, however, all interested actors need also to (1) consider the issues and five recommendations noted above, which reflect a deeper understanding of diasporas and their current engagement than the prevailing one; and (2) begin to directly address the six identified impediments. Clearly, this is an agenda that requires proaction on the part of many and diverse actors. The stakes for quality of life in the homelands and among the diasporas are high and merit this commitment.

Notes

1. There are a range of definitions; for example, one is "groupings of migrants who participate on a routine basis in a field of relationships, practices and norms that include both places of origin and destination" (Roberts, Frank, and Lozano-Ascencio 1999, 239).

2. Most studies assume there is a relationship but do not specify it conceptually or methodologically. Some efforts to do so include Nyberg-Sørensen (2004b); Gundel (2002); and Maimbo and Ratha (2005).

3. Remittances often do not reach the poorest of the poor, who may be less likely to have links to diaspora communities (Massey et al., 1999).

4. This section draws on Orozco (2005a).

5. IFAD has also worked in other areas of funding to hometown associations.

6. GDA's first remittance specialist, Thomas Debass, was hired in 2007.

Acronyms and Abbreviations

AACC	Afghan-American Chamber of Commerce
ABC	Armenian Business Corporation
ABF	Armenian Business Forum
AFME	Agence Française pour la Maitrise de l'Energie
A4T	Afghans4Tomorrow
AICC	Afghan International Chamber of Commerce
AISA	Afghanistan Investment Support Agency
BME	black and minority ethnic
BSTDB	Black Sea Trade and Development Bank
CFDT	Confédation Française Démocratique du Travail
CPA	Coalition Provisional Authority
CSO	civil-society organization
DAAS	Dominica Academy of Arts and Sciences
DBS	diaspora business support
DFID	Department for International Development
DIP	diaspora Iraqi professional
DO	diaspora organization
DOD	US Department of Defense
DOS	US Department of State
DSC	Dominica State College
DSEC	Dominica Sustainable Energy Corporation
EDF	Electricité de France
EEC	European Economic Community
EPO	export promotion organization
EU	European Union
FDI	foreign direct investment

FDIC	Federal Deposit Insurance Corporation
FINCA	Foundation for International Community Assistance
FOCAL	Canadian Foundation for the Americas
GATS	General Agreement on Trade in Services
GDA	Global Development Alliance
GDP	gross domestic product
GNP	gross national product
GOA	government of Armenia
GTZ	German bilateral aid agency
HTA	hometown association
IADB	Inter-American Development Bank
IAF	Inter-American Foundation
IFAD	International Fund for Agricultural Development
IOM	International Organization for Migration
IPA	investment promotion agency
IRDC	Iraqi Reconstruction and Development Council
IRS	Internal Revenue Service
IT	information technology
ITIN	Individual Taxpayer Identification Number
JNBS	Jamaica National Building Society
KBC	Kirkuk Business Center
LAC	Latin America and Caribbean
LED	Local Economic Development
LGP	Local Governance Program
M/D	Migration and Development
MIF	Multilateral Investment Fund
MMPW	Ministry of Municipalities and Public Works
MNC	multinational corporation
MOF	Ministry of Finance
MTO	money transfer operation
NAMLP	New Alliance Model Loan Product
NATF	New Alliance Task Force
NCCS	National Center for Charitable Statistics
NGO	nongovernmental organization
NMCP	Netherlands Management Cooperation Programme
NRI	nonresident Indian
OCP	overseas Chinese professional
OECD	Organization for Economic Cooperation and Development
ONE	National Office of Electricity
PERG	Programme d'Electricifation Rurale Globale
PRC	People's Republic of China
PVO	private voluntary organization
RRG	rapid-response grant

RTI	Research Triangle Institute
SMEs	small- and medium-sized enterprises
TOKTEN	Transfer of Knowledge Through Expatriate Nationals
UNDP	United Nations Development Programme
USAID	United States Agency for International Development
USG	US government
WOCCU	World Council of Credit Unions, Inc.

Bibliography

AACC (Afghan-American Chamber of Commerce). *2005 Annual Report.* http://www.a-acc.org/docs/2005%20Annual%20Reportwcover.pdf (accessed May 31, 2007).

Abusharaf, Rogaia Mustafa. *Wanderings: Sudanese Migrants and Exiles in North America.* Ithaca, NY: Cornell University Press, 2002.

Acosta, Pablo. "Labor Supply, School Attendance, and Remittances from International Migration: The Case of El Salvador." *Policy Research Working Paper* 3903. Washington, DC: World Bank, 2006.

Adams, Richard H., Jr. "Remittances, Poverty, and Investment in Guatemala." In *International Migration, Remittances and the Brain Drain*, edited by Çağlar Özden and Maurice Schiff, 53–80. Washington, DC: World Bank, 2005.

Adebajo, Adekeye. *Liberia's Civil War.* Boulder, CO: Lynne Rienner, 2002.

AFME (Agence Française pour la Maitrise de l'Energie), Ambassade de France/Service de la Coopération Technique, et al. *Programme pilote de pre-électrification rurale: Dossier de projet préliminaire.* Rabat: AFME, 1988.

Aharoni, Yahir. "How to Market a Country." *Columbia Journal of World Business* 1, no. 2 (1966): 41–49.

Ahmed, Zafar U., et al. "Export Promotion Programs of Malaysian Firms: An International Marketing Perspective." *Journal of Business Research* 55, no. 10 (2002): 831–854.

AICC (Afghan International Chamber of Commerce). http://www.aicc-online.org (accessed May 31, 2007).

AISA (Afghanistan Investment Support Agency). http://www.aisa.org.af/ (accessed May 31, 2007).

Akenson, Donald Harman. *The Irish Diaspora: A Primer.* Toronto: P.D. Meany Company, 1996.

Alarcon, Rafael. "The Development of Hometown Associations in the United States and the Use of Social Remittances in Mexico." Working paper. Washington, DC: Inter-American Dialogue, 2000.

Alburo, Florian A., and Danilo I. Abella. "Skilled Labour Migration from

Developing Countries: Study on the Philippines." *International Migration Papers* 51. Geneva: ILO, 2002.

Alexseev, Mikhail A. "Desecuritizing Sovereignty: Economic Interest and Responses to Political Challenges of Chinese Migration in the Russian Far East." In *How Governments Respond: Sovereignty Under Challenge*, edited by John D. Montgomery and Nathan Glazer, 261–289. New Brunswick, NJ, and London: Transaction Publishers, 2002.

Allen, Tim, and Hubert Morsink. "Introduction: When Refugees Go Home." In *When Refugees Go Home: African Experiences*, edited by Tim Allen and Hubert Morsink, 1–13. Trenton, NJ: Africa World Press, 1994.

Anderson, Mary. *Do No Harm: How Aid Can Support Peace—or War*. London: Lynne Rienner, 1999.

Anonymous. "Diaspora Humanitarian Assistance to Armenia in the Last Decade." Paper presented at the "Armenia Diaspora Conference," Yerevan, Armenia, September 22–23, 1999. www.armeniadiaspora.com/conference99/humanitarian.html (accessed January 17, 2008).

Archibold, Randal C. "Armenian Furor over PBS Plan for Debate." *New York Times*, Feburary 25, 2006, B1, B16.

Armstrong, John A. "Mobilized and Proletarian Diasporas." *American Political Science Review* 70, no. 2 (1976): 393–408.

Association of Foundations. *Good News for the Poor: Diaspora Philanthropy by Overseas Filipinos*. Quezon City: Association of Foundations, 2005.

Atash, Nadir. *Business Climate in Afghanistan*. Washington, DC: Afghan-American Chamber of Commerce, 2004.

Ayón, David R. "Long Road to the *Vota Postal*: Mexican Policy and People of Mexican Origin in the US." *Policy Paper* 6. Berkeley, CA: Center for Latin American Studies, University of California, Berkeley, 2006. http://socrates.berkeley.edu:7001/Publications/workingpapers/policypapers/AyonWeb.pdf (accessed July 26, 2006).

Baghdasaryan, Edik. "On the Trail of the Lincy Lending Project." *Association of Investigative Journalists: Hetq Online*. December 16, 2003. http://www.hetq.am/en/h-1203-lincy.html.

Bakalian, Anny. *Armenian-Americans: From Being to Feeling Armenian*. New Brunswick, NJ: Transaction Press, 1993.

Barakat, Sultan. "Post-Saddam Iraq: Deconstructing a Regime, Reconstructing a Nation." *Third World Quarterly* 26, nos. 4–5 (2005): 571–591.

Barkan, Joel D., Michael L. McNulty, and M. A. O. Ayeni. "'Hometown' Voluntary Associations, Local Development, and the Emergence of Civil Society in Western Nigeria." *Journal of Modern Africa Studies* 29, no. 3 (1991): 457–478.

Barro, Robert J., and Jong-Wha Lee. "International Data on Educational Attainment: Updates and Implications." *CID Working Paper* 42. Cambridge, MA: Center for International Development, Harvard University, 2000.

Barton, Frederick. "Failed and Failing States: The Current Approach to Development." Presentation to the Development Management Network annual workshop, Washington, DC, George Washington University, October 30, 2004.

Basch, Linda G., Nina Glick-Schiller, and Cristina Szanton Blanc. *Nations Unbound: Transnational Projects, Postcolonial Predicaments, and De-territorialized Nation-States*. Amsterdam: Gordon and Breach, 1994.

Bechky, Beth A. "Sharing Meaning Across Occupational Communities: The Transformation of Understanding on a Production Floor." *Organization Science* 14, no. 3 (2003): 312–330.

Beck, Thorsten, Ross Levine, and Norman Loayza. "Finance and the Sources of Growth." *Journal of Financial Economics* 58, nos. 1–2 (2000): 261–300.

Beine, Michel, Frédéric Docquier, and Hillel Rapoport. "Brain Drain and Economic Growth: Theory and Evidence." *Journal of Development Economics* 64, no. 1 (2001): 275–289.

Benhabib, Seyla. "Citizens, Residents and Aliens in a Changing World: Political Membership in the Global Era." *Social Research* 66, no. 3 (1999): 709–744.

Bentaleb, Nadia. *Energie rurale pour le développement: Etude de cas Africains.* Paris: Editions Publisud, 2002.

Berdai, Mohamed, and Vincent Butin. "Dynamique institutionelle et mobilisation des populations: Le PPER au Maroc." *Liason Energie-Francophonie* 23 (1994): 28–29.

———. *Mettre en oeuvre l'électrification décentralisée dans une demarche participative: Un nouveau service et une stratégie d'équipment rural: Le cas de Programme Pilote d'Electrification Rurale Décentralisée (PPER) au Maroc.* Rabat, Morocco: Ministère de l'Intérieur, 1993.

Berg, Elliott J. *Rethinking Technical Cooperation: Reforms for Capacity Building in Africa.* New York: United Nations Development Programme and Development Alternatives, Inc., 1993.

Beyan, Amos Jones. *The American Colonization Society and the Creation of the Liberian State.* Lanham, MD: University Press of America, 1991.

Bhagwati, Jagdish, and Koichi Hamada. "The Brain Drain, International Integration of Markets for Professionals and Unemployment: A Theoretical Analysis." *Journal of Development Economics* 1, no. 1 (1974): 19–42.

Biao, Xiang. "Promoting Knowledge Exchange Through Diaspora Networks (The Case of the People's Republic of China)." In *Converting Migration Drains into Gains: Harnessing the Resources of Overseas Professionals*, edited by Clay Wescott and Jennifer M. Brinkerhoff, 33–72. Manila: Asian Development Bank, 2006.

Biswas, Bidisha. "Nationalism by Proxy: A Comparison of Social Movements Among Diaspora Sikhs and Hindus." *Nationalism and Ethnic Politics* 10, no. 2 (2004): 269–295.

Black, Richard. "Return and Reconstruction in Bosnia-Herzegovina: Missing Link, or Mistaken Priority?" *SAIS Review* 21, no. 2 (2001): 177–199.

Blair, Harry. "Rebuilding and Reforming Civil Services in Post-Conflict Societies." In *Governance in Post-Conflict Societies: Rebuilding Fragile States*, edited by Derick W. Brinkerhoff, 161–184. Oxford, UK: Routledge, 2007.

Blanchard, Christopher M. *Afghanistan: Narcotics and US Policy.* Washington, DC: Congressional Research Service, Library of Congress, 2006.

Bolt, Paul J. "Looking to the Diaspora: The Overseas Chinese and China's Economic Development, 1978–1994." *Diaspora: A Journal of Transnational Studies* 5, no. 3 (1996): 467–497.

Bournoutian, George A. *A Concise History of the Armenian People.* Costa Mesa, CA: Mazda Publishers, 2003.

Braakman, Marije. "Roots and Routes. Questions of Home, Belonging and Return in an Afghan Diaspora." Masters thesis, University of Leiden, 2005. http://www.ag-afghanistan.de/files/braakman_roots_a_routes.pdf (accessed January 19, 2008).

Brainard, Lori A., and Jennifer M. Brinkerhoff. "Sovereignty Under Siege or a Circuitous Path to Strengthening the State?: Digital Diasporas and Human

Rights." *International Journal of Public Administration* 9, no. 8 (2006): 595–618.

———. "Lost in Cyberspace: Shedding Light on the Dark Matter of Grassroots Organizations." *Nonprofit and Voluntary Sector Quarterly* 33, no. 3 (Supplement) (2004): 32S–53S.

Brinkerhoff, Derick W. "Technical Cooperation for Building Strategic Policy Management Capacity in Developing Countries." *International Journal of Technical Cooperation* 2, no. 1 (1996): 1–18.

Brinkerhoff, Derick W., and James Mayfield. "Democratic Governance in Iraq? Progress and Peril in Reforming State-Society Relations." *Public Administration and Development* 25, no. 1 (2005): 59–73.

Brinkerhoff, Jennifer M. "Diaspora Identity and the Potential for Violence: Toward an Identity-Mobilization Framework." *Identity: An International Journal of Theory and Research* 8, no. 1 (2008a): 67–88.

———. "Diaspora Philanthropy in an At-Risk Society: The Case of Coptic Orphans in Egypt." *Nonprofit and Voluntary Sector Quarterly* 37, no. 3 (2008b), forthcoming.

———. "Exploring the Role of Diasporas in Rebuilding Governance in Post-Conflict Societies." In *Africa's Finances: The Contribution of Remittances.* Newcastle upon Tyne, UK: Cambridge Scholars Publishing, 2008c, forthcoming.

———. "Contributions of Digital Diasporas to Governance Reconstruction in Post-Conflict and Fragile States: Potential and Promise." In *Rebuilding Governance in Post-Conflict Societies: What's New, What's Not,* edited by Derick W. Brinkerhoff, 185–203. London: Routledge, 2007.

———. "Digital Diasporas and Conflict Prevention: The Case of Somalinet.com." *Review of International Studies* 32, no. 1 (2006a): 25–47.

———. "Digital Diasporas' Challenge to Traditional Power: The Case of Tibetboard." Paper presented at the annual meeting for the American Political Science Association, Philadelphia, August 31–September 3, 2006b.

———. "Diasporas, Skills Transfer, and Remittances: Evolving Perceptions and Potential." In *Converting Migration Drains into Gains: Harnessing the Resources of Overseas Professionals*, edited by Clay Wescott and Jennifer M. Brinkerhoff, 1–32. Manila: Asian Development Bank, 2006c.

———. "Diasporas, Information Technology and Base of the Pyramid Market Development: What Can We Learn from Thamel.com?" Paper presented at the annual meeting of the Academy for International Business, Quebec City, July 9–12, 2005.

———. "Digital Diasporas and International Development: Afghan-Americans and the Reconstruction of Afghanistan." *Public Administration and Development* 24, no. 5 (2004): 397–413.

———. *Partnership for International Development: Rhetoric or Results?* Boulder, CO: Lynne Rienner, 2002.

———. *Digital Diasporas: Identity and Transnational Engagement.* London and New York: Cambridge University Press, forthcoming.

Brinkerhoff, Jennifer M., and Derick W. Brinkerhoff. "Government-Nonprofit Relations in Comparative Perspective: Evolution, Themes, and New Directions." *Public Administration and Development* 22, no. 1 (2002): 3–18.

Brossard, Hubert. "Importance of Organizations for Investment Promotion During an Investment Decision Process: An Exploratory Study." *Management International Review* 38, no. 3 (1998): 203–213.

Burgess, Katrina. "Migrant Philanthropy and Local Governance in Mexico." In *New Patterns for Mexico: Observations on Remittances, Philanthropic Giving, and Equitable Development,* edited by Barbara J. Merz, 99–156. Cambridge, MA: Harvard University Press, 2006.

Burnett, Victoria. "Seeking the Most Hardy Investors: A Coke Bottling Plant Is the Biggest Investment Yet by a Member of the Afghan Diaspora." *Financial Times,* September 30, 2004, 31.

Butin, Vincent, and M/D. "Electrification rurale décentralisée: Eléctrification par groupe lectrogène et Mini-Réseau Local." Rabat, Morocco: M/D. Unpublished mimeo, 1993.

Byman, Daniel, et al. *Trends in Outside Support for Insurgent Movements.* Santa Monica, CA: Rand Corporation, 2001.

Callon, Michel. "Techno-Economic Networks and Irreversibility?" In *A Sociology of Monsters: Essays on Power, Technology and Domination,* edited by John Law, 132–161. London: Routledge, 1991.

Carlile, Paul. "Transferring, Translating, and Transforming: An Integrative Framework for Managing Knowledge Across Boundaries." *Organizational Science* 15, no. 5 (2004): 555–569.

Carr, Stuart C., Kerr Inkson, and Kaye Thorn. "From Global Careers to Talent Flow: Reinterpreting 'Brain Drain.'" *Journal of World Business* 40, no. 4 (2005): 386–401.

Carrington, William J., and Enrica Detragiache. "How Extensive Is the Brain Drain?" *Finance and Development* 36, no. 2 (1999): 46–49.

———. "How Big Is the Brain Drain?" *IMF Working Paper* WP/98/102. Washington, DC: International Monetary Fund, 1998.

Center for International Disaster Information. "Afghanistan—Drought." *OCHA Situation Report* 4 (July 19, 2000). http://iys.cidi.org/disaster/00b/0014.html (accessed May 30, 2007).

Central Intelligence Agency. *The World Factbook.* https://www.cia.gov/library/pub-lications/the-world-factbook/geos/af.html (accessed May 31, 2007).

Central Statistics Office. *Dominica: 2005 Population and Housing Census.* Roseau, Dominica: Ministry of Finance, 2006a.

———. *Foreign Trade Statistics: 1990–2005.* Roseau, Dominica: Ministry of Finance, 2006b.

———. *Demographic Statistics* 2. Roseau, Dominica: Ministry of Finance, 1996.

Chang, Wen-Chin. "Guanxi and Regulation in Networks: The Yunnanese Jade Trade Between Burma and Thailand, 1962–1988." *Journal of Southeast Asian Studies* 35, no. 3 (2004): 479–501.

Chapin, Frances W. "Channels for Change: Emigrant Tourists and the Class Structure of Azorean Migration." *Human Organization* 51, no. 1 (1992): 44–62.

Chaudhry, Kiren Aziz. "The Price of Wealth: Business and State in Labor Remittance and Oil Economies." *International Organization* 43, no. 1 (1989): 101–145.

Chesterman, Simon, Michael Ignatieff, and Ramesh Thakur. "Making States Work: From State Failure to State-Building." New York: International Peace Academy and United Nations University, 2004. http://www.ipacademy.org/Publications/Publications.htm (accessed October 17, 2006).

Cheung, Gordan C.K. "Chinese Diaspora as a Virtual Nation: Interactive Roles Between Economic and Social Capital." *Political Studies* 52, no. 4 (2004): 664–686.

Christian, Gabriel J. "The History of a Nationalist Movement: Education and

Ideology." In *In Search of Eden 2—Essays on Dominican History*, edited by Irving W. Andre and Gabriel J. Christian, 527–556. Toronto: Pond Case Press, 2002.

Clemens, Michael. "Do Visas Kill? Health Effects of African Health Professional Emigration." *Center for Global Development Working Paper* 114. Washington, DC: Center for Global Development, March 9, 2007. http://www.cgdev.org/content/publications/detail/13123/ (accessed June 6, 2007).

Cohen, Jeffrey H. "Remittance Outcomes and Migration: Theoretical Concepts, Real Opportunities." *Studies in Comparative International Development* 40, no. 1 (2005): 88–112.

Cohen, Robin. *Global Diasporas: An Introduction*. London: UC London Press, 1997.

———. "Diasporas and the Nation State: From Victims to Challengers." *International Affairs* 72, no. 3 (1996): 507–520.

Coleman, James S. *Foundations of Social Theory*. Cambridge, MA: Belknap–Harvard University Press, 1990.

———. "Social Capital in the Creation of Human Capital." *American Journal of Sociology* 94 (Supplement) (1988): S95–S120.

Collier, Paul, and Anke Hoeffler. "Greed and Grievances in Civil War." *Policy Research Working Paper* 2355. Washington, DC: World Bank, 2001.

Commission on the Private Sector and Development. *Unleashing Entrepreneurship: Making Business Work for the Poor. Report to the Secretary-General of the United Nations*. New York: United Nations Development Programme, 2004.

Connections for Development. "CfD. Connections for Development. Connecting Black and Minority Ethnic Communities to Their World." http://www.cfdnetwork.co.uk/ (accessed July 19, 2007).

Cook, Beth, Chris Dodds, and William Mitchell. "Social Entrepreneurship—False Premises and Dangerous Forebodings." *Australian Journal of Social Issues* 38, no. 4 (2003): 57–72.

Cook, Scott D.N., and John Seeley Brown. "Bridging Epistemologies: The Generative Dance Between Organizational Knowledge and Organizational Knowing." *Organization Science* 10 (1999): 381–400.

Coser, Louis. *The Functions of Social Conflict*. Glencoe, IL: Free Press, 1956.

Czinkota, Michael R. "Why National Export Promotions?" *International Trade Forum* 2 (1996): 10–13.

Dade, Carlo. "Policy Considerations for Working with Diaspora Populations." Keynote speech to "Diasporas as Wealth Creators Workshop," Jönköping, Sweden, April 6–7, 2006. http://www.diwec.org/Downloads.htm (accessed July 23, 2006).

Daoud, Zakya. *Marocains de l'autre rive*. Casablanca: Editions Maghrébines, 2005.

———. *Marocains des deux rives*. Paris: Editions Ouvrières, 1997.

Davis, Lee. *The NGO-Business Hybrid: Is the Private Sector the Answer?* Baltimore, MD: Johns Hopkins University, 1997.

de Haas, H. *Migration and Development in Southern Morocco: The Disparate Socio-Economic Impacts of Out-Migration on the Todgha Oasis Valley*. Amsterdam: CERES, 2003.

de la Garza, Rodolfo, and Briant Lindsay Lowell, eds. *Sending Money Home: Hispanic Remittances and Community Development*. Lanham, MD: Rowman & Littlefield, 2002.

Dees, J. Gregory. "Enterprising Nonprofits." *Harvard Business Review*, January–February (1998): 55–67.

DFID (Department for International Development). *The 1997 White Paper: International Development, Eliminating World Poverty.* London: DFID, 1997.

DGIS (Dutch Ministry of Foreign Affairs). *Preparation of the 2007 EU Report on Policy Coherence for Development. Response of the Netherlands to the Questionnaire.* The Hague: DGIS, 2007. http://www.minbuza.nl/binaries/en-pdf/pcd-questionnaire-nederland-final.pdf (accessed July 19, 2007).

Diamantopoulos, Adamantios, Bodo B. Schlegelmilch, K.Y. Katy Tse. "Understanding the Role of Export Marketing Assistance: Empirical Evidence and Research Needs." *European Journal of Marketing* 27, no. 4 (1993): 5–18.

Dichter, Thomas. *Despite Good Intentions: Why Development Assistance in the Third World Has Failed.* Amherst and Boston: University of Massachusetts Press, 2003.

Dick, Shelly. "FMO Country Guide: Liberia. Forced Migration." Online, 2003. http://www.forcedmigration.org/guides/fmo013/fmo013.pdf (accessed July 18, 2007).

———. "Liberians Living in Ghana: Living Without Humanitarian Assistance." *UNHCR Working Paper* 29. Oxford, UK: Oxford University Refugee Studies Programme, 2002.

Docquier, Frédéric, and Abdeslam Marfouk. "International Migration by Education Attainment, 1990–2000." In *International Migration, Remittances and the Brain Drain*, edited by Çağlar Özden and Maurice Schiff, 151–200. Washington, DC: World Bank, 2005.

———. "Measuring the International Mobility of Skilled Workers." *World Bank Policy Research Working Paper* 3381. Washington, DC: World Bank, 2004.

Dominica Academy of Arts and Sciences. *Diaspora Policy Paper.* http://www.da-academy.org/draft_intro.html (accessed January 21, 2008).

Dougherty, Deborah. "Interpretive Barriers to Successful Product Innovation in Large Firms." *Organizational Science* 3, no. 2 (1992): 179–202.

Duff, John B. *The Irish in the United States.* Belmont, CA: Wadsworth Publishing, 1971.

Durand, Jorge, Emilio A. Parrado, and Douglas A. Massey. "Migradollars and Development: A Reconsideration of the Mexican Case." *International Migration Review* 30, no. 2 (1996): 423–444.

Dustmann, Christian, and Oliver Kirchkamp. "The Optimal Migration Duration and Activity Choice After Re-migration." *Journal of Development Economics* 67, no. 2 (2001): 351–372.

Edwards, Alejandra Cox, and Manuelita Ureta. "International Migration, Remittances, and Schooling: Evidence from El Salvador." *NBER Working Paper* 9766, June 2003.

Eisenhardt, Kathleen M. "Building Theories from Case Study Research." *Academy of Management Review* 14, no. 4 (1989): 532–550.

Ellis, Stephen. *The Mask of Anarchy: The Destruction of Liberia and the Religious Dimension of an African Civil War.* New York: NYU Press, 1999.

Esman, Milton J. "Diasporas and International Relations." In *Modern Diasporas in International Politics*, edited by Gabriel Sheffer, 333–349. London and Sydney: Croom Helm, 1986.

Ezz Al Deen, Mohammad. "Afghan Expatriates Remit About $300M Annually from the UAE." *Gulf News,* January 22, 2006.

Fagen, Patricia. "Remittances in Crisis: A Haiti Case Study." *Humanitarian Policy Group Background Paper.* London: Humanitarian Policy Group, Overseas Development Institute, April 2006. http://www.odi.org.uk/hpg/papers/BG_Haiti_remittances.pdf (accessed June 9, 2007).

Fagen, Patricia Weiss, and Micah N. Bump. "Remittances in Conflict and Crises: How Remittances Sustain Livelihoods in War, Crises and Transitions to Peace." *International Peace Academy Policy Paper*. International Peace Academy, Security-Development Nexus Program, February 2006. http://www.ipacademy.org/pdfs/Remittances_ERPT.pdf (accessed March 28, 2007).

Farhadi, Torek (Senior strategy officer, Middle East North Africa Department, International Finance Corporation). Personal interview, April 14, 2006.

FinFacts, Ireland. "Finfacts: Irelands Business and Finance Portal." http://www.finfacts.ie/ (accessed November 28, 2005).

Fowler, Alan. "NGDOs as a Moment in History: Beyond Aid to Social Entrepreneurship or Civic Innovation." *Third World Quarterly* 21, no. 4 (2000): 637–654.

Francis, June, and Colleen Collins-Dodd. "Impact of Export Promotion Programs on Firm Competencies, Strategies, and Performance: The Case of Canadian High-Technology SMEs." *International Marketing Review* 21, nos. 4–5 (2004): 474–495.

Freedman, Amy. "Politics from Outside: Chinese Overseas and Political and Economic Change in China." In *International Migration and the Globalization of Domestic Politics*, edited by Rey Koslowski, 130–147. New York: Routledge, 2005.

Gamlen, Alan. "The Brain Drain Is Dead, Long Live the New Zealand Diaspora." *Working Paper* 10. Oxford: University of Oxford, Centre on Migration, Policy and Society, 2005.

Gardner, Katy. *Global Migrants, Local Lives: Travel and Transformation in Rural Bangladesh*. Oxford, UK: Clarendon Press, 1995.

Geithner, Peter F., Lincoln C. Chen, and Paula D. Johnson. *Diaspora Philanthropy and Equitable Development in China and India*. Cambridge, MA: Harvard University Press, 2005.

Gelbard, Enrique. "Armenia After a Decade of Reforms." Paper presented at the "Third Annual AIPRG Conference on Armenia"; World Bank; Washington, DC; January 15–16, 2005.

Gevorkyan, Aleksandr V., and David A. Grigorian. "Armenia and Its Diaspora: Is There a Scope for a Stronger Economic Link?" *Armenian Forum* 3, no. 2 (2003): 1–35.

Giddens, Anthony. *The Constitution of Society: Outline of the Theory of Structuration*. Berkeley: University of California Press, 1984.

Gillespie, Kate. "The Globalization of Indian IT." In *Global Marketing*, edited by Kate Gillespie, J. Jeannet, and H.D. Hennessey, 521–523. New York: Houghton Mifflin, 2007.

———. *The Tripartite Relationship: Government, Foreign Investors, and Local Investors During Egypt's Economic Opening*. New York: Praeger, 1984.

Gillespie, Kate, and Anna Adrianova. "Diaspora Support for Business Development in Armenia: Examining Paradigms of Social Entrepreneurship." Paper presented at the 2nd "Armenian International Policy Research Group Conference"; Washington, DC; January 17–18, 2004.

Gillespie, Kate, and Liesl Riddle. "Export Promotion Organization Emergence and Development: A Call to Research." *International Marketing Review* 21, nos. 4–5 (2004): 462–473.

Gillespie, Kate, Edward Sayre, and Liesl Riddle. "Palestinian Interest in Homeland Investment." *Middle East Journal* 55, no. 22 (2001): 237–255.

Gillespie, Kate, et al. "Diaspora Homeland Investment." *Journal of International Business Studies* 30, no. 3 (1999): 623–635.

Giuliano, Paolo, and Marta Ruiz-Arranz. "Remittances, Financial Development and Growth." *IMF Working Paper* 05/234. Washington, DC: International Monetary Fund, 2005.

Glick-Schiller, Nina, and George Fouron. *Georges Woke Up Laughing: Long-Distance Nationalism and the Search for Home.* Durham, NC: Duke University Press, 2001.

Global Commission on International Migration. *Migration in an Interconnected World: New Directions for Action.* Geneva: Global Commission on International Migration, 2005. http://www.gcim.org/en/ (accessed February 3, 2006).

Goldring, Luin. "The Mexican State and Transmigrant Organizations: Negotiating the Boundaries of Membership and Participation." *Latin American Research Review* 37, no. 3 (2002): 55–99.

Government of the Kingdom of Belgium, the International Organization for Migration, the European Commission, and the World Bank. *Migration and Development Conference: Final Report.* Brussels: International Organization for Migration Regional Liaison and Coordination Office to the European Union. March 2006.

Greeley, Andrew. *The American Catholic: A Social Portrait.* New York: Basic Books, 1977.

Green, Richard (Acting assistant secretary of state, Bureau of Population, Refugees and Migration). "Remarks on Strategic Consultations on Afghan Refugees." Press release, US Mission to the United Nations in Geneva, October 7, 2005. http://www.us-mission.ch/Press2005/1007Greene.htm (accessed January 19, 2008).

Grigorian, David A. "Banking Sector in Armenia: What Would It Take to Turn a Basket Case into a Beauty Case?" *Armenian Journal of Public Policy* 1 (2003): 55–77.

Grosclaude, Michel. *Maroc: Mission de suivi des projets "pré-électrification rurale" et télédetection; Compte-rendu de mission au Maroc.* Paris: Ambassade de France à Rabat, 1990.

Grubel, Herbert G., and Anthony Scott. "The International Flow of Human Capital." *American Economic Review* 56, nos. 1–2 (1966): 268–274.

Guarnizo, Luis Edwardo. "The Economics of Transnational Living." *International Migration Review* 37, no. 3 (2003): 666–699.

Gundel, Joakim. "The Migration-Development Nexus: Somalia Case-Study." *International Migration* 40, no. 5 (2002), 255–279.

Gunter, Michael M. *Transnational Armenian Activism.* London: Research Institute for the Study of Conflict and Terrorism, 1970.

Hakobyan, Anna. "Armenia's Light and Protection?" *Transitions Online.* November 11, 2003. http://www.tol.cz.

Hall, Peter. "Brain Drains and Brain Gains: Causes, Consequences, Policy." *International Journal of Social Economics* 32, no. 11 (2005): 939–951.

Hammond, Laura. *This Place Will Become Home: Refugee Repatriation to Ethiopia.* Ithaca, NY: Cornell University Press, 2004.

Hanifi, Shah Mahmoud. "Material and Social Remittances to Afghanistan." In *Converting Migration Drains into Gains: Harnessing the Resources of Overseas Professionals,* edited by Clay Wescott and Jennifer M. Brinkerhoff, 98–120. Manila: Asian Development Bank, 2006.

———. "National Building and the Afghan Diaspora." Presentation at the "Special Conference—Afghanistan Promise and Fulfillment"; Washington, DC; Middle East Institute; May 25, 2004. www.mideasti.org/articles/doc214.html (accessed January 19, 2008).

Harbom, Lotta, Stina Högbladh, and Peter Wallensteen. "Armed Conflict and Peace Agreements." *Journal of Peace Research* 43, no. 5 (2006): 617–631.

Hart, Gillian. *Disabling Globalization: Places of Power in Post-Apartheid South Africa.* Berkeley: University of California Press, 2002.

Hill, Charles W.L. *International Business.* 6th edition. New York: McGraw-Hill, 2007.

Honig, Benson. "Who Gets the Goodies? An Examination of Microenterprise Credit in Jamaica." *Entrepreneurship and Regional Development* 10, no. 4 (1998): 313–334.

Huband, Mark. *The Liberian Civil War.* London: Frank Cass, 1988.

Hulme David, and Michael Edwards, eds. *NGOs, States and Donors: Too Close for Comfort?* New York: St. Martin's Press/Save the Children, 1997.

Human Rights Watch. "Afghanistan, Iran, Pakistan: A Closed Door Policy." *Human Rights Watch* 14 (2002). http://hrw.org/reports/2002/pakistan/index.htm (accessed January 19, 2008).

Hunger, Uwe. "Indian IT Entrepreneurs in the US and in India: An Illustration of the 'Brain Gain Hypothesis.'" *Journal of Comparative Policy Analysis: Research and Practice* 6, no. 2 (2004): 99–109.

———. "The 'Brain Gain' Hypothesis: Third-World Elites in Industrialized Countries and Socioeconomic Development in Their Home Country." *Working Paper* 47. Muenster, Germany: Center for Comparative Immigration Studies, University of Muenster, January 2002.

IADB-MIF (Inter-American Development Bank, Multilaterial Investment Fund). "RG-M1019: MIF-IFAD Partnership Facility for Rural Private Sector Dev-LAC." Washington, DC: IADB-MIF, 2006a. http://www.iadb.org/projects/Project.cfm?project=RG-M1019&Language=English (accessed July 18, 2007).

———. "Multilateral Investment Fund Projects." Washington, DC: IADB-MIF, 2006b. http://www.iadb.org/projects/mif_project.cfm?language=English (accessed July 18, 2007).

———. *Receptores de remesas en Bolivia, Peru.* Washington, DC: IADB-MIF, September 2005.

———. *Receptores de remesas en Republica Dominicana.* Washington, DC: IADB-MIF, September 2004.

———. *Receptores de remesas en Guatemala, El Salvador y Honduras.* Washington, DC: IADB-MIF, September 2003a.

———. *Receptores de remesas en Ecuador.* Washington, DC: IADB-MIF, May 2003b.

———. *Receptores de remesas en Mexico.* Washington, DC: IADB-MIF, October 2003c.

ICG (International Crisis Group). "The Next Iraqi War? Sectarianism and Civil Conflict." *Middle East Report* 52. Brussels: ICG, February 2006.

IMF (International Monetary Fund). *Balance of Payments Statistics Yearbook.* Washington, DC: IADB-MIF, 2005.

IOM (International Organization for Migration). *World Migration 2005: Costs and Benefits of International Migration.* Geneva: IOM, 2005.

———. *World Migration Report 2000,* Geneva: IOM, 2000.

Iredale, Robyn. "The Migration of Professionals: Theories and Typologies." *International Migration* 39, no. 5 (2001): 7–26.

IRS (Internal Revenue Service). Form 990 Instructions for 2001. Washington, DC: Department of the Treasury, 2001.

ITC (International Trade Centre). *Trade Promotion Institutions: Monograph on the Role and Organisation of Trade Promotion.* Geneva: International Trade Centre, UNCTAD/GATT, 1986.

Jabar, Faleh A. "Postconflict Iraq: A Race for Stability, Reconstruction, and Legitimacy." *Special Report* 120. Washington, DC: US Institute of Peace, May 2004.

Jazayery, Leila. "The Migration-Development Nexus: Afghanistan Case Study." *International Migration* 40, no. 5 (2002): 231–252.

Johnson, Paula. "Diaspora Philanthropy: Existing Models, Emerging Applications." *Alliance* 10, no. 4 (2005): 8.

Kanaiaupuni, Shawn Malia, and Katherine M. Donato. "Migradollars and Mortality: The Effects of Migration on Infant Survival in Mexico." *Demography* 36, no. 3 (1999): 339–353.

Kapur, D. "Diasporas and Technology Transfer." *Journal of Human Development* 2, no. 2 (2001): 265–286.

Kastoryano, Riva. "Muslim Diaspora(s) in Western Europe." *South Atlantic Quarterly* 98, nos. 1–2 (1999): 191–202.

Kaukab, Shahana. "Situation of Migration and Potential Available to Reverse the Brain Drain—Case from Pakistan." *Public Personnel Management* 34 (2005): 103–112.

Kellogg, Katherine C., Wanda J. Orlikowski, and Joanne Yates. "Life in the Trading Zone: Structuring Coordination Across Boundaries in Postbureaucratic Organizations." *Organizational Science* 17, no. 1 (2006): 22–48

Kent, Gregory. "Diaspora Power: Network Contributions to Peacebuilding and the Transformation of War Economies." Paper presented at the seminar "Transforming War Economies," Plymouth, UK, June 16–18, 2005.

Kerlin, Janelle A., and Elizabeth Reid. "Federal Policy Shifts and Nonprofits: Foreign Policy Change and Its Effect on U.S. International NGOs." Paper presented at the 34th annual "ARNOVA Conference"; Washington, DC; November 17–19, 2005.

Khachaturyan, Arman. "Corporate Governance in Armenia: A Legal Perspective." Paper presented at the "Second International Armenian International Policy Research Group Conference on Armenia: Challenges of Sustainable Development"; World Bank; Washington, DC; January 17–18, 2004.

King, Brian E., and M. Ari Gamage. "Measuring the Value of the Ethnic Connection: Expatriate Travelers from Australia to Sri Lanka." *Journal of Travel Research* 33, no. 2 (1994): 46–51.

King, Charles, and Neil J. Melvin. "Diaspora Politics: Ethnic Linkages, Foreign Policy, and Security in Eurasia." *International Security* 24, no. 3 (1999/2000): 108–138.

King, Robert G., and Ross Levine. "Finance Entrepreneurship and Growth: Theory and Evidence." *Journal of Monetary Economics* 32, no. 3 (1993): 513–542.

Klandermans, Bert, and Dirk Oegema. "Potentials, Networks, Motivations, and Barriers: Steps Towards Participation in Social Movements." *American Sociological Review* 52, no. 4 (1987): 519–531.

Kogut, Bruce, and Udo Zander. "Knowledge of the Firm, Combinative Capabilities and the Replication of Technology." *Organization Science* 3, no. 3 (1992): 383–397.

Koser, Khalid, and Richard Black. "The End of the Refugee Cycle." In *The End of The Refugee Cycle: Refugee Repatriation and Reconstruction*, edited by Richard Black and Khalid Koser, 1–17. New York: Berghahn Books, 1999.

Koslowski, Rey, ed. *International Migration and the Globalization of Domestic Politics.* New York: Routledge, 2005a.

Koslowski, Rey. "International Migration and the Globalization of Domestic Politics: A Conceptual Framework." In *International Migration and the Globalization of Domestic Politics*, edited by Rey Koslowski, 5–32. New York: Routledge, 2005b.

Kulaksiz, Sibel, and Andrea Purdekova. "Somali Remittance Sector: A Macroeconomic Perspective." In *Remittances and Economic Development in Somalia: An Overview*, edited by Samuel Munzele Maimbo, 5–8. Social Development Papers, Conflict Prevention and Reconstruction Series. Washington, DC: World Bank, 2006. http://siteresources.worldbank.org/ EXTCPR/Resources/WP38_web.pdf?resourceurlname=WP38_web.pdf (accessed March 28, 2007).

Kunz, Egon F. "Exile and Resettlement: Refugee Theory." *International Migration Review* 15, nos. 1–2 (1981): 42–51.

Kuznetsov, Yevgeny, Adolfo Nemirovsky, and Gabriel Yoguel. "Argentina: Burgeoning Networks of Talent Abroad, Weak Institutions at Home." In *Diaspora Networks and the International Migration of Skills*, edited by Yevgeny Kuznetsov, 153–170. Washington DC: World Bank, 2006.

Kwok, Viem, and Hayne Leland. "An Economic Model of the Brain Drain." *American Economic Review* 72, no. 1 (1982): 91–100.

Kyle, David. "The Otavalo Trade Diaspora: Social Capital and Transnational Entrepreneurship." *Ethnic and Racial Studies* 22, no. 2 (1999): 422–427.

Lacroix, Sumner J., Michael Plummer, and Keun Lee, eds. *Emerging Patterns of East Asian Investment in China.* Armonk, NY: M.E. Sharpe, 1995.

Lal, Vinay. "The Politics of History on the Internet: Cyber-Diasporic Hinduism and the North American Hindu Diaspora." *Diaspora: A Journal of Transnational Studies* 8, no. 2 (1999): 137–172.

Lammers, Cornelis Jacobus, and David John Hickson, eds. *Organizations Alike and Unlike: International and Interinstitutional Studies in the Sociology of Organizations.* London: Routledge and Kegan Paul, 1979.

Landolt, Patricia. "Salvadoran Economic Transnationalism: Embedded Strategies for Household Maintenance, Immigrant Incorporation, and Entrepreneurial Expansion." *Global Networks* 1, no. 3 (2001): 217–242.

Landolt, Patricia, Lilian Autler, and Sonia Baires. "From 'Hermano Lejano' to 'Hermano Mayor': The Dialectics of Salvadoran Transnationalism." *Ethnic and Racial Studies* 22, no. 2 (1999): 290–315.

Lapointe, Michelle. "Diasporas in Caribbean Development." Washington, DC: Inter-American Dialogue and the World Bank, 2004.

Lave, Jean, and Etienne Wenger. *Situated Learning: Legitimate Peripheral Participation.* Cambridge, UK: Cambridge University Press, 1991.

Leatherman, Janie, et al. *Breaking Cycles of Violence: Conflict Prevention in Intrastate Crises.* West Hartford, CT: Kumarian Press, 1999.

Levitt, Jeremy I. *The Evolution of Deadly Conflict in Liberia.* Durham, NC: Carolina Academic Press, 2005.

Levitt, Peggy. "Transnational Migration: Taking Stock and Future Directions." *Global Networks* 1, no. 3 (2001a): 195–216.

———. *The Transnational Villagers.* Berkeley: University of California Press, 2001b.

———. "Social Remittances: A Local-Level, Migration-Driven Form of Cultural Diffusion." *International Migration Review* 32, no. 4 (1998): 926–949.

Levy, Hernan. *Rural Roads and Poverty Alleviation.* Washington, DC: World Bank, 2004.

Li, Feng, and Jing Li. *Foreign Investment in China.* New York: St. Martin's Press, 1999.

Lindley, Anna. "Migration and Financial Transfers: UK-Somalia." *Refuge* 23, no. 2 (2006a): 20–27.

———. "The Influence of Migration, Remittances and Diaspora Donations on Education in Somali Society." In *Remittances and Economic Development in Somalia: An Overview,* edited by Samuel Munzele Maimbo, 9–18. Social Development Papers, Conflict Prevention and Reconstruction Series. Washington, DC: World Bank, 2006b. http://siteresources.worldbank.org/ EXTCPR/Resources/WP38_web.pdf?resourceurlname=WP38_web.pdf (accessed March 28, 2007).

Lowell, Lindsay, and Allan Findlay. "Migration of Highly Skilled Persons from Developing Countries: Impact and Policy Responses—Synthesis Report." *International Migration Papers* 44. Geneva: International Labour Office, 2002.

Lowell, B. Lindsay, Allan Findlay, and Emma Stewart. "Brain Strain: Optimising Highly Skilled Migration from Developing Countries." *Asylum and Migration Working Paper* 3. London: Institute for Public Policy Research, 2004.

Lowell, B. Lindsay, and Rodolofo O. de la Garza. *The Developmental Role of Remittances in U.S. Latino Communities and in Latin American Countries: A Final Project Report.* Washington, DC: Inter-American Dialogue and the Tomas Rivera Policy Institute, 2000.

Lubkemann, Stephen C. *Culture in Chaos: An Anthropology of the Social Condition in War.* Chicago: University of Chicago Press, 2007.

———. "Possibilities and Perils of Indigenous Humanitarianism: A Critical Framework for Examining a 'Third Humanitarian Space.'" Paper presented at the 9th "Biennial Conference of the International Association for the Study of Forced Migration," São Paulo, Brazil, January 9–11, 2005a.

———. "Migratory Coping in Wartime Mozambique: An Anthropology of Violence and Displacement in 'Fragmented Wars.'" *Journal of Peace Research* 42, no. 4 (2005b): 493–508.

———. "Diasporas and Their Discontents—Return Without Homecoming in the Forging of Liberian and African-American Identity." *Diaspora: A Journal of Transnational Studies* 13, no. 1 (2004a): 123–128.

———. "Global Locals and Political Process in War-Torn Nations: The Liberian Diaspora in War-Making and Peace-Building." Paper presented at the annual meeting of the African Studies Association, New Orleans, November 11, 2004b.

———. "Situating Migration in Wartime and Post-War Mozambique: A Critique of Forced Migration Research." In *Categories and Contexts: Anthropological Studies in Critical Demography—IUSSP Studies in Social Demography,* edited by Simon Szreter, A. Dharmalingam, and Hania Sholkamy, 371–399. Oxford, UK: Oxford University Press, 2004c.

Lugan, Bernard. *Histoire du Maroc: Des origines à nos jours.* Paris: Criterion, 1992.

Lyon, Alynna J., and Emek M. Uçarer. "Mobilizing Ethnic Conflict: Kurdish Separatism in Germany and the PKK." In *International Migration and the Globalization of Domestic Politics,* edited by Rey Koslowski, 62–82. New York: Routledge, 2005.

Lyons, Terrence. "Diasporas and Homeland Conflict." In *Globalization, Territoriality and Conflict,* edited by Miles Kahler and Barbara F. Walter, 111–131. Cambridge, UK: Cambridge University Press, 2006.

———. "Engaging Diasporas to Promote Conflict Resolution: Transforming Hawks into Doves." Washington, DC: Working paper of the Institute of Conflict Analysis and Resolution, George Mason University, 2004.

M/D (Migration et Développement). *Evaluation capitalisation des initiatives locales, 2000.* Taroudant, Morocco: Migration et Développement, 2002.

———. "Projet Maroc: Chantier d'électrification, région de talioune." Nice: Unpublished document, 1992.

M/D and Migration et Développement Local. *Programme d'electrification décentralisée sur initiative locale.* Marseille, France, and Rabat, Morocco: M/D and Migration et Développement Local, 1996.

Maimbo, Samuel Munzele, ed. *Remittances and Economic Development in Somalia: An Overview.* Social Development Papers, Conflict Prevention and Reconstruction Series. Washington, DC: World Bank, 2006. http://siteresources. worldbank.org/EXTCPR/Resources/WP38_web.pdf?resourceurlname=WP38_ web.pdf (accessed March 28, 2007).

Maimbo, Samuel Munzele, and Dilip Ratha, eds. *Remittances: Development Impact and Future Prospects.* Washington: DC: World Bank, 2005.

Maimbo, Samuel Munzele, Mayank Patel, Walter Mahler, and Hussein Siad. "Financial Sector Development in Somalia: Central Banking and Financial Services in an Uncertain Environment." In *Remittances and Economic Development in Somalia: An Overview*, edited by Samuel Munzele Maimbo, 38–49. Social Development Papers, Conflict Prevention and Reconstruction Series. Washington, DC: World Bank, 2006. http://siteresources.worldbank.org/ EXTCPR/Resources/WP38_web.pdf?resourceurlname=WP38_web.pdf (accessed March 28, 2007).

Manda, Gilbert. "Brain Drain or Brain Gain?" *New African* 435 (2004): 74.

Mandel, Maud S. *In the Aftermath of Genocide: Armenians and Jews in Twentieth Century France.* Durham, NC: Duke University Press, 2003.

Marcus, Aliza. "Kurdish TV from Britain Is Nationalist Voice." *Reuters World Service*, May 15, 1995.

Margolis, Mac, with Sudip Mazumdar et al. "Brain Gain; Sending Workers Abroad Doesn't Mean Squandering Minds." *Newsweek,* March 8, 2004: 30.

Martin, Susan F. "Remittance Flows and Impact." Paper presented at the regional conference "Remittances as a Development Tool"; organized by the Multilateral Investment Fund and the Inter-American Development Bank; Washington, DC; May 17–18, 2001. http://www.iadb.org/mif/v2/files/ susanmartin.doc (accessed January 9, 2006).

Massey, Douglas, Luin Goldring, and Jorge Durand. "Continuities in Transnational Migration: An Analysis of Nineteen Mexican Communities." *American Journal of Sociology* 99, no. 6 (1994): 1492–1533.

Massey, Douglas S., et al. *Worlds in Motion: Understanding International Migration at the End of the Millennium.* New York: Oxford University Press, 1999.

Matsouka, Atusko, and John Sorenson. *Ghosts and Shadows: Construction of Identity and Community in an African Diaspora.* Toronto: University of Toronto Press, 2001.

McCaffrey, Lawrence J. *The Irish Catholic Diaspora in America.* Washington, DC: Catholic University Press, 1997.

McSpadden, Lucia Ann. "Negotiating Masculinity in the Reconstruction of Social Place: Eritrean and Ethiopian Refugees in the United States and Sweden." In *Engendering Forced Migration: Theory and Practice*, edited by Doreen Marie Indra, 242–260. New York: Berghahn Books, 1999.

Mernissi, Fatema. *ONG rurales de haut-atlas: les ait débrouille*. Marrakech: Editions le Fennec, 1998.

Meyer, Jean-Baptiste. "Network Approach Versus Brain Drain: Lessons from the Diaspora." *International Migration* 39, no. 5 (2001): 91–110.

Meyer, John-Baptiste, and Mercy Brown. "Scientific Diasporas: A New Approach to the Brain Drain." Paper presented at the "World Conference on Science," UNESCO-ICSU. Budapest, June 26–July 1, 1999. http://www.unesco.org/most/meyer.htm (accessed January 19, 2008).

Meyer, John-Baptiste, et al. "Turning Brain Drain into Brain Gain: The Colombian Experience of the Diaspora Option." *Science-Technology and Society*, no. 2 (1997). http://sansa.nrf.ac.za/documents/stsjbm.pdf (accessed January 9, 2006).

Miller, Donald E., and Lorna Touryan Miller. *Armenia: Portraits of Survival and Hope*. Berkeley: University of California Press, 2003.

Milman, Ady, Arieh Reichel, and Abraham Pizam. "The Impact of Tourism on Ethnic Attitudes: The Israeli-Egypt Connection." *Journal of Travel Research* 29, no. 2 (1990): 45–50.

Minear, Larry. *The Humanitarian Enterprise: Dilemmas and Discoveries*. Bloomfield, CT: Kumarian Press, 2002.

Ministry of External Affairs (India). "Report of the High Level Committee on the Indian Diaspora." New Delhi: Ministry of External Affairs, 2001.

Ministry of the Interior, Kingdom of Morocco, and AFME (Agence Française pour la Maitrise de l'Energie). *Programme de pre-electrification rurale en coopération franco-marocaine*. Rabat, Morocco: Kingdom of Morocco, Ministry of the Interior, 1987.

Minoglou, Ioanna Pepelasis, and Helen Louri. "Diaspora Entrepreneurial Networks in the Black Sea and Greece, 1870–1917." *Journal of European Economic History* 26, no. 1 (1997): 69–105.

Mishra, Prachi. "Emigration and Brain Drain: Evidence from the Caribbean." *IMF Working Paper* 06/25. Washington, DC: International Monetary Fund, 2006.

Missaoui, Rafik. *Le secteur informel de l'énergie dans les pays en développement: Cas du Maghreb*. Doctoral diss., Paris École Centrale, 1996.

Miyagiwa, Kaz. "Scale Economies in Education and the Brain Drain Problem." *International Economic Review* 32, no. 3 (1991): 743–759.

Mohamoud, Awil A. *Mobilising African Diaspora for the Promotion of Peace in Africa*. Amsterdam: African Diaspora Policy Centre, 2005. http://www.diaspora-centre.org/documents/MobilisingAfricanDiaspora.pdf (accessed March 28, 2007).

Moini, Abdol H. "An Inquiry into Successful Exporting: An Empirical Investigation Using a Three-Stage Model." *Journal of Small Business Management* 33, no. 3 (1995): 9–25.

Mora, Jorge, and J. Edward Taylor. "Determinants of Migration, Destination, and Sector Choice: Disentangling Individual, Household, and Community Effects." In *International Migration, Remittances and the Brain Drain*, edited by Çağlar Özden and Maurice Schiff, 21–52. Washington, DC: World Bank, 2005.

Moran, Mary. *Liberia: The Violence of Democracy*. Philadelphia: University of Pennsylvania Press, 2006.

———. "Time and Place in the Anthropology of Events: A Diaspora Perspective on the Liberian Transition." Special Issue: Warscape Ethnography in West Africa, edited by Daniel Hoffman and Stephen C. Lubkemann. *Anthropological Quarterly* 78, no. 2 (2005): 457–464.

Moran, Theodore H., Edward M. Graham, and Magnus Blomstrom. *Does Foreign*

Investment Promote Development? New Methods, Outcomes, and Policy Approaches. Washington, DC: Institute for International Economics, 2005. ·

Morarjee, Rachel. "Karzai Aims to Lure Investors into 'Needy, Greedy Market,'" *Financial Times,* May 10, 2006: 2.

Morisset, Jacques. "Does a Country Need a Promotion Agency to Attract Foreign Direct Investment?: A Small Analytical Model Applied to 58 Countries." *World Bank Policy Research Working Paper* 3028. Washington, DC: World Bank, 2003.

Morisset, Jacques, and Kelly Andrews-Johnson. "The Effectiveness of Promotion Agencies at Attracting Foreign Direct Investment." *Foreign Investment Advisory Service Occasional Paper* 16. Washington, DC: International Finance Corporation and Multinational Investment Guarantee Agency, 2004.

Mort, Gillian Sullivan, Jay Weerawardena, and Kashonia Carnegie. "Social Entrepreneurship: Towards Conceptualization." *International Journal of Nonprofit and Voluntary Sector Marketing* 8, no. 1 (2003): 76–88.

Mossadeq, Fahim. "Electrification rurale décentralisée: Un programme pilote est prévu pour 3600 foyers." *L'Economiste,* January 11, 1996a. http://www. leconomiste.com (accessed February 5, 2005).

———. "La réorganisation de l'ONE démarre." *L'Economiste,* March 7, 1996b. http://www.leconomiste.com (accessed February 5, 2005).

Moya, Jose C. "Immigrants and Associations: A Global and Historical Perspective." *Journal of Ethnic and Migration Studies* 31, no. 5 (2005): 833–864.

Multilateral Investment Guarantee Agency. "2005 IPA Performance Benchmarking Program: Investor Inquiry Handling (Overview of the Study and Analysis of the Results)." Washington, DC: World Bank, 2005.

Mundra, Kusum. "Immigration and International Trade: A Semi-parametric Empirical Investigation." *Journal of International Trade & Economic Development* 14, no. 1 (2005): 65–91.

Natsios, Andrew. "Reconstruction in Iraq." Remarks before the Chaldean American Chamber of Commerce, West Bloomfield, MI, September 9, 2005. http://www.usaid.gov/press/speeches/2005/sp050909.html (accessed February 11, 2006).

Nenova, Tatiana, and Tim Harford. "Anarchy and Invention: How Does Somalia's Private Sector Cope Without Government?" *Public Policy for the Private Sector* 280. Washington, DC: Private Sector Development Vice Presidency, World Bank Group, 2004. http://rru.worldbank.org/Documents/publicpolicyjournal/280-nenova-harford.pdf (accessed March 28, 2007).

Neuman, Gerald L. *Strangers to the Constitution: Immigrants, Borders, and Fundamental Law.* Princeton, NJ: Princeton University Press, 1996.

Newland, Kathleen, and Erin Patrick. *Beyond Remittances: The Role of Diasporas in Poverty Reduction in Their Country of Origin.* Washington, DC: Migration Policy Institute, 2004.

Nuijten, Monique. *In the Name of the Land: Organization, Transnationalism, and the Culture of the State in a Mexican Ejido.* Wageningen, Netherlands: Ponsen en Looijen, 1998.

Nyberg-Sorenson, Ninna. "Migration and Development: Transnational Networks, Remittances, Civil Society and Human Capital Potential." Paper presented at the International Forum on Remittances, Washington, DC, June 30, 2005.

———. "Migrant Remittances as a Development Tool: The Case of Morocco." *Migration Policy Research Working Paper Series* 2. Geneva: IOM, 2004a.

———. "The Development Dimension of Migrant Remittances." *Migration Policy*

Research Working Paper Series 1. Geneva: IOM, 2004b. http://www.iom.int//
DOCUMENTS/PUBLICATION/EN/mpr1.pdf (accessed January 9, 2006).
———. "The Development Dimension of Migrant Transfers." *DIIS Working Paper*
16. Copenhagen: Danish Institute of International Studies, 2004c.
Nyberg-Sorensen, Ninna, Nicholas Van Hear, and Poul Engberg-Pedersen. "The
Migration-Development Nexus: Evidence and Policy Options." *IOM Migration
Research Series* 8. Geneva: IOM, 2002.
O'Grada, Cormac. *A Rocky Road: The Irish Economy Since the 1920s.* Manchester,
UK: The Manchester University Press, 1997.
Ogden, Denise, James R. Ogden, and Hope Jensen Schau. "Exploring the Impact of
Culture and Acculturation on Consumer Purchase Decisions: Toward a
Microcultural Perspective." *Academy of Marketing Science Review* no. 3
(2004): 1–3.
Ögelman, Nedim. "Immigrant Organizations and the Globalization of Turkey's
Domestic Politics." In *International Migration and the Globalization of
Domestic Politics*, edited by Rey Koslowski, 33–61. New York: Routledge,
2005.
Olesen, Henrik. "Migration, Return and Development: An Institutional Perspective."
In *The Migration-Development Nexus*, edited by Nicholas Van Hear and Ninna
Nyberg-Sorensen, 133–158. Geneva: IOM, 2003.
ONE (Office National de l'Electricité). Home page. http://www.one.org.ma
(accessed November 15, 2004).
———. *Le Programme d'Electrification Rurale Globale: L'Electricité pour tous.*
Casablanca: ONE, 2002.
———. *PERG: Programme d'Electrification Rurale Globale. Megawatt: La lettre
des cadres de l'Office National de l'Electricité.* Casablanca: ONE, 1999.
Opiniano, Jeremaiah, and Tricia Anne Castro. "Promoting Knowledge Transfer
Activities Through Diaspora Networks: A Pilot Study of the Philippines." In
*Converting Migration Drains into Gains: Harnessing the Resources of
Overseas Professionals*, edited by Clay Wescott and Jennifer M. Brinkerhoff,
54–71. Manila: Asian Development Bank, 2006.
Orlikowski, Wanda J. "Knowing in Practice: Enacting a Collective Capability in
Distributed Organizing." *Organization Science* 13, no. 3 (2002): 249–273.
Orozco, Manuel. "International Flows of Remittances: Cost, Competition and
Financial Access in Latin America and the Caribbean—Toward an Industry
Scorecard." Report presented at the meeting "Remittances and Transnational
Families"; sponsored by the Multilateral Fund of the Inter-American
Development Bank (IADB) and the Annie E. Casey Foundation; Washington,
DC; May 12, 2006a.
———. *Remittances and the Local Economy in Latin America: Between Hardship
and Hope.* Washington, DC: Inter-American Dialogue (study commissioned by
IADB, July 2006b).
———. *International Financial Flows and Worker Remittances: Issues and Lessons.*
Washington, DC: Inter-American Dialogue (commissioned by United Nations),
2005a.
———. *Transnational Engagement, Remittances and Their Relationship to
Development in Latin America and the Caribbean.* Washington, DC: Institute
for the Study of International Migration, Georgetown University, July 2005b.
———. *Hometown Associations and Their Present and Future Partnerships: New
Development Opportunities?* Washington, DC: Inter-American Dialogue (com-
missioned by US Agency for International Development), 2003.

―――. "Globalization and Migration: The Impact of Family Remittances in Latin America." In *Approaches to Increasing the Productive Value of Remittances*, edited by Inter-American Foundation, 19–38. Washington, DC: Inter-American Foundation, 2001.

―――. "Latino Hometown Associations as Agents of Development in Latin America." Washington, DC: Inter-American Dialogue/Tomas Rivera Policy Institute, 2000.

―――, with Rachel Fedewa. "Regional Integration? Trends and Patterns of Remittance Flows Within South East Asia. South East Asia Report." Washington, DC: Inter-American Dialogue, August 2005.

Orozco, Manuel, Lindsay Lowell, Micah Bump, and Rachel Fedewa. "Transnational Engagement, Remittances and Their Relationship to Development in Latin America and the Caribbean." Final report submitted to the Rockefeller Foundation for grant 2003 GI 050. Washington, DC: Institute for the Study of International Migration, Georgetown University, 2005.

Orozco, Manuel, with Michelle Lapointe. "Mexican Hometown Associations and Development Opportunities." *Journal of International Affairs* 57, no. 2 (2004): 31–49.

Orozco, Manuel, with Micah Bump, Rachel Fedewa, and Katya Sienkiewicz. *Diasporas, Development, and Transnational Integration: Ghanaians in the US, UK, and Germany*. Washington, DC: Institute for the Study of International Migration, Georgetown University, and the Inter-American Dialogue. Report commissioned for Citizens International for US Agency for International Development, October 3, 2005.

Ostergaard-Nielsen, Eva. "Diasporas and Conflict Resolution: Part of the Problem or Part of the Solution?" Copenhagen: Danish Institute of International Studies, 2006. http://www.diis.dk/graphics/Publications/Briefs2006/%F8stergaard-nielsen_diaspora_conflict_resolution.pdf (accessed July 18, 2007).

Ostrom, Elinor. *Governing the Commons: The Evolution of Institutions for Collective Action*. New York: Cambridge University Press, 1990.

Özden, Çağlar, and Maurice Schiff, eds. *International Migration, Remittances and the Brain Drain*. Washington, DC: World Bank, 2005.

Özerdem, Alpaslan. "The Mountain Tsunami: Afterthoughts on the Kashmir Earthquake." *Third World Quarterly* 27, no. 3 (2006): 397–419.

Page, John, and Richard H. Adams, Jr. "International Migration, Remittances, and Poverty in Developing Countries." *Policy Research Working Paper* 3179. Washington DC: World Bank, 2004.

Palumbo, Frederick, and Ira Teich. "Market Segmentation Based on Level of Acculturation." *Marketing Intelligence & Planning* 22, no. 4 (2004): 472–484.

Pandey, Abhishek, Alok Aggarwal, Richard Devane, and Yevgeny Kuznetsov. "The Indian Diaspora: A Unique Case?" In *Diaspora Networks and the International Migration of Skills*, edited by Yevgeny Kuznetsov, 71–97. Washington DC: World Bank, 2006.

Panossian, Razmik. "Between Ambivalence and Intrusion: Politics and Identity in Armenia-Diaspora Relations." *Diaspora: A Journal of Transnational Studies* 7, no. 2 (1998): 149–196.

Parameswaran, Ravi, and R. Mohan Pisharodi. "Assimilation Effects in Country Image Research." *International Marketing Review* 19, no. 3 (2002): 259–278.

Paul, Rachel Anderson. "Grassroots Mobilization and Diaspora Politics: Armenian Interest Groups and the Role of Collective Memory." *Nationalism and Ethnic Politics* 6, no. 1 (2000): 24–47.

Pellegrino, Adela. "Trends in Latin American Skilled Migration: 'Brain Drain' or 'Brain Exchange'?" *International Migration* 39, no. 5 (2001): 111–132.

Phillips, David L. *Losing Iraq: Inside the Postwar Reconstruction Fiasco*. Boulder, CO: Westview Press, 2005.

Pieke, Frank N., Nicholas Van Hear, and Anna Lindley. *Synthesis Study: Informal Remittance Systems in African, Caribbean and Pacific Countries*. Oxford, UK: Economic and Society Research Council (ESRC) Centre on Migration, Policy and Society (COMPAS) for Department of International Development (DFID) UK, European Community's Poverty Reduction Effectiveness Programme, and Deloitte & Touch, 2005.

Pires-Hester, Laura. "The Emergence of Bilateral Diaspora Ethnicity Among Cape Verdean–Americans." In *The African Diaspora: African Origins and New World Identities*, edited by Isidore Okpewho, Carole Boyce Davies, and Ali A. Mazrui, 485–503. Bloomington: Indiana University Press, 1999.

Polanyi, Michael. *The Tacit Dimension*. New York: Doubleday, 1967.

Popkin, Eric. "Transnational Migration and Development in Postwar Peripheral States: An Examination of Guatemalan and Salvadoran State Linkages with Their Migrant Populations in Los Angeles." *Current Sociology* 51, nos. 3–4 (2003): 347–374.

Poros, Maritsa V. "The Role of Migrant Networks in Linking Local Labor Markets: The Case of Asian Indian Migration to New York and London." *Global Networks* 1, no. 3 (2001): 243–260.

Portes, Alejandro. "Globalization from Below: The Rise of Transnational Communities." In *The Ends of Globalization: Bringing Society Back In*, edited by Don Kalb, Marci van der Land, and Richard Staring, 253–270. Boulder, CO: Rowman & Littlefield, 1999.

Portes, Alejandro, and Julia Sensenbrenner. "Embeddedness and Immigration: Notes on the Social Determinants of Economic Action." *American Journal of Sociology* 98, no. 6 (1993): 1320–1350.

Portes, Alejandro, Cristina Escobar, and Alexandria Walton Radford. "Immigrant Transnational Organizations and Development: A Comparative Study." Princeton, NJ: Center for Migration and Development, Princeton University. Unpublished manuscript, 2005.

Pottier, Johan. "The 'Self' in Self-Repatriation: Closing Down Mugunga Camp in Eastern Zaire." In *The End of the Refugee Cycle*, edited by Richard Black and Khalid Koser, 142–170. New York: Berghahn Books, 1999.

Pries, Ludger. "The Approach of Transnational Social Spaces: Responding to New Configurations of the Social and the Spacial." In *New Transnational Social Spaces: International Migration and Transnational Companies in the Early Twenty-First Century*, edited by Ludger Pries, 3–33. London: Routledge, 2001.

Rai, Amit S. "India On-Line: Electronic Bulletin Boards and the Construction of Diasporic Hindu Identity." *Diaspora: A Journal of Transnational Studies* 4, no. 1 (1995): 31–57.

Ramamurti, Ravi. "Developing Countries and MNEs: Extending and Enriching the Research Agenda." *Journal of International Business Studies* 35, no. 4 (2004): 277–285.

Ratha, Dilip. "Workers' Remittances: An Important Source of External Development Finance." In *Remittances: Development Impact and Future Prospects*, edited by Samuel Munzele Maimbo and Dilip Ratha, 19–52. Washington, DC: World Bank, 2005.

———. "Workers' Remittances: An Important and Stable Source of External

Development Finance." In *Global Development Finance 2003*, edited by the International Monetary Fund, 157–175. Washington DC: International Monetary Fund, 2003.

Redding, S. Gordon. *The Spirit of Chinese Capitalism*. Berlin: Walter DeGruyter, 1990.

Reid, Elizabeth, and Janelle A. Kerlin. "The International Nonprofit Subsector in the United States: International Understanding, International Development and Assistance, and International Affairs." Washington, DC: Urban Institute, 2005.

Reid, Stan D. "Information Acquisition and Export Entry Decisions in Small Firms." *Journal of Business Research* 12, no. 2 (1984): 153–155.

Reno, William. "The Business of War in Liberia." *Current History* 95, no. 601 (1996): 211–215.

Renshon, Stanley A. "Dual Citizens in America: An Issue of Vast Proportions and Broad Signficance." Washington, DC: Center for Immigration Studies Backgrounder, 2000. http://www.cis.org/articles/2000/back700.html#20 (accessed November 28, 2007).

Republic of Ireland, Central Statistics Office. *Annual Migration Estimates, 2005*. Dublin: Republic of Ireland, Central Statistics Office, 2005.

Richards, Paul. *Fighting for the Rainforest: War, Youth and Resources in Sierra Leone*. Oxford, UK: James Currey, 1996.

Richards, Paul, et al. "Community Cohesion in Liberia: A Rapid Post-War Assessment." *Social Development Papers, Conflict Prevention and Reconstruction* 21. Washington DC: World Bank, 2005.

Riddle, Liesl. "The Social Embeddedness of Export Promotion Organization in the Turkish Clothing Industry." Ph.D. diss., University of Texas at Austin, 2001.

Riddle, Liesl A., and Kate Gillespie. "Information Sources for New Ventures in the Turkish Clothing Export Industry." *Small Business Economics* 20, no. 1 (2003): 105–120.

Roberts, Bryan R., Reanne Frank, and Fernando Lozano-Ascencio. "Transnational Migrant Communities and Mexican Migration to the United States." *Ethnic and Racial Studies* 22, no. 2 (1999): 240–266.

Roberts, Bryan W., et al. *Remittances to Armenia*. Yerevan, Armenia: USAID-Armenia, October 1, 2004.

Robinson, Jenny. *Development and Displacement*. Oxford, UK: Oxford University Press, 2002.

Rosenau, James. *Distant Proximities: Dynamics Beyond Globalization*. Princeton, NJ: Princeton University Press, 2003.

Ross, Jack C. *An Assembly of Good Fellows: Voluntary Associations in History*. Westport, CT: Greenwood Press, 1976.

Russell, Sharon S., and Michael S. Teitelbaum. *International Migration and International Trade*. Washington, DC: World Bank, 1992.

Safdari, Cyrus, Nancy J. Scannell, and Rubina Ohanian. "A Statistical Approach to Peer-Groupings: The Case of Banks in Armenia." *Journal of American Academy of Business, Cambridge* 6, no. 2 (2005): 24–31.

Safran, William. "Diasporas in Modern Societies: Myths of Homeland and Return." *Diaspora: A Journal of Transnational Studies* 1, no. 1 (1991): 83–99.

Salamon, Lester M. "Of Market Failure, Voluntary Failure, and Third-Party Government: Toward a Theory of Government–Nonprofit Relations in the Modern Welfare State." *Journal of Voluntary Action Research* 16, nos. 1–2 (1987): 29–49.

Sawyer, Amos. *The Emergence of Autocracy in Liberia: Tragedy and Challenge*. San Francisco, CA: Institute of Contemporary Studies Press, 1992.

Saxenian, AnnaLee. "From Brain Drain to Brain Circulation: Transnational Communities and Regional Upgrading in India and China." Berkeley: Univeristy of California at Berkeley, School of Information, 2005. http://www.sims.berkeley.edu/~anno/papers/ (accessed January 6, 2006).

———. "Brain Circulation: How High-Skill Immigration Makes Everyone Better Off." *The Brookings Review* 20, no. 1 (2002a): 28–31.

———. "Transnational Communities and the Evolution of Global Production Networks: The Cases of Taiwan, China, and India." *Industry and Innovation* 9, no. 3 (2002b): 183–204.

———. *Silicon Valley's New Immigrant Entrepreneurs*. San Francisco: Public Policy Institute of California, 1999.

Schiff, Maurice. "Brain Gain: Claims About Its Size and Impact on Welfare and Growth Are Greatly Exaggerated." In *International Migration, Remittances and the Brain Drain*, edited by Çağlar Özden and Maurice Schiff, 201–226. Washington, DC: World Bank, 2005.

Schrecker, Ted, and Ronald Labonte. "Taming the Brain Drain: A Challenge for Public Health Systems in Southern Africa." *International Journal of Occupational and Environmental Health* 10, no. 4 (2004): 409–415.

Schwartz, Jordan, Shelly Hahn, and Ian Bannon. "The Private Sector's Role in the Provision of Infrastructure in Post-Conflict Countries: Patterns and Options." *Social Development Papers, Conflict Prevention and Reconstruction* 16. Washington, DC: World Bank, 2004.

Seguin, Beatrice, Leah State, and Peter A. Singer. "Scientific Diasporas as an Option for Brain Drain: Recirculating Knowledge for Development." *International Journal of Biotechnology* 8, nos, 1–2 (2006): 78–88.

Seiranyan, Lilit. "Lincy Foundation in Armenia." *Association of Investigative Journalists: Hetq Online,* October 8, 2001a. http://www.hetq.am/am/h-1001-lins1.html.

———. "Loan Programs of Lincy Foundation in Armenia." *Association of Investigative Journalists: Hetq Online*, December 11, 2001b. http://www. hetq.am/am/h-1101-lins2.html.

Seringhaus, F.H. Rolf. "Export Promotion in Developing Countries: Status and Prospects." *Journal of Global Marketing* 6, no. 4 (1993): 7–29.

———. "Export Promotion: The Role and Impact of Government Services." *Irish Marketing Review* 2 (1987): 106–116.

———. "Impact of Government Export Marketing Assistance" *International Marketing Review* 3, no. 2 (1986): 55–66.

———. "Government Export Marketing Assistance to Small and Medium-Sized Ontario Manufacturing Firms: The Role and Impact of Trade Missions on Firm's Offshore Market Involvement." Ph.D. diss., New York University, 1984.

Seringhaus, F.H. Rolf, and Guenther Botschen. "Cross-National Comparison of Export Promotion Services: The Views of Canadian and Austrian Companies." *Journal of International Business* 22, no. 1 (1991): 115–134.

Seringhaus, F.H. Rolf, and Philip J. Rosson. *Government Export Promotion: A Global Perspective*. London: Routledge, 1990.

Sfeir-Younis, Alfredo. "The Spiritual Entrepreneur." *Reflections* 3, no. 3 (2002): 43–45.

Shain, Yossi. "The Role of Diasporas in Conflict Perpetuation or Resolution." *SAIS Review* 22, no. 2 (2002): 115–144.

————. *Marketing the American Creed Abroad: Diasporas in the US and Their Homelands.* Cambridge, UK: Cambridge University Press, 1999.

————. "Ethnic Diasporas and US Foreign Policy." *Political Science Quarterly* 109, no. 5 (1994–1995): 811–841.

————. "Democrats and Secessionists: US Diasporas as Regime Destabilizers." In *International Migration and Security,* edited by M. Weiner, 287–322. Boulder, CO: Westview, 1993.

Shandy, Dianna J. "Global Transactions: Sudanese Refugees Sending Money Home." *Refuge* 23, no. 2 (2006): 28–35.

Sheffer, Gabriel. *Diaspora Politics: At Home Abroad.* Cambridge, UK: Cambridge University Press, 2003.

————. "A New Field of Study: Modern Diasporas in International Politics." In *Modern Diasporas in International Politics,* edited by Gabriel Sheffer, 1–15. London and Sydney: Croom Helm, 1986.

Smillie, Ian, ed. *Patronage or Partnership: Local Capacity Building in Humanitarian Crisis.* Bloomfield, CT: Kumarian Press, 2001.

Smith, Constance E., and Anne E. Freedman. *Voluntary Associations: Perspectives on the Literature.* Cambridge, MA: Harvard University Press, 1972.

Smith, Michael Peter. *Transnational Urbanism: Locating Globalization.* Oxford, UK: Blackwell, 2001.

Smith, Robert C. "Migrant Membership as an Instituted Process: Transnationalization, the State and the Extra-Territorial Conduct of Mexican Politics." In *International Migration and the Globalization of Domestic Politics,* edited by Rey Koslowski, 105–129. New York: Routledge, 2005.

————. "Los ausentes siempre presentes: The Imagining, Making and Politics of a Transnational Community Between Ticuani, Puebla, Mexico, and New York City." PhD diss., Columbia University, New York, 1995.

Sökefeld, Martin. "Alevism Online: Re-imagining a Community in Virtual Space." *Diaspora: A Journal of Transnational Studies* 11, no. 1 (2002): 85–123.

Somers, Margaret, and Fred Block. "From Poverty to Perversity: Ideas, Markets, and Institutions over 200 Years of Welfare Debate." *American Sociological Review* 70, no. 2 (2005): 260–287.

Stark, Oded. "Rethinking Brain Drain." *World Development* 32, no. 1 (2004): 15–22.

Stark, Oded, Christian Helmenstein, and Alexia Prskawetz. "A Brain Gain with a Brain Drain." *Economics Letters* 55, no. 2 (1997): 227–234.

Stigter, Elca, and Alessandro Monsutti. "Transnational Networks: Recognizing a Regional Reality." AREU Briefing Paper Series. Kabul: Afghanistan Research and Evaluation Unit, 2005.

Sweeney, Paul. *The Celtic Tiger: Ireland's Economic Miracle Explained.* Dublin: Oak Tree Press, 1996.

Taylor, J. Edward. "Earnings and Mobility of Legal and Illegal Immigrant Workers in Agriculture." *American Journal of Agricultural Economics* 74, no. 4 (1992): 889–896.

Taylor, J. Edward, et al. "International Migration and Community Development." *Population Index* 62, no. 3 (1996a): 397–418.

————. "International Migration and National Development." *Population Index* 62, no. 2 (1996b): 181–212.

Thomas-Hope, Elizabeth. "Skilled Labour Migration from Developing Countries: Study on the Caribbean Region." *International Migration Paper* 50. Geneva: ILO International Migration Programme, 2002.

Thompson, John, Geoff Alvy, and Ann Lees. "Social Entrepreneurship—A New

Look at the People and the Potential." *Management Decision* 38, no. 5 (2000): 328–338.

Tölölyan, Kachig. "Rethinking Diaspora(s): Stateless Power in the Transnational Moment. *Diaspora: A Journal of Transnational Studies* 1, no. 1 (1996): 3–36.

Torres, Federico, and Yevgeny Kuznetsov. "Mexico: Leveraging Migrants' Capital to Develop Hometown Communities." In *Diaspora Networks and the International Migration of Skills*, edited by Yevgeny Kuznetsov, 99–128. Washington DC: World Bank, 2006.

Triki, Latif. "Déficit électrique: Des délestages jusqu'au deuxième semestre 1994." *L'Economiste*, October 13, 1994. http://www.leconomiste.com (accessed February 5, 2005).

———. "Electricité: Calendrier des coupures à Ain Sébaa-Hay Mohammadi." *L'Economiste*, September 9, 1993a. http://www.leconomiste.com (accessed February 5, 2005).

———. "Electricité: Le ministre de l'Energie et des mines 'dénone les reticences des industriels' à la réorganisation." *L'Economiste*, January 7, 1993b. http://www.leconomiste.com (accessed February 5, 2005).

Turkish Daily News. "Limits on Kurdish Movies and Music Lifted." *Turkish Daily News,* June 13, 2006. http://www.turkishdailynews.com.tr/article.php?enewsid=46049&mailtofriend=1 (accessed July 23, 2006).

Uduku, Ola. "The Socio-economic Basis of a Diaspora Community: Igbo bu ike." *Review of African Political Economy* 92, no. 29 (2002): 301–342.

Ul Haque, Nadeem, and Se-Jik Kim. "Human Capital Flight: Impact of Migration on Income and Growth." *IMF Staff Papers* 42. Washington, DC: International Monetary Fund, 1995.

UNDP (United Nations Development Programme). *Human Development Report 2006. Beyond Scarcity: Power, Poverty, and the Global Water Crisis*. New York: UN Development Programme, 2006. http://hdr.undp.org/hdr2006/statistics/indices/tools.cfm (accessed June 11, 2007).

———. "The Potential Role of Remittances in Achieving the Millennium Development Goals—An Exploration." Roundtable on Remittances and the MDGs. New York: UNDP, October 10, 2005. http://tcdc2.undp.org/SSC_TEST/Take2/asp/Remittances_Oct102005B.pdf (accessed June 19, 2007).

US Agency for International Development (USAID). "Elections Assistance." Washington, DC: USAID, December 29, 2005. http://www.usaid.gov/iraq/accomplishments/elections.html (accessed May 30, 2007).

———. *Foreign Aid in the National Interest: Promoting Freedom, Security, and Opportunity*. Washington, DC: USAID, 2002.

USAID, Armenia. *Strategy for 2004–2008*. Yerevan, Armenia: USAID, 2004.

US Census Bureau. *2000 Census of Population and Housing*. Washington, DC: Census Bureau, 2000. http://www.census.gov/prod/cen2000/ (accessed June 18, 2007).

US Committee for Refugees. *World Refugee Survey 2005*. Washington, DC: US Committee for Refugees, 2006. http://www.refugees.org/data/wrs/06/docs/principal_sources_of_refugees.pdf (accessed July 28, 2006).

US Department of State. 2005. "Strategic Consultations on Afghan Refugees." Remarks by Richard Greene, acting assistant secretary of state, Bureau of Population and Migration, October 7. http://www.us-mission.ch/Press2005/1007Greene.htm.

US Office of Immigration Statistics. *2005 Yearbook of Immigration Statistics*. Washington, DC: US Office of Immigration Statistics, 2006. http://www.uscis.gov/graphics/shared/statistics/yearbook/index.htm (accessed July 28, 2006).

van de Walle, Dominique. *Do Basic Services and Poverty Programs Reach Morocco's Poor?* Washington, DC: World Bank, 2004.

Van Hear, Nicholas. *New Diasporas: The Mass Exodus, Dispersal, and Regrouping of Migrant Communities.* Seattle: University of Washington Press, 1998.

Van Hear, Nicholas, Frank Pieke, and Steven Vertovec, with assistance of Anna Lindley, Barbara Jettinger, and Meera Balarajan. "The Contribution of UK-Based Diasporas to Development and Poverty Reduction." Oxford, UK: Economic and Society Research Council (ESRC) Centre on Migration, Policy and Society, University of Oxford (for the Department for International Development), 2004.

Verrier, Michel. "From the Bush to the Television Studio: A Trump Card for Turkey's Kurdish Guerillas." *Le Monde Diplomatique*, December 13, 1997. http://mondediplo.com/1997/12/pkk (accessed July 23, 2006).

Vertovec, Steven. "Transnational Networks and Skilled Labour Migration." Paper presented at the conference "Ladenburger Diskurs 'Migration' Gottlieb Daimier-und Karl Benz-Stiftung," Ladenburg, Germany, February 14–15, 2002.

Vidal, Jean-Pierre. "The Effect of Emigration on Human Capital Formation." *Journal of Population Economics* 11, no. 4 (1998): 589–600.

von Hippel, Eric. "Sticky Information and the Locus of Problem Solving: Implications for Innovation." *Management Science* 40, no. 4 (1994): 429–439.

Waldo, Mohamed Abshir. "Somali Remittances: Myth and Reality." In *Remittances and Economic Development in Somalia: An Overview*, edited by Samuel Munzele Maimbo, 19–23. Social Development Papers Conflict Prevention and Reconstruction Series. Washington, DC: World Bank, 2006. http://siteresources.worldbank.org/EXTCPR/Resources/WP38_web.pdf?resourceurlname=WP38_web.pdf (accessed March 28, 2007).

Wallace, Sherri L. "Social Entrepreneurship: The Role of Social Purpose Enterprises in Facilitating Community Economic Development." *Journal of Developmental Entrepreneurship* 4, no. 2 (1999): 153–174.

Wang, Hongying. *Weak States, Strong Networks: The Institutional Dynamics of Foreign Direct Investment in China.* Oxford, UK: Oxford University Press, 2001.

Wee, Chow Hou, David T.E. Lim, and Gilbert Y.W. Tan. "The Image of Countries as Locations for Investment." In *Product-Country Images: Impact and Role in International Marketing*, edited by Nicolas G. Papadopoulous and Louise A. Heslop. New York: International Business Press, 1992.

Weiner, Myron. "Introduction: Security, Stability, and International Migration." In *International Migration and Security*, edited by M. Weiner, 1–35. Boulder, CO: Westview, 1993.

Wells, Louis T., and Alvin G. Wint. "Marketing a Country: Promotion as a Tool for Attracting Foreign Investment." *Foreign Investment Advisory Service Occasional Paper* 13. Washington, DC: International Finance Corporation, the Multinational Investment Guarantee Agency, 2000.

———. "The Public-Private Choice: The Case of Marketing a Country to Investors." *World Development* 19, no. 7 (1990): 749–761.

Wescott, Clay, and Jennifer M. Brinkerhoff, eds. *Converting Migration Drains into Gains: Harnessing the Resources of Overseas Professionals.* Manila: Asian Development Bank, 2006. http://www.adb.org/Documents/Books/Converting-Migration-Drains-Gains (accessed January 19, 2008).

Williams, Allan M., and Vladimir Baláz. "What Human Capital, Which Migrants?

Returned Skilled Migration to Slovakia from the UK." *International Migration Review* 39, no. 2 (2005): 439–468.

Wint, Alvin G. "Investment Horizons: Afghanistan: An Analysis of Foreign Direct Investment Costs and Conditions in Four Industries." Washington, DC: World Bank, 2005.

———. "Promoting Transnational Investment: Organizing to Service Approved Investors." *Transnational Corporations* 2, no. 1 (1993): 71–90.

World Bank. *Global Economic Prospects (GEP): Economic Implications of Remittances and Migration.* Washington, DC: World Bank, 2006a.

———. *Protecting Investors, Doing Business.* Washington, DC: World Bank, 2006b.

———. "Investment Horizons: Afghanistan: An Analysis of Foreign Direct Investment Costs and Conditions in Four Industries." Washington, DC: World Bank, 2005a.

———. *World Development Indicators 2005.* Washington, DC: World Bank, 2005b.

———. "Morocco—Recent Economic Development in Infrastructure (REDI): Water Supply and Sanitation Sector." *Sector Report* 29634. Washington, DC: World Bank, 2004a.

———. *World Development Indicators 2004.* Washington, DC: World Bank, 2004b.

———. *Morocco—Social Development Agency.* Project ID no. MAPE73531. Washington, DC: World Bank, 2001.

———. *Implementation Completion Report: Morocco, Second Rural Electrification Project.* Report no. 17551. Washington, DC: World Bank, 1998.

———. *Staff Appraisal Report: Morocco, Second Rural Electrification Project.* Loan no. 8426–MOR. Washington, DC: World Bank, 1990.

———. *Project Completion Report: Morocco, Village Electrification Project.* Washington, DC: World Bank, 1988.

Zelizer, Viviana. *The Social Meaning of Money: Pin Money, Paychecks, Poor Relief, and Other Currencies.* Princeton, NJ: Princeton University Press, 1997.

The Contributors

Anna Andriasova is assistant professor and program director for marketing courses at the University of Maryland, University College.

Derick W. Brinkerhoff is senior fellow in international public management with RTI International (Research Triangle Institute) and associate faculty member at George Washington University's Trachtenberg School of Public Policy and Public Administration.

Jennifer M. Brinkerhoff is associate professor of public administration and international affairs at George Washington University, as well as founding director of the university's interdisciplinary Diaspora Research Program.

Milton J. Esman is John S. Knight Professor of International Studies and professor emeritus of government at Cornell University.

Thomson Fontaine, currently an economist at the International Monetary Fund (IMF), previously lectured at Clemson University and the University of the West Indies.

Kate Gillespie is associate professor of international business in the Marketing Department at the University of Texas at Austin.

Natasha Iskander is assistant professor of public policy at New York University's Wagner School of Public Service.

Janelle A. Kerlin is assistant professor of public administration and urban studies at Georgia State University's Andrew Young School of Policy Studies.

Stephen C. Lubkemann is associate professor of anthropology and international affairs at George Washington University and cofounder of the University's Diaspora Research Program.

Valentina Marano is a doctoral fellow in international business at the University of South Carolina.

Manuel Orozco is director of remittances and development at the Inter-American Dialogue. He also teaches at Georgetown University and George Washington University.

Liesl Riddle is associate professor of international business and international affairs at George Washington University and cofounder of the university's Diaspora Research Program.

Samuel Taddesse has more than thirty years of professional experience in policy analysis, strategic planning, monitoring and evaluation, and information management. He served in Iraq as national program policy and information director for the Iraq Local Governance Program implemented by RTI International (Research Triangle Institute).

Index

About the Book

For some time in diaspora studies, attention to remittances has overshadowed the growing impact of emigrant groups both within the social and political arenas in their homelands and with regard to fundamental economic development. The authors of *Diasporas and Development* redress this imbalance, focusing on three core issues: the responses of diasporas to homeland conflicts, strategies for mobilizing effective homeland investment, and the positive role of direct diaspora participation in development efforts.

The book combines detailed case studies with theoretical frameworks to provide a valuable foundation for further research.

Jennifer M. Brinkerhoff is associate professor of public administration and international affairs at George Washington University. She is author of *Digital Diasporas: Identity and Transnational Engagement* as well as numerous articles on diaspora-related issues.